GENDERED COMMUNITY

GENDERED COMMUNITY

ROUSSEAU, SEX, AND POLITICS

PENNY A. WEISS

NEW YORK UNIVERSITY PRESS
New York and London

NEW YORK UNIVERSITY PRESS
New York and London

Copyright © 1993 by New York University
All rights reserved

Library of Congress Cataloging-in-Publication Data
Weiss, Penny A.
Gendered community : Rousseau, sex, and politics / Penny A. Weiss.
 p.   cm.
Includes bibliographical references (p. 177) and index.
ISBN 0-8147-9263-4 (acid-free paper)
1. Rousseau, Jean-Jacques, 1712–1778—Views on sex role. 2. Sex role.   I. Title.
HQ1075.W437   1993
305.3—dc20   93-23909
                       CIP

New York University Press books are printed on acid-free paper,
and their binding materials are chosen for strength and durability.

Manufactured in the United States of America

10   9   8   7   6   5   4   3   2   1

From and to "Team Weiswerda"

CONTENTS

Acknowledgments   ix

Abbreviations   xvii

PART ONE

1 Introduction: Gender, Rousseau, and Politics   3

2 Producing Gender: Sex, Freedom, and Equality in Rousseau's *Emile*   10

3 Anatomy and Destiny: Rousseau, Antifeminism, and Woman's Nature   36

4 Families and Politics: Sex Roles and Community   54

5 The Justice of Sex Roles: "Rousseau, Judge of Jean-Jacques"   75

6 Rousseau and Feminist Revolution: The Impossibility of Gendered Community   90

PART TWO

7 Feminism and Communitarianism: Exploring the Relationship   121

8 Gender Bias in Political Theory: (Un)Seeing and (Un)Doing   149

Notes   163

Bibliography   177

Index   185

ACKNOWLEDGMENTS

Somehow I always thought that sitting down to write about debts incurred in the preparation of this book would be both easy and pleasurable. It is neither. I find it difficult to name what some people have meant to this project. I find it unpleasant to think of the obstacles I have encountered, both institutional and personal. I find myself uncomfortable with aspects of the self-revelation involved. I can't figure out how to avoid writing an autobiography when much of what got me here has roots far back in time. I'm not completely certain for whom I'm writing this. Myself? Those acknowledged within? Some broader audience? I even find it eerie to be undertaking the task that marks the end of the book with which I have been living for so (too) long.

I turn back to a talk I gave last year, "Feminism and Collaborative Research." When writing it I sat down and read the "Acknowledgments" sections of dozens of feminist books which happened to be at hand in my office. At the time I found this—itself a collaborative process—a helpful way of getting to what was distinctive about feminist collaboration. Now I look back at it to see if it can help me reflect on the debts incurred in my own writing. I scan the six items that caught my attention as revealing something about collaborative scholarship among feminists. I only sketch them here, for I am just using them as an opportunity for self-reflection.

1. The first feature I noted is the frequent acknowledgment of intellectual debts to the women's movement. In *Money, Sex, and Power*, for example, Nancy Hartsock expresses her debt to "the political arguments within the feminist movement and the work of feminist theorists," as well as to the

political activists with whom she had worked a decade earlier on the journal *Quest: A Feminist Quarterly*. Carole Pateman, in *The Sexual Contract*, says "my deepest intellectual debt is to the arguments and activities of the feminist movement, which has transformed my view both of political theory and of political life."

I owe almost everything I love about academia to the women's movement. It was feminism that first got me asking big questions about the world, as an undergraduate at the University of South Florida, and it is feminism that continues to motivate me today to grapple with such things as Rousseau's sexual politics (and other, more obviously interesting issues!). Nothing else has provided similar or comparable intellectual, personal, and political challenges all rolled up into one. I am indebted to those who have worked and continue to work to blur the supposedly sacred line separating intellectual and political endeavors, who keep feminist theory grounded in and engaged with people's actual lives. I thank the long line of people who have made it possible to pursue a feminist agenda in academic life and in general, and who know that the political is intellectual and the intellectual isn't "only academic." Because of them, I am forever kept on my toes.

In my own history I see the impossibility of separating out the personal, the political, and the institutional in the women's movement to which I owe so much. I think simultaneously of the Women's Center and Women's Peer Counseling Program at South Florida, and of the women there with whom I first explored feminism, Nancy Klimas, Maria Carroll, and Susan Sandweiss. I think of Women's Studies programs with which I have been affiliated as a teacher, and I also immediately conjure up the treasured colleague-friends I have met through them, especially Diane Finnerty, Dorothy Leland, Marilyn Friedman, Dena Targ, Berenice Carroll, and Heidi Gottfried. I cannot ignore my personal debt to institutional Affirmative Action programs, for surely they have been critical in getting me where I am today; they motivated my current department to hire a feminist theorist, me.

2. A second feature I found interesting in feminist "Acknowledgments" is a rejection of marking oneself as original, solitary, unique or, best of all, "definitive." In *Gyn/Ecology: The Metaethics of Radical Feminism*, Mary Daly admits to her work's being "so intertwined with" that of another individual that "it has often been impossible to tell whose ideas are whose." Patricia Hill Collins, author of *Black Feminist Thought: Knowledge, Consciousness, and the Politics of Empowerment*, aims not to close a line of thought but to bring more people into the discussion. She writes: " 'How

can I as one person speak for such a large and complex group as African-American women?' . . . In the course of writing the book I came to see my work as being part of a larger process, as one voice in a dialogue among people who had been silenced. . . . [M]y hope is that others who were formerly and are currently silenced will find their voices. I, for one, certainly want to hear what they have to say." And, in general, feminist authors want their work to be considered, as Hester Eisenstein puts it in *Contemporary Feminist Thought*, only as "a contribution to the ongoing debate over the future of feminist theory and the women's movement."

I have learned from every person who has written on Rousseau and gender, including those with whom I disagree. It is not so common to thank those with whom one is not familiar, but truly I owe great thanks to writers only some of whom I know personally: Joel Schwartz, Susan Moller Okin, Zillah Eisenstein, Lynda Lange, Nanerl Keohane, Anne Harper, Jean Elshtain, and Jane Roland Martin. I know from the use I have made of their work that there is a common project in which we are engaged, one that makes our current disagreements valuable and tractable. After all this time I still find problems in my text, things unclearly expressed or unsatisfactorily resolved. It has been difficult to let go of an imperfect creation. I have gained perspective by coming to see the work as one constructive voice in a larger conversation.

3. A third feature I found interesting in the "thank you" sections of feminist texts is that instead of acknowledging only influences that confer prestige upon oneself, feminist authors often do almost the opposite. For example, proudly placing themselves in a tradition of women theorists and essayists does not bring with it the obvious tag of legitimacy that aligning oneself with the history of male philosophers does; in fact, such placement is the author's contribution to creating the legitimacy of that other tradition. Mary Daly, in *Gyn/Ecology*, expresses gratitude to her foresisters, "Matilda Joslyn Gage, Virginia Woolf, and many whose names I do not know, many of whom were probably burned as witches." Genuine indebtedness to students is also admitted freely in such acknowledgments—another influence not conferring prestige. In *Feminist Thought: A Comprehensive Introduction*, Rosemarie Tong thanks a student by name for her "spirit of collaboration" and the "experience of intellectual partnership."

I noted these examples because it seemed to me that there's a pattern to the kinds of collaboration usually acknowledged by authors and those often unnoted and unappreciated. It is not only acceptable but a bonus to thank those people, practices, and institutions highly esteemed in academia: grant-giving foundations, well-known scholars, prestige-conferring presses and journals, fellowships at noteworthy universities, commentators at national or international conferences, and so forth. These things show that the authors have already received the academic seal of approval, for others previously deemed noteworthy have spread their legitimacy and influence to include them. Thanking journals for allowing us to reprint our articles in a book—not exactly a major sacrifice—is a feather in our cap. What we are acknowledging is that we have already been blessed, we have previously passed muster, we already have access to big names and big audiences and big presses. Acknowledgment of these forms and sources of collaboration make the author look important. Citing them is pulling out credentials. To acknowledge them is easy. (As I spread my feathers, I thank Sage Publications, Inc., publisher of *Political Theory* for chapter 3, *Polity* for chapter 2, and Indiana University Press, publisher of *Hypatia* for chapter 4. I also thank Niko Pfund at New York University Press for his interest in feminist publications and for breaking me of the habit of saying "I have just argued that . . . I will now argue that . . . " I was also fortunate to have an excellent copyeditor, Victoria Wilson-Schwartz. In all humility, and in the name of forming realistic expectations in those still struggling to get published, let me note that an early version of chapter 7 was rejected, chapter 3 was reworked and reworked before *Hypatia* took it, and *Polity* was the second place to which I sent chapter 1. Don't give up.)

There is also something academically acceptable about thanking secretaries. Our access to and thus our acknowledgment of them, I fear, shows our elevated place in hierarchies. So do the kinds of tasks assigned them. But the secretaries in my department have been important actors in this book, and I wish to acknowledge that in ways that make clear my respect, esteem, and affection for them. They waited with me for publishers' verdicts. They celebrated with me when the acceptance came. They rushed jobs for me, even when my perpetual disorganization was the cause of the rush. They read parts and told me they liked them. They supported me when illness dramatically slowed completion of this project. Barbara Bergner, Beth Turner, Betty Hartman, and, most especially, Claire Windler, thank you, thank you.

4. A fourth feature of acknowledgments in feminist texts is the appreciation given colleagues, friends, and groups for the contributions they make which are not, narrowly understood, exclusively intellectual. Judith Baer,

in *Equality under the Constitution*, thanks one who helped her get a foot in the door by inviting her to present a conference paper, something that may be more of a hurdle for women than men, given the mentoring system in operation today. Bell Hooks, in *Ain't I a Woman: Black Women and Feminism*, thanks her fellow black women workers whose belief in her and her project still sustains her and acknowledges those who helped her face the ridicule she received in response to writing about black women. Judith Plaskow, author of *Standing Again at Sinai: Judaism from a Feminist Perspective*, expresses thanks to her Jewish feminist spirituality collective. Hester Eisenstein thanks the members of her New York women's group and her sisters in the Sydney feminist community.

Indebtedness to these individuals and groups shows Michèle Le Doeuff to be correct when she states, "[W]hen you are a woman and a philosopher it is useful to be a feminist in order to understand what is happening to you." The acknowledgments in feminist texts indicate that if you are an academic and a feminist you had better find sources of support and collaboration outside the university, not only because you will encounter hostility within it, which you will, but also because the models of collaboration and support operating there are often grossly inadequate, recalling the definition of collaboration as "cooperation with the enemy."

I have not had an easy time finding or creating a stable group of scholars with whom to travel. Of course, going to graduate school at Notre Dame was not exactly an auspicious start. I am proud of myself for overcoming the obstacles placed before me there, from lack of funding to obvious skepticism about my abilities. (Really, shouldn't a school named "Our Lady" provide a more hospitable environment?) Having three small children has not exactly left me a lot of time to nurture friendships. Perhaps the community I envision is harder to come by than I imagined, or perhaps I still don't understand the rules of the game. I do, however, have some graduate students at Purdue to thank for both support and stimulation: Loretta Kensinger, Diane Gruber, Brenda MacIntyre, and Gina Scuteri. Even at Notre Dame, several people were of immeasurable worth: Edward Goerner was a splendid dissertation director (using a word he might employ), a wise guide, perceptive critic, and enthusiastic supporter; Lynne Suzanne was a partner and colleague who made a difference; Mike Francis and Susan Roberts were friends; my soccer team kept me sane. Knowing so little about academic life when I entered it professionally, I thank those who got me on panels, who answered questions about academic customs and rituals, and gave encouragement during the early years of my career: Anne Harper, Maria Falco, and Lee Wilson. And I thank Harry Targ for the perspective he gave me one day as we stood by our mailboxes and I opened my first rejection notice, from *Ethics*: "Oh, I've been rejected by better journals than that!" he said.

5. On a slightly different point, there is also evident in feminist acknowledgments collaboration with and dependence on explicitly feminist grants, libraries, and societies. In *Reason's Disciples*, Hilda Smith writes: "I would first like to thank collectively that group of women historians which has, over the last decade, come together to form feminist organizations within the profession and labored to create the current field of women's history. Without the help of these historians, scholars such as myself, both as graduate students and as faculty, would have had to pursue the nearly impossible task of developing careers and research in a vacuum." Judith Plaskow, author of *Standing Again at Sinai*, expresses deep gratitude to the Women and Religion section of the American Academy of Religion and the New York Feminist Scholars in Religion as "crucial to my development as a feminist and a theologian." Ann Ferguson, author of *Sexual Democracy: Women, Oppression, and Revolution*, thanks SOFPHIA, the Socialist Feminist Philosophers Association. Marilyn Frye, in *The Politics of Reality: Essays in Feminist Theory*, thanks the Society for Women in Philosophy (SWIP). Such organizations enhance the possibilities of collaborative research among their members, and are themselves collaborative actors in their crucial role of encouraging, airing, and rewarding feminist scholarship.

In this vein I am grateful for the Women and Politics section of the American Political Science Association, through which I have presented all of my APSA papers and which provides me with the opportunity to hear just about all the papers I choose to hear at the conventions. I have seen live models of feminist cooperation at Midwest SWIP meetings. I have enjoyed feminist theory reading groups and learned much at the ever-present Women's Studies brown bag lunches. The existence of feminist journals such as *Hypatia* has been critical to my development as a scholar.

6. Finally, since most acknowledgments end with thanks to families, I close with the note that feminist thank-yous do not seem to evince the same kinds of collaboration within families as do nonfeminist ones. While male authors are notorious for thanking their wives for help in research, typing, editing, and childcare, I have thus far found no woman who does precisely the reverse. Perhaps such women, if they exist, credit those men with coauthorship? Still found are thanks for and sometimes, implicitly, apologies to

families for putting up with a dirty house and fast-food dinners. Zillah Eisenstein, in *The Female Body and the Law*, thanks, not a male partner, but the staff of the childcare center for the care bestowed upon her daughter; to such workers I am also deeply indebted. There are a surprising number of thanks to mothers and sisters. Eisenstein thanks her mother "for everything." Bell Hooks closes her acknowledgments by thanking her mother for teaching "all her daughters, that Sisterhood empowers women by respecting, protecting, encouraging, and loving us." Dale Spender, in *Women of Ideas*, stresses how much the actors in her life have helped in ordinary, and ordinarily overlooked, ways. And she does this with style and "originality," promising her mother a visit and a conversation about Elizabeth Cady Stanton and offering her sister a year of research help like that the sister had just given. Note there, too, the mutuality, the lack of hierarchy. Marilyn Frye, similarly, thanks her partner for "intelligent and knowledgeable collaboration, encouragement and criticism," and promises "I will make sure she gets as much as she has given."

In my family of origin, my siblings Wendy and Jerry were the first to attend college, and Janie was the first to graduate. The precedents they set were important to me. Like me, however, they were never quite sure what I was doing in graduate school all those years. Nonetheless, I received support from members of my family, and was taught, especially by my mother, to have esteem for education or, more precisely, for reading, for formulating positions, for being knowledgeable. My mother was more than once the "first woman" in the jobs she held, something about which I recall being proud even as a child and which had influence on my own career decisions. I wish my father had lived to see some of the fruits of my labor, but I know aspects of his spirit live in them and in me. I still hear him asking, half sarcastically and half searchingly, "*What's* political theory?" I owe both my parents thanks for their confidence and pride in me.

It is to my family today that this book is dedicated: Bob Strikwerda, and Linden, Brennin, and Avian Weiswerda. They have taught me firsthand about the positive potential of community. My children give me perspective, pleasure, and purpose, even while they exhaust me. There is nothing like building with Legos or playing in a sandbox to keep one alive to various ways of seeing and being in the world. Linden's imagination and sensitivity keep life enchanting. Brennin's honesty and gusto keep life challenging. Avian's easy affection and toddler humor keep life balanced. I owe my partner thanks for being a wonderful father who has done his share to sustain our family, for assistance with word processors that tax my no-tech soul, and for love in the lean years. Only helping each other as we do makes it possible to keep going.

Finally, I will say that I detest it when someone tells me, "I don't know how you do it, with three small children, blah, blah, blah." I feel obliged to answer, honestly, "I don't do it, or not as easily or as well as I could. I'm tired and grumpy, blah, blah, blah." Make no mistake: the system in place does not work. I am lucky to have loved ones with whom to muddle through.

ABBREVIATIONS

The following is a list of editions of Jean-Jacques Rousseau's works for which abbreviations are used in the text. Extremely accurate English translations exist for all of Rousseau's major writings, and I have relied heavily upon them. For many words subject to multiple translations, or central to my argument, I also include the original French, taken from *Oeuvres Complètes*.

d'Alembert Letter to M. d'Alembert on the Theatre. Translated by Allan Bloom. In *Politics and the Arts*. Ithaca, N.Y.: Cornell University Press, 1968.
Emile Emile, or, On Education. Translated by Allan Bloom. New York: Basic Books, 1979.
FD First Discourse. *The First and Second Discourses*. Translated by Roger D. Masters and Judith R. Masters. New York: St. Martin's Press, 1964.
OC Oeuvres Complètes. 4 vols. Edited by Bernard Gagnebin and Marcel Raymond. Paris: Gallimard, Bibliothèque de la Pléiade, 1959–69.
SC On the Social Contract. *On the Social Contract with Geneva Manuscript and Political Economy*. Translated by Judith R. Masters. Edited by Roger D. Masters. New York: St. Martin's Press, 1978.
SD Second Discourse. *The First and Second Discourses*. Translated by Roger D. Masters and Judith R. Masters. New York: St. Martin's Press, 1964.

PART ONE

ONE

INTRODUCTION: GENDER, ROUSSEAU, AND POLITICS

Rousseau's fame for writing in apparent inconsistencies and paradoxes is indisputably well deserved. He confronts the reader with ironies of all sorts. There are contrasts between his life and his written words: Rousseau the educational theorist failed as a private tutor, and Rousseau the supporter of traditional familial obligations left to foundling homes the children born to him and Thérèse Levasseur.[1] There are apparent contradictions within his ideas themselves as well: Rousseau speaks of masters as themselves enslaved and, most famously, of a general will that forces people to be free. Yet readers must exercise extra caution lest something be judged an inconsistency that is in fact only a puzzle, for he tells us "I do not believe that . . . I contradict myself in my ideas; but I cannot gainsay that I often contradict myself in my expressions" (*Emile*, 108n.).

It is also incontestable that any single work of an author of Rousseau's intellect and breadth is best understood in light of general ideas which inform and are further explored in other works. The ideas he treats at length range from human evolution to the political role of education and from the antithesis between contemporary society and human nature to the structure of a legitimate government. Yet Rousseau informs us that many of his essays work together to form a whole, and that all are informed by the same principles (*OC*, 4:928).

A final difficulty in interpreting Rousseau is that his association with, among other things, Enlightenment thought, social contract theory, individualism, romanticism, and totalitarianism tempts readers to force him into categories which he may not fit. On the other hand, Rousseau's own understanding of himself as an independent writer speaking to humanity may allow readers to miss linkages between his ideas and those of others.

The substance, style, and sheer volume of Rousseau's writing require, then, that his thought be interpreted carefully and that some of his essays be used as a check on our understanding of others. In wrestling here with issues of gender, I confront what seems, by all appearances, to be an inconsistency in Rousseau that runs through many of his works, and I attempt to resolve it by placing it in the context of themes and principles, sometimes reassessed here, that provide the framework of his political philosophy.

An examination of Rousseau's views on differential treatment of the sexes seems to expose numerous and serious inconsistencies in his thought. The principles of male education found in the first four books of the *Emile* (which are usually commented upon favorably and thought to be in accord with Rousseau's general philosophical positions) appear to have little in common with the (less favorably viewed) educational program recommended for women in book 5. In the *Social Contract* Rousseau asserts that one necessary condition of political legitimacy is that laws be made by all; yet female citizens are excluded from direct participation in the assembly. The *Second Discourse* demonstrates that human nature is almost infinitely malleable, affected by forces ranging from the climatic and economic to the educational and legal; yet Rousseau seems to treat the sexes as radically different by nature. And while so often characterized as an egalitarian and liberal thinker, Rousseau seems to subordinate women to the rule of men and to leave women few avenues for individual development or self-expression. Those searching for consistency in his thought thus find no small hurdle in his remarks on the roles and relations of the sexes, and those searching the history of philosophy for treatment of women as equal to men or as full citizens would seem well advised to look elsewhere.

It is tempting to attribute Rousseau's remarks on the sexes, as many have done, to the sexist times in which he wrote[2] or to his personal idiosyncratic preferences, so starkly do they seem to conflict with his principled commitments to freedom and equality. There are, however, three related problems standing in the way of such resolutions. First of all, ascribing sexism to personal predilection denies sexism's social character, ignoring its embeddedness in social practices and institutions and removing it from political scrutiny. As Le Doeuff has written of Sartre, "If we continue to regard [his presuppositions] as psychologically motivated and personal, we have to see them as peculiar to him, related to the idiosyncrasy of Jean-Paul Sartre. . . . And the analysis stops there."[3] In a similar way, racism is often depoliticized: "the rhetoric of increased privatization, in response to racial issues, functions as the rationalizing agent of public unaccountability and, ultimately, irresponsibility."[4] Further, even were it correct to attribute Rousseau's sexism to his era or to his individual personality, these understandings of the *causes* of his remarks do nothing to alleviate their *effects* on his politics. In general, that is to say, even when an appeal to someone's era or personality is put forth as a conclusion to one inquiry, regarding causes, another more important one, regarding effects, remains: "How are sexist assumptions manifested in that person's politics, and with what consequences?" Last, there are good reasons for thinking that something more than philosophical shortsightedness or personal prejudice is involved here. The sheer number of times that discussions about the sexes arise in Rousseau's thought is itself remarkable,[5] and in strong contrast with the amount of attention given such themes by most male figures in the history of political philosophy.[6] Equally noteworthy is the fact that his insistent advocacy of a radically sex-roled society survived his acquaintance with feminist ideas,[7] ideas associated with what today is called liberal feminism.[8] It seems reasonable to infer both that Rousseau knew the relations and positions of the sexes to be of great political significance, and that his opinions on the subject were the product of reflection. I will argue that Rousseau's position on gender roles and relations is very consciously selected, and for political reasons. The stance he adopted was understood by him as reflecting and supporting, rather than contradicting, his central philosophical and political priorities; in fact, using gender as a way into Rousseau's thought can bring to light priorities often otherwise overlooked or underemphasized. Those who treat Rousseau's words on women as an inconsistent but detachable appendage to his "real" thought thus misread both.

My aims in this book are twofold. For Rousseau scholars I hope to contribute to debates about his internal consistency and his understandings of gender, justice, freedom, community, and equality. The literature on Rousseau has generally misrepresented both the substance and the relevance of his sexual politics, a subject of scant interest until the current wave of the women's movement helped bring significant numbers of feminists into academic positions. Further, analysis of his statements concerning the sexes provides an opportunity to see his thought from a relatively fresh perspective, one which leads here to a new interpretation of the *Emile* and which has implications for interpretations of his other works. I hope, too, that analysis of Rousseau's views on gender might persuade nonfeminist Rousseau scholars of the elevated understanding attention to gender brings to the history of political theory and, ultimately, might help some to see the need for a politics that takes sexual equality as a priority.

My second aim is connected more directly to feminist theory. Why do feminists continue to study the "major" historical figures of philosophy? Documenting the sexual inegalitarianism in their thought seems to be a project of limited usefulness for feminist theory and practice. It would appear, for example, that there are endless tasks for feminist scholars more pressing and more relevant to the attainment of sexual equality than reconstructing the arguments of Rousseau—an eighteenth-century, white, male, European intellectual writing in defense of socially enforced sexual differentiation.

Feminist study of historical philosophers can have diverse ends. A first goal may be to clarify someone's thoughts on gender, on what has long been ignored or misrepresented by translators and commentators. Unquestionably, the tendency until very recently has been to see, for example, studies of Aquinas's views of angels or miracles or politics as worthwhile, but examination of his views on women as trivial, inessential, beside the point, and not even philosophical.[9] Because of this, much work is often needed even to discover what has been said about gender in the history of political philosophy, and why. Part of this book is devoted to reconstructing Rousseau's views on the positions and relations of the sexes and unraveling the grounds on which they are defended. "Indifference" to such projects is a "formidable form of resistance" to sexual equality,[10] an expression of the opinion that like women themselves, ideas about women are not worth bothering about.

A second object of feminist attention to thinkers in the traditional history of political theory is to reveal the centrality of their views on gender. To neglect someone's words about sex may be to misunderstand or miss central elements of their general philosophy. Revealing the role of women in a philosopher's scheme of thought can lead to a new, more complete picture of that scheme, and a reevaluation of it. Aristotle's often-admired politically active citizens, for example, look less attractive when it is shown that their existence requires the existence of male and female slaves and of confined wives. Much of this book is aimed at recovering the connection between

Rousseau's sexual politics and his political theory. I will argue that far from being marginal, Rousseau's views on gender are central to his politics; for example, his sexually differentiated educations are largely responsible for turning individuals into citizens. One cannot cleanse Rousseau of his ideas about women, cannot pretend that the "good parts" can still be endorsed without dragging the rest along. His politics comprise a package in need of a more careful and honest evaluation than that. His political strategies give rise to a range of important contemporary questions regarding families, citizens, and communities.

A third goal of feminist inquiry into the philosophers of the past may be to discover arguments which, though not originally applied to issues of sex, may fruitfully be so applied. For example, while Marx's main concern was class and not sex, his work on ideology, relations of production, and the division of labor have been instructively used in feminist analyses. Surprising as it may seem, I will argue that some of Rousseau's ideas can be used by feminists, though not without some modification and adaptation, including his critique of individualism and his story of the development of human beings and institutions. Too, the understanding of Rousseau suggested here chips away at the myth that gender has "always" been looked at in one way by (male) philosophers.

My own attraction to Rousseau has always been only partly about Rousseau qua Rousseau. I was drawn to him at first because of the seemingly obvious contradiction between his general philosophy and his views on gender, which I originally set out years ago simply to highlight and condemn in what I thought would be an uncomplicated and straightforward exercise. But the attraction persisted, because as I studied, I saw in Rousseau an antifeminism I had not heard or thought much about. The main argument of this book is that Rousseau's defense of sexual differentiation is based on the contribution he perceives it can make to the establishment of community, and not on an appeal to some version of "natural" sex differences. In teaching courses on feminist theory over the years, I have in fact found that my students have an initial attachment to gender roles rooted in a Rousseauesque understanding of their inherent harmlessness and of the benefits they bring.

As a feminist I am committed to understanding the opposition to feminism, because I think it necessary for the coherence of our theories and the success of our politics to hear and answer its concerns and questions. Rousseau was not a simple misogynist, determined to interpret nature or history or culture in such a way as to bless male supremacy with the aura of inevitability or justifiability. The concerns that led him to support sexual differentiation, especially the concern with moving beyond self-interest to real community, are often laudable and shared by many feminists. Thus, Rousseau's resistance to feminism is not based on the same morally offensive principles and logically flawed reasoning as are many other antifeminisms. But because Rousseau's antifeminism is as troubling in its implications as are the others, it is one that deserves to be heard and responded to.[11] And that is what I hope to contribute here.

I use Rousseau's sexually differentiated educations as a point of departure. Chapter 2 of this study compares the educational programs recommended for Emile and Sophie, representatives of their genders. While the two programs obviously differ in content, and do so for the sake of gender differentiation and what it supposedly brings in its wake, I take issue with the argument that they are guided by different and wholly incompatible principles. My focus on the theoretical consistency between women's and men's educations not only leads to a more coherent interpretation of the text considered by Rousseau to be his best but also shows how Rousseau's views on women cohere with and form a part of, rather than contradict, his political philosophy in general.

The main argument of chapter 3 is directed against the claim that Rousseau, or any antifeminist, educates the sexes differently solely or simply because he believes that they have different natures. I show that possible sex differences in physical strength, mental capacities, interests, and reproductive functions are all insufficient, by Rousseau's own account, to explain the differences in the educations and lives of women and men. That is, Rousseau's antifeminism is not an application of biological determinism.

Having shown that Rousseau does not believe sex roles to be mandated by nature, I turn in chapter 4 to an exploration of the ends that lead him to advocate a radically sex-differentiated society. Looking at his arguments in favor of the sex-roled, affectionate family, and against bourgeois and aristocratic families, it is possible to see that his position is based on the perceived political benefits of the former and the negative repercussions of the latter. Sexual differentiation in general, and within the family in particular, is advocated by Rousseau as a means to community.

In chapter 5 I complete the textual exegesis with reflections on the internal consistency of Rousseau's work. By giving "Rousseauean" responses to some arguments against him, I show how he might have perceived his sexual politics to be compatible with his general philosophical and political principles, including his understanding of justice.

I begin the sixth chapter showing how important elements of Rousseau's thought can be understood as consistent with insights of contemporary feminist political theory. Despite this, however, I argue that Rousseau's system of enforced sex differences will actually undermine the community he so desires, the community in whose interest he advocates sexual differentiation in the first place. Looking in particular at women's public and private restriction to indirect power, I conclude that in practice the scheme is ultimately self-defeating. Like those before and after him, Rousseau fails to make the sexes different and equal. The resources invested in maintaining enforced sexual differentiation are misspent, the accumulated costs obscene.

In chapter 7 I move from a sole focus on Rousseau to communitarianism in general. I explore why it is that while feminists are very interested in community, communitarians, from Plato to Rousseau to MacIntyre, are generally uninterested in or hostile to feminism. I compare the arguments each makes against liberalism as a way of finding the sources and substance of the differences between feminists and communitarians. I argue that while feminists and communitarians understand liberalism similarly, and so have a common opponent, their grounds for rejecting it reflect fundamentally different political commitments that do not necessarily intersect.

In the concluding chapter I gaze upon the dreadful sexism so pervasive in the (standard) history of political theory. Using the device of a sex-role reversal, I hope to shed light on the often unseen and always costly sexism in political ideas and practices.

A note about style and content. Chapters 2 through 5 are mostly concerned with an internal analysis of Rousseau that proceeds through textual exegesis. I try to note contemporary feminist concerns throughout, but these get much more consideration in the final three chapters, as part of the critique of Rousseau, other communitarians, and the traditional history of political theory. I have tried to make all of the chapters accessible and useful to Rousseau scholars who are not well versed in feminist theory, to feminist theorists not well versed in Rousseau, and to others interested in the general issues of gender equality, freedom, and community. I regret any failures on this score.

TWO

PRODUCING GENDER: SEX, FREEDOM, AND EQUALITY IN ROUSSEAU'S *EMILE*

Although the book bearing his name was written in 1750, Rousseau's Emile could pass for a "sensitive, new-age, guy" according to portraits of him in the secondary literature. He's strong, yet caring. He's bright and resourceful, without being pedantic. He's a reliable worker, but not overly fond of money. He stays in shape and gives to the needy. Why he's even acquainted with sexual responsibility and imposes no sexual double standard on women, whose respect he seeks.

Rousseau's Sophie, on the other hand, seems completely out of place in the late twentieth century. An eighteenth-century "total woman," she's the eternal caregiver. Portrayed as modest and motherly, unschooled and unskilled, she strikes many as more a plaything than a partner to Emile. Sophie gets her way through feminine wiles and is too consumed with appearance and reputation to survive as an appealing role model.

Practically since the ink dried on the pages of Rousseau's *Emile*, commentators have been disturbed by the substance of Sophie's education and perplexed by its apparent inconsistency with the more favorably received program of male education. From Wollstonecraft, Voltaire, and Formey in the eighteenth century to late twentieth-century feminist critics, comments abound alluding to the defects of Rousseau's scheme of female education and the ways in which it contradicts his own principles.[1] The following comments are representative:

Emile was to be a critical, self-reliant citizen, entitled to an elaborate education and full equality with his peers. Sophie, on the other hand, was to be trained only as a wife to Emile and as a mother to his children.[2]

Sophy's [sic] education could not be more different than Emile's. His education is aimed at freedom and independence, while her education is directed toward making her able to please man and be subjected to him.[3]

Rousseau is a paradigm case of this differential application of the axiomatic principles on which most political philosophy has been built since the seventeenth century. His primary "human" values—equality and freedom—are swept aside entirely when he discusses the proper place and role of the female sex.[4]

Until very recently, however, even when noted, the inconsistency between women's and men's education in Rousseau was often downplayed and excused, written off as an easily understandable and relatively minor, if unfortunate, aberration. The inconsistency was ascribed to the prejudice of the time or of the author and, given the lack of further attention, was not seen as raising any serious substantive problems. These resolutions, however, rest on questionable assumptions and cause more difficulties in interpretation than they resolve. They treat Rousseau's statements on the sexes as unreflective of and unimportant to his philosophy, without proving that such is the case. The ease with which inattention to Rousseau's views on the sexes has been justified is itself an obstacle to understanding them and their central place in his politics. At least as much can be learned about Rousseau from studying his comments on female education as on male education. In large part because of the lack of attention to women's education, the principles behind Rousseau's education for *both* sexes have frequently been misrepresented.[5] The two educations can, in fact, be reconciled, and in a way that demonstrates the consistency of Rousseau's views on women with other elements of his political philosophy.

In arguing for the theoretical consistency of Rousseau's sexually differentiated educational programs, I am *not* claiming that the programs are substantive twins—they cannot be, because they are intended to create sex differences—but I am arguing that they are not contradictory either. That is, Rousseau's values are not "swept aside" in discussions of the female sex. The sexes are educated to become different, but the training of both generally appeals to an identical understanding of the human condition and of what problems political arrangements, including education, must address. In presenting evidence for this interpretation, I compare it to evidence for the view that Sophie's education and Emile's are totally dissimilar. I conclude with some thoughts about the causes of misinterpretation, about the significance of the similarities in women's and men's educations in Rousseau, and about questions a feminist perspective raises for Rousseau's educational schemes.

EDUCATION AND FREEDOM

Rousseau establishes one principle that goes a great distance toward explaining his practical programs of education.

> The truly free man wants only what he can do and does what he pleases. That is my fundamental maxim. It need only be applied to childhood for all the rules of education *[les règles de l'éducation]* to flow from it. (*Emile*, 84)

Rousseau's assertion that "all the rules of education" flow from his conception of freedom indicates the very political nature of his educational scheme and provides a standard by which to assess the education of each sex. While not every particular of education must be aimed solely at freedom, each must at least be compatible with it.

In the conditions Rousseau portrays as characterizing the earliest stages of human development, a prepolitical state of nature, people live freely, being without the authority of a master and without need for the services, companionship, or esteem of others. The needs of natural savages are limited, and their powers are sufficient to satisfy them independently. This vision of each individual determining and satisfying minimal needs without particular or sustained dependencies is the purest and most influential portrayal of freedom in Rousseau's thought. And it is here, Rousseau says, "in this original state," that we can find an example of a condition where "power and desire [are] in equilibrium *[l'équilibre]* and man is not unhappy" (*Emile*, 80). While the regular interdependence that defines civil society decisively alters the human condition in such a way that freedom can no longer be associated with independence and self-sufficiency, the ideal of equilibrium is maintained in the *Emile*. As Roger Masters notes, "The natural man is not here primitive man, nor even merely the abstraction of what is common to all socialized men, but the man who is not in contradiction with himself and whose faculties are in 'equilibrium.' " [6]

The freedom that informs educational practices in modern society is still concerned with the development of one's powers and the restriction of one's desires to the realm of that which can be obtained without becoming a master or a slave. Happiness is the result, or concomitant, of this balance. This formal definition only requires an equilibrium between two factors, not necessarily a certain "amount" or "kind" of either one. Thus, although people may lead quite different lives, freedom and happiness are within the grasp of all who can maintain the powers-desires equilibrium. But do the two sexes have comparable chances of establishing this balance, of being socially free, based on their different Rousseauean educations? To answer this, both facets of freedom and happiness need investigating: the development of powers and the restriction of desires.

POWERS

Rousseau's notion of what counts as powers—what "empowers" people—is a broad one, and failure to attend to *his* understanding of what does and does not empower people is the source of much misinterpretation. Based on commentaries on Emile's education, an education which virtually all interpret as fostering strength and self-sufficiency, the "powers" component of the freedom ratio is thought to include at least physical fitness, economic independence, and freedom from public opinion. This list need not, and indeed should not, be considered exhaustive. It is sufficient that the items on it are representative of and significant in interpretations of the text. In discussing each, I first lay out the obvious contrasts between Emile's and Sophie's training, and the standard way of interpreting these contrasts as leading to freedom only for Emile, and then offer some textually based corrections and challenges to both.

PHYSICAL FITNESS

Without question, Emile's education places heavy emphasis on strengthening his body and accustoming him to physical hardships. No activities are forbidden Emile; nothing is too taxing, too dangerous, or too adventurous. He is constantly in motion, and the tutor is advised not to oppose such "restlessness" ("inquiétude") (*Emile*, 64). But of girls it is said, "They must first be exercised in constraint [contrainte]" (Emile, 369). For Sophie's "fair sex," only "agreeable, moderate, and salutary exercises" are urged (Emile, 366), and they play no games which bruise or harden their skin.

These differences can easily be interpreted as contributing to Emile's self-sufficiency and Sophie's dependency: the weak need assistance and protection, while the strong can take care of themselves or command the services of others. Further, the psychological training of men to be active and women to be constrained reinforces and is reinforced by the differences in physical training. While Emile was frequently injured during his physical trials, Rousseau held that "the well-being of freedom makes up for many wounds" (Emile, 78). Sophie, it seems, has neither wounds nor freedom.

Such an interpretation is marred, however, by three related problems. First, it omits mention of those similarities that do exist in the educational philosophy of the two programs; second, it pays insufficient attention to the ends of physical education; and third, it fails to place physical education in the broader context of Rousseau's politics.

Three similarities in the two programs provide evidence that they are informed by the same philosophy of education. First, Rousseau asserts that for both sexes "since the body is born, so to speak, before the soul, the body ought to be cultivated first" (Emile, 365). For girls as for boys, Rousseau acknowledges the developmental stages through which they pass (emotional and intellectual as well as physical) and urges that these stages be treated as a constraint upon the educator. Further, Rousseau recognizes individual variations within these developmental periods, a lesson being relearned in educational reform today.[7]

Second, Rousseau criticizes

the paternal household, where a girl—delicately fed, always pampered or scolded [flatée ou tancée], always seated within range of her mother's eyes, shut up in a room —does not dare stand up, walk, speak, or breathe, and does not have a moment of freedom to play, jump, run, shout, or indulge in the petulance natural to her age. (Emile, 366)

This condemnation coincides with principles found in Emile's education. Rousseau regards childhood not only as a distinct state but also as one which ought to be more appreciated in its own right. He rejects a conception of children as "miniature adults" and its practical consequences of subjecting youngsters to strict discipline and early formal intellectual education. He also casts aside a conception of children as "imperfect adults," a view which leads either to neglect or to overprotection. With childhood as but a prelude to adulthood, and worthless in itself, youngsters are either indulged and mollycoddled, carefully shielded from the world to preserve them for healthy adulthood, or merely tolerated until they become useful adults. Rousseau allows for the energy and pleasures properly characteristic of youth, male and female. He does not devalue any developmental stages, however immature children in them may be, much as the similarly limited life of the natural savage is not depreciated. In fact, one implication of Rousseau's argument is that we may need to turn more to children for lessons about how to structure adult life.

Lastly, in the training of both sexes Rousseau rejects education which is guided only by the needs of the future adult and which ignores present happiness and interests. But for neither sex does he embrace education which cares *only* for present happiness. Rousseau's program for *both* sexes can be understood in this query: "Why do you give him more ills than his condition entails without being sure that these present ills are for the relief of the future?" (*Emile*, 80). That is, *if* there is reasonable certainty that one is preparing a child for events or situations she or he will encounter as an adult and that less suffering is involved in advance preparations than in facing the difficulty upon adulthood, then (and only then) such focus on the future is justifiable to Rousseau. Lessons which pass such a test are given to Sophie *and* Emile. Because the adult lives of men and women differ, so do their educations. But each *is* prepared for their "Rousseauean destiny," and neither is given training which is of no particular use to them.

While Emile seems to be created to be the ultimate Boy Scout—prepared for anything and dependent on no one—Rousseau's program is misrepresented if it is thought to include preparation for every possible fate that might befall a person. Rather, people are prepared for events which are most reasonably likely to occur, and which need or benefit from preparation far in advance. According to Rousseau, as a citizen of a republic Emile will be in the army and, should there be a war, must possess the strength and endurance to participate in battle. Sophie will not be expected to do military service. Hence, because of the different lives they will lead, Emile must undergo different physical training than Sophie, but the lessons of both are determined by future utility.

To understand the other important similarities in Emile's and Sophie's educations it is necessary to see that in Emile's physical training strength is not sought as an end in itself. Rousseau mentions at least four important consequences for Emile of constant exercise and exposure.

First, he applauds the fact that physical activity (rather than forced intellectual education) develops the mind. Children learn most easily through movement, experimentation, and confrontation with the consequences of their actions: "Since he is constantly in motion, he is forced to observe many things, to know many effects. . . . the more he makes himself strong and robust, the more he becomes sensible and judicious" (*Emile*, 119). Second, Rousseau notes that the physical health born from exercise allows one to be a useful person. This is opposed to Rousseau's hard image of the sickly person as "useless to himself and others, involved uniquely with preserving himself" (*Emile*, 53), and dependent upon that detested art of medicine. Third, Rousseau sees a healthy body as a necessary condition of freedom (*Emile*, 54, 118, 125). The weak require assistance, while those like Emile, "able to do more by themselves, . . . need to have recourse to others less frequently" (*Emile*, 78).

Lastly, physical fitness relates to a recurring theme of the *Emile*: preparedness in the face of the changing or the unknown. The physical element of preparedness is represented by the book's frontispiece of Thetis submerging her child in the water of the Styx.[8] Rousseau's goal is to "harden their bodies against the intemperance of season, climates, elements; against hunger, thirst, fatigue" (*Emile*, 47). Given the flux of modern life, Rousseau prepares Emile to survive in any environment and to be capable of conquering or ignoring physical discomfort. Even the many accidents young, active Emile is sure to have are an asset, for they decrease sensitivity to the greater injuries adults must bear. One's environment is a given—a part of the "world of things" outside one's control. Rousseau's intent is that Emile be able to accept and bear this given.

Emile is exposed to activity and hardship in order to create a person who understands cause and effect relationships, who is able to remain healthy and active in various environments and situations, and who can both transcend self-concern and be free from certain debilitating dependencies. Rousseau's sexually differentiated programs of education would thus be inconsistent if none of these goals were sought in Sophie's education, either through physical training or some other means (assuming there is more than one possible means to the ends). But Sophie's education does not render her stupid, frail, inflexible, self-absorbed, or helpless. She may, for example, be learning causal relations in a more domesticated setting, but this need not involve less experimentation or mental development. Similarly, she participates in enough exercise to maintain good health and learns of other contributors to physical well-being, such as proper diet and food preparation. Emile's education aims at taking him outside of himself while avoiding slavish dependence on others; the goal is something between slavery and mastery, and between self-absorption and total dependence. The same may be said of Sophie's education: in this respect the two programs are identical.

It is crucial to note a final similarity in the two regimes of physical training. Both sexes are being physically prepared for certain *social* roles, roles which involve responsibilities to others and which show that Rousseau does not intend either Sophie or Emile to be a free and independent savage. For example, Emile's training enables him to be a citizen-soldier, a social role involving obligations and loyalties to political and familial communities. He will be strong for others, not simply for himself. Similarly, in writing that "[w]omen ought not to be robust *like* men, but they should be robust *for* men, so that the men born from them will be robust too" (*Emile*, 366), Rousseau shows that Sophie's strength matches a certain role she must fulfill for others, not simply for herself. For neither sex is the need for strength considered in isolation from social needs. The two educations are guided by the same political framework, making it more likely that what Rousseau considers necessary social tasks will be performed.

Sophie's relative physical weakness does indeed place her in a condition different from that of social men, and of men and women in the state of nature. But there are two reasons we should not yet conclude that Rousseau thus makes all and only women dependent. First, as a look at the history of feminist theory reveals, belief in or advocacy of women's relative physical weakness does not lead to advocacy of sexual inequality or even sexual differentiation as a necessary consequence. Perhaps none have gone so far in conceding women's relative physical weakness as Simone de Beauvoir, yet de Beauvoir denied any necessary connection to social inferiority.

Woman is weaker than man; she has less muscular strength, fewer red blood corpuscles, less lung capacity; she runs more slowly, can lift less heavy weights, can compete with man in hardly any sport; she cannot stand up to him in a fight. . . . Certainly these facts cannot be denied—but in themselves they have no significance . . . [W]henever the physiological fact (for instance, muscular inferiority) takes on meaning, this meaning is at once seen as dependent on a whole context . . . [I]t is not upon physiology that values can be based. . . . Thus we must view the facts of biology in the light of an ontological, economic, social, and psychological context.[9]

Second, while physical weakness is a form of weakness that can under certain circumstances leave one in need of others, as will become clearer in the next three chapters, Rousseau is trying to encourage interdependence. He believes that two people with like strengths and weaknesses will not have a predictable need for each other.[10] Similarly, the fact that men are trained to be physically strong in no way can be taken to mean that they have no need for others. The strengths and weaknesses of the sexes will differ, and must differ in Rousseau's scheme, because only then will each reliably be drawn to the other, overcoming their natural isolation. For example, in another context Rousseau writes:

> If woman could ascend to general principles as well as man can, and if man had as good a mind for details as woman does, they would always be independent of one another, they would live in eternal discord, and their partnership [société] could not exist. (*Emile*, 377)

The freedom that should, according to Rousseau, inform educational practices requires a balance between desires and powers. What Rousseau establishes in physical education is a corresponding balance between duties and abilities, between what one has to do socially and what one is capable of doing. Other elements of the *Emile* are directed at shaping people who will want to engage in these social tasks. Thus seen, the different physical programs have several principles in common and do relate, for both sexes, to social freedom. These themes receive further elaboration below.

ECONOMIC INDEPENDENCE

A second aspect of Emile's self-sufficiency is economic independence; he can provide for himself. The possession of marketable skills has a seemingly obvious relationship to freedom. Money earned is purchasing power that gives one the option of satisfying certain needs and desires. Perhaps most importantly, earning power also frees one from degrading and dangerous dependencies, the compulsion to prostitute oneself to those whose money one needs. Emile learns many trades, following the self-sufficient and ingenious hero of the sole book presented to the young boy—*Robinson Crusoe*.

In this context Rousseau again returns to the theme of fate, of fortune's impartial and imperial unconcern with individual destinies.

Do you not see that in working to form him exclusively for one station you are making him useless for any other . . . ? You trust in the present order of society without thinking that this order is subject to inevitable revolutions. . . . Are the blows of fate so rare that you can count on being exempted from them? (*Emile*, 194)

Rousseau is attacking both class-specific and apprentice education. The former leaves one unprepared to meet the challenges presented by social and political changes. The antiaristocratic Rousseau finds this especially true among the wealthy. A narrow apprentice education is rejected for neglecting the person qua person in its quest for education of the person qua artisan.

Emile is prepared to support himself under a variety of conditions. His happiness is independent of the availability of any one specific vocation, and as an artisan he is most independent of others. It is for these reasons that Rousseau claims Emile's work "brings him closest to the state of nature" (*Emile*, 195).

Similar training for Sophie receives no mention at all. She is taught only the skills of household management, including cooking, sewing, cleaning, and keeping accounts. If Emile's training furthers his independence and flexibility, Sophie's seems to render her dependent and unprepared in the face of change. What if her husband, on whom she appears to be economically dependent, dies, is temporarily or permanently disabled, or cannot sell his labor or products at all or at a price sufficient to support his family? Perhaps Rousseau does not consider it necessary to teach Sophie a flexible trade, since her fortune and position will always depend directly on that of a man, and only indirectly on political conditions. But this only presents a larger problem. For Rousseau insists that "dependence on things, since it has no morality, is in no way detrimental to freedom and engenders no vices . . . [but] dependence on men, since it is without order [*désordonnée*], engenders all the vices, and by it, master and slave are mutually corrupted [*dépravent*]" (*Emile*, 85). It looks as though in Emile's education, as in politics, Rousseau goes to great lengths to banish dependence on particular individuals, in line with the lessons about freedom learned from the state of nature. But Sophie, the unfortunate representative of everywoman, appears to be left in a state of personal dependence, with no autonomous source of income and no skills with which to secure one if accidental circumstances should require it. And this is a condition that feminists, from Charlotte Perkins Gilman to Virginia Woolf to Betty Friedan, have readily and rightly condemned. The familiar arguments against it are that male "providers" possess disproportionately large shares of power and control over family matters, that women ill-treated by their husbands have more difficulty extricating themselves from the relationship due to economic constraints, and that women's economic dependence is a central element of her general dependence on men, contributing to the creation of a relationship between them that often is structurally more like that of adult and child than of two equal adults.

It is too early yet to draw conclusions about the applicability of such arguments to Rousseau's sexual politics; the extent to which the situation that they address and that Rousseau endorses are the same is not yet sufficiently clear. For the present, I will show how the usual account of the inequality of the two sexes regarding a trade can be challenged on several grounds from within the context of Rousseau's own politics. First, while there is a sense in which Emile's occupations make him freer, from Rousseau's perspective the very need for a trade, and the division of labor upon which it rests, signals a loss of freedom. Even one involved in the stablest of crafts must be sensitive to the market, scientific advances, and customers' desires. Rousseau writes elsewhere, "An author who would brave the general taste would soon write for himself alone" (d' Alembert, 19). One with useless or outmoded products, or unsatisfied customers, fails to make a living. Emile is caught in the "chains" of society by his dependence on science, the market, and other individuals. While given relatively stable means of supporting himself, and crafts not subject to much division of labor, Emile stands at quite a distance from the perfectly free, self-sufficient natural savage.

The opposite argument can be made regarding Sophie. That is, the fact that Emile's trade thrusts him more deeply into the social world and thus makes him more dependent on others raises the interesting and perhaps surprising issue of whether Sophie might not actually be freer than Emile. In her distance from the public world and its division of labor, Sophie is closer to the happy state of nature than is Emile. Her work is more connected with satisfaction of true needs and less dependent on others for its completion. The most coherent interpretation of the text comes from seeing the difference here as part of an attempt by Rousseau to distribute fairly between the sexes what he sees as the benefits and burdens of social life. Each has less freedom in certain areas, more in others, just as each is rendered dependent on the other in different ways. This theme will receive further elaboration later, especially in chapter 5.

The perception of Emile as free because of his access to a trade, and of Sophie as enslaved by her lack thereof, can be challenged in a second way. It can be argued that Sophie's training in household management is comparable to Emile's training as a craftsperson. With her skills, Sophie is prepared to perform her social duty, managing a household, and to do so under any conditions, just as Emile is prepared to perform his. Further, there seems to be no basis for saying that as "housewives" women are dependent while as "breadwinners" men are self-sufficient. It is an unjustifiable assumption, and one not obviously made by Rousseau, that in their sex-specific roles women contribute less to their own survival, the maintenance of the household, the welfare of offspring, or the well-being of society, than do men. Simply consider the life of Rousseau's woman. She grows, preserves, and prepares food, weaves material and turns it into clothing, nurses, manages, keeps accounts, and educates. It is not obvious that with these skills she is really more dependent on a man than he is on her, is less prepared than he to adapt to a changing world, or is any less a contributor to society.

Lastly, when Rousseau discusses the trades he would like Emile to learn, he rejects some that do not "suit his sex." While the topic arises only indirectly and is not given much emphasis, there are some means of earning an income, such as "sewing and the needle trades" (*Emile*, 199) which are not inappropriate for women. Rousseau does not encourage women to engage in them, but they do exist. Moreover, Sophie needs no additional training for such work, for as a wife and mother she is equipped with skills marketable in the paid labor force.

Both sexes are thus prepared for the roles they will adopt in Rousseau's legitimate state. Neither sex is, can be, or ought to be made totally self-sufficient. According to him, each is given a set of equally useful, and thus equally valuable, skills necessary for the survival and well-being of familial and political communities. From Rousseau's nonacquisitive, nonindividualistic standpoint, for both sexes possession of these skills is in some ways liberating, in other ways enchaining. For both, preparation for their "vocational duties" involves denaturing, direction, and limitation, as well as perfection of hitherto dormant capacities and the possibilities of community.

FREEDOM FROM PUBLIC OPINION AND AUTHORITY

He is taught to be able to think free from the binding prejudices of society, but she is taught to accept authority without thinking.[11]

Perhaps no theme in the *Emile* seems more pervasive and central, or more passionately advocated, than that of Emile's independence from public opinion. In Rousseau's writings conformity to opinion and unquestioning acquiescence to authority are linked with everything from superficial and deceitful personal relations to self-interested and despotic politics. Scorn is thus duly heaped upon their influence, in education as in everyday life.[12]

Resistance to authority relates to independence and power in several ways. First, if people are accustomed simply to accept the word of others, as opposed to finding out for themselves, they "believe much and never . . . know anything" (*Emile*, 125). One need not reason or experiment if another is willing simply to reveal the answer, or if one can resort to following directions. The consequences of this, Rousseau thinks, are startling. If so raised, Emile would fail to learn to take responsibility for himself; "habit and obedience [would] take the place of [his] reason" (*Emile*, 118), and he would be unable to distinguish between good and bad advice, leaving him an easy prey. He would, finally, be not only in need of others but at their mercy.

Operating by habit and obedience rather than reason also leaves one less able to respond to new situations. Yet we have seen Rousseau stress preparedness in the face of the changing and unknown. So important is this that he sees the harm of learning from opinion and authority as greater than ignorance: "I prefer a hundred times over his being ignorant . . . to your having to tell . . . him" (*Emile*, 148).

The goal of "authenticity" also seems to have a part in Rousseau's condemnation of opinion, authority, and prejudice. Concerned with avoiding education that produces people "appearing to relate everything to others and never relating anything except to themselves alone" (*Emile*, 41), he writes that "to be oneself and always one, a man must act as he speaks" (*Emile*, 40). A connection seems to exist between authenticity and harmony on the one hand, and refusal to be a slave of fashion on the other. This link between honesty and independence is evident in Rousseau's educational practices: "It is quite clear that the more I make his [Emile's] well-being independent of either the will or the judgments of others, the more I reduce any interest in him to lie" (*Emile*, 103).

On the practical level, Emile learns by trial and error, by experimentation rather than by memorization or reading and listening to authorities. Habituated to thinking for himself, Emile knows that it is in fact possible to solve problems by himself, and sees such a procedure as the norm in daily life. This training encourages independence, autonomy, and authenticity.

This indifference to authority, opinion, and prejudice is a cornerstone of Emile's preparation for freedom. Yet Rousseau practically boasts that it is an indifference appropriate to males only:

When a man acts well, he depends only on himself and can brave public judgment; but when a woman acts well, she has accomplished only half of her task, and what is thought of her *[ce que l'on pense d'elle]* is no less important to her than what she actually is *[ce qu'elle est en effet]*. . . . Opinion is the grave of virtue among men and its throne among women. (*Emile*, 364–65)

Unlike Emile, in deciding upon a course of action Sophie must not only consult her reason and conscience but must consider what others will think as well. She lacks that radical freedom which arises from exercising the power to decide for oneself how to think and act and is described as having "been taught from her childhood nothing so much as to adjust herself *[s'accommoder]* to the people with whom she had to live" (*Emile*, 404).

In Emile's training Rousseau rejects education using appeals to authority and giving answers before the student first tries to secure them independently. But Sophie's education seems to exclude practices bolstering independent thought and self-reliance. Take her religious education as an example:

Due to the very fact that in her conduct woman is enslaved *[asservie]* by public opinion, in her belief she is enslaved by authority. Every girl ought to have her mother's religion, and every woman her husband's. . . . Since authority ought to rule the religion of women, the issue is not so much one of explaining to them the reasons there are for believing as of explaining distinctly what we believe. (*Emile*, 377–78)

That is (despite the Savoyard Vicar's argument that objective reasons for belief do not exist), Emile has the opportunity to wonder and decide for himself about such issues, while Sophie is merely told to follow the religion of her parents and husband.

Sophie's careful training in sensitivity to others implies that the lesson of submitting to the necessity of things but never to the wills of others is intended for males only. In an apparently radical departure from his earlier position, Rousseau states that women must submit to the wills of others; "they have—or ought to have—little freedom" (*Emile*, 369–70). Emile is taught that the "world of things" is beyond his control, but that otherwise he is captain of his ship. Sophie is taught to believe she has no freedom to exert against the world of things or against other people's wills. Rousseau writes of women that

> they never cease to be subjected either to a man or to the judgments of men and they are never permitted to put themselves above these judgments. . . . [S]he ought to learn early to endure even injustice and to bear a husband's wrongs *[supporter les torts]* without complaining. (*Emile*, 370)

It looks as if Emile's education is structured to produce a resourceful person of independent thought and action, as immune to external influences as possible, while Sophie's is devised to produce a person sensitive and submissive to the views of others, especially their views of her—a person possessing as little independence of thought and action as possible. Yet it is still possible to argue that the contrast here is in fact only superficial.

First of all, the bald statement that Emile is trained to be free from all opinion flies in the face of the fact that he is to be a citizen. As Leo Strauss writes, opinion

> is the basis of society. . . . According to Rousseau, civil society is essentially a particular, or more precisely a closed, society. . . . Civil society requires conformance . . . compared with man's [*sic*] natural independence, all society is therefore a form of bondage.[13]

Rousseau writes in the *Social Contract*: "Man was/is born free, and everywhere he is in chains. . . . How did this change occur? I do not know. What can make it legitimate? I believe I can answer this question" (*SC*, 46). His goal is not to break all social "chains" but to allow only those which are "legitimate." As a citizen of a closed society, Emile must be subjected to opinions that attach people to their community. "Adam was sovereign of the world, like Crusoe of his island, [only] as long as he was its only inhabitant" (*SC*, 48).

It is erroneous to suppose that Rousseau simply dismisses opinion across the board. While without doubt he wants to limit or destroy its more pernicious manifestations and effects, he knows that opinion, especially in the form of *les moeurs,* is essential to society.

> [One form of law is] the most important of all; which is not engraved on marble or bronze, but in the hearts of the citizens; which . . . preserves a people in the spirit of its institution, and imperceptibly substitutes the force of habit for that of authority. I am speaking of mores, customs, and especially of opinion—a part of the laws unknown to our political theorists, but on which the success of all the others depends. (SC, 77)

Operating almost invisibly through habit, opinion both reduces the need for resort to external authority and positively attaches citizens to their communities. It is utterly indispensable for both sexes.

Emile's submission to opinion does not begin when he becomes an adult citizen. Even as a child he is subjected to others' wills. "Children, even in the state of nature, enjoy only an imperfect freedom, similar to that enjoyed by men in the civil state" (*Emile,* 85). Emile is as manipulated by his education as Sophie is by hers. All Rousseau does is take pains to conceal this fact from him.

> There is no subjection so perfect as that which keeps the appearance of freedom. . . . Doubtless he ought to do only what he wants; but he ought to want only what you want him to do. He ought not to make a step without your having foreseen it; he ought not to open his mouth without your knowing what he is going to say. (*Emile,* 120; also 171, 185)

One could hardly desire a bolder admission of conscious manipulation and control. As Allan Bloom remarks, "The tutor and his helpers must disappear, as it were, and everything that happens to the child must *seem* to be an inevitable effect of nature."[14] The tutor systematically tricks Emile into thinking, for instance, that nature rather than the tutor has disciplined him, or that refusals are always based entirely on the impossibility of satisfying the request rather than on changeable human will.[15]

As Emile is much more subject to opinions than has often been thought, so Sophie is not so totally subjected to them as she is frequently portrayed. Rousseau says that "*up to the age* when reason is enlightened, and when nascent sentiment makes the conscience speak, what is good or bad for young girls is what the people around them have decided it to be" (*Emile,* 381, emphasis added). Sophie has early exposure to the mores of her culture, but this does not mean that she is left with no means by which to question opinion or convention. "Finally the moment comes when [girls] begin to judge things by themselves, and then it is time to *change the plan* of their education" (*Emile*, 382, emphasis added).

Rousseau clearly states that for both sexes inner sentiment judges convention, and that if the two conflict inner sentiment is authoritative (*Emile*, 382–83). His position on Sophie's subjection to opinion seems more moderate, and more similar to his position on Emile's subjection, when he says

As soon as she depends on both her own conscience and the opinions of others, she has to learn to compare these two rules, to reconcile them, and to prefer the former only when the two are in contradiction. She becomes the judge of her judges. (*Emile*, 383)

Saying she is to prefer the dictates of conscience to those of opinion *only* when the two disagree amounts to saying she is to prefer conscience *whenever* the two conflict and, further, implies that her conscience is always active and critical. Thus, one could conclude that Sophie, like Emile, is never to follow opinion when she judges it to be in error and, again like Emile, is to listen to and consider it respectfully, out of affection, habit, and obligation. If for no other reasons than that the trends of a given time may corrupt them, and that part of their task is to shield children from the "crushing force of social conventions," Rousseau absolutely rejects an educational program for women that gives them no law but convention or prejudice.[16]

Rousseau's position acknowledges that as social and political creatures, it is both impossible and undesirable for either women or men to be completely impervious to the forces of opinion and authority. His strategy seems to be one that, given the force of self-interest, trains people to bestow the benefit of the doubt upon the community. But, given the destructive potential of authority and opinion, it is also a strategy that grants both sexes the means and the right to challenge them in the name of morality and integrity. Checks on self-interestedness do not always assume the same form for both sexes, since the forms their self-interestedness take vary according to their different social roles. Similarly, the same check does not always exist to the same degree for the two sexes, since other checks operating on one sex may make it unnecessary. Still, the ends for both are the same, and the means are similar.

DESIRES

Thus far I have examined only the "powers" half of the happiness ratio; the other part, "desires," remains. Rousseau warns, "[D]o not fancy that in extending your faculties you extend your strength. On the contrary, you diminish your strength if your pride is extended farther than it" (*Emile*, 81). To be free and happy it is necessary not only to develop one's powers, which are finite, but also to limit one's potentially unlimited desires in due proportion. Rousseau assumes that, like powers, desires are greatly influenced by social forces, and he sees their training as a legitimate and crucial political task. It may well be that in discussions of Rousseau's sexual politics this subject is especially important and revealing.

Controlling Emile's desires is achieved in part by teaching him to submit to or accept the inevitable and immovable. He must "at an early date feel the harsh yoke which nature imposes on man, the heavy yoke of necessity under which every finite being must bend. Let him see this necessity in things, never in the caprice of men" (*Emile*, 91).

As we now know, while Emile is only to see this necessity in things, in fact it comes from the wills of others as well. If seen as such, however, Emile is likely to resist it. He learns to resign himself to what is presented and *perceived* as necessity. His training goes beyond lessons, for example, about accepting disease and death, to understandings about property and sex —explicitly social constructions in Rousseau's political thought. Whatever the lessons of necessity, in teaching them as such to Emile Rousseau says, "you will make him patient, steady, resigned, calm, even when he has not got what he wanted, for it is in the nature of man [sic] to endure patiently the necessity of things but not the ill will of others" (*Emile*, 91).

Rousseau also discusses curbing Emile's potentially boundless imagination for the sake of happiness. Imagination can make us miserable in numerous ways. We can be frustrated by imagining things as other than they must be. Imagination can exaggerate risks and damages, leaving us immobile and overly fearful. And as an escape, imagination can steer us away from hardships which we in fact can and ought to overcome. While not discouraging curiosity and inventiveness, Rousseau directs Emile's imaginings in a way compatible with maintaining the equilibrium between what he wants and what is in his power to obtain in a given situation.

Disparaging luxury and wealth is yet another means toward reducing and controlling desires. Rousseau's rejection of modes of living which revolve around the procurement of wealth is in part a rejection of insecure social status and uncertain power. The potentially fleeting nature of riches and, therefore, of social status derived from their possession leads Rousseau to advocate a "maximin" strategy. None should feel immune to crises and revolutions in the social order, and everyone should be prepared to ground their status in more certain and secure personal qualities, such as inner strength, goodness, and ingenuity. Rousseau thus advocates a secular version of "There but for the grace of God go I"; he extends the range in which pity will operate from the natural condition to the political and economic world. This, like the admonition to "Accept that which you cannot change," limits the range and number of Emile's desires.

Lastly, to keep the number of Emile's desires at a minimum, Rousseau attempts to foster only "true" needs in the child. This includes needs which have as their object the necessities of life, needs which can be satisfied without the assistance of others, and needs whose object is something useful. While this conception of true needs arises from Rousseau's portrayal of the state of nature, even in civil society his intent is to exclude needs arising only from pride, from a desire to be esteemed and to see oneself and be seen as superior to others in honor, wealth, or reputation. The attempt to satisfy such needs can cause one either to exploit others or to become dependent on them in debilitating and degrading ways. Rousseau's project of restraining those desires at the outset is one founded on the requirements of stable and legitimate social relations. It is a project vastly different from that of Hobbes and Locke, who agree that such desires cause conflict but who nevertheless invite them into civil society, and then offer governmental protection against their most severe personal consequences.

Practically speaking, the educator trains Emile to know and accept the limits of his own powers and the limits imposed by the existence of other individuals and the community. He is taught that not all desires are realizable or legitimate, whether they arise from within or from the latest flux in popular opinion.

The project of restraining desires, one half of the balance necessary for freedom and happiness, proceeds in much the same way for the two sexes. Statements pulled from the *Emile*, such as "[Girls] must be exercised in constraint, so that it never costs them anything" (369), are frequently cited as quick and easy proof of Rousseau's harsh brand of antifeminism.[17] These citations are problematical, however, for they fail to address the fact that

Rousseau consistently makes similar statements with respect to males, political statements that reflect his understanding of the human condition.

This fact ought to receive more attention, because it reveals that both sexes are being directed, limited, and generally prepared for social life by education. While it often seems on the surface that Emile is to be left as free as nature presented him, and Sophie alone is to be channeled and restrained, it is to Emile that the tutor offers the following words of wisdom:

Restrain your heart within the limits (bournes) of your condition. Study and know these limits. However narrow they may be, a man is not unhappy as long as he closes himself up within them. (*Emile*, 445)

Rousseau seems to assume that the desires of both sexes can and must be manipulated and that such manipulation and limitation is compatible with happiness. Both sexes are taught to see such channeling as "natural" and thus are more apt to accept it and proceed from there. The channeling, again, is often different: men, for instance, are steered away from pursuit of wealth, women from the "public" sphere. The guiding principle, however, is the same: both are directed to learn to care for and be responsible to others. The condition of *both* sexes is marked by limitations. Restraint is the consequence and condition of social life. All that can and must be done is to make the necessary chains more legitimate and less painfully obvious.

Rousseau's perspective on the training of desires is more complicated and more hopeful than that of Hobbes. Rousseau insightfully notes that extended faculties are often accompanied by extended pride which, in practice, actually diminishes one's strength. Hobbes makes an interesting observation about pride: vainglory "is most incident to young men."[18] Males are more likely, according to Hobbes, to think more highly of themselves than is warranted and to want others to agree with their overinflated self-perceptions. Since Hobbes treats vainglory as one of the primary causes of war, the prideful male turns out to be the most common troublemaker. Rousseau's solution to this differs from that of Hobbes. By trying to train desires themselves, Rousseau aims to control vainglory and thereby to change the now competitive character of human relations, founded on the model of the Hobbesian male. Among other things, given Hobbes's observation about men and pride, Rousseau's strategy can be read as a positive "feminization" of men.

CONCLUSION

The argument that the educations of Sophie and Emile are totally dissimilar in philosophy as well as in practice is a weak one. While the discussion here does not add up to a comprehensive treatment of Rousseau's educational schemes, the themes I have addressed are representative, significant, and popular in secondary literature. They are adequate to reveal the fundamental flaws in the familiar view this quote represents:

> Between Emile's education and that which Sophie receives, there is more than a contrast, there is an abyss. Rousseau emancipated Emile; he enslaves Sophie. To the same degree that he showed himself bold in his views on the "foundation" of men, is he timid, backward and conservative in his ideas on woman's education.[19]

Establishing the important similarities and connections between the educations of women and men allows for a more coherent interpretation of Rousseau's work. Both sexes are acknowledged to go through various developmental stages that must be respected in education. For both, the limits and wonder of childhood are respected, and both are taught that which will be useful in their (different) adult lives. Each is given both sensitivity to opinion and some means of resisting it. Both are resourceful, neither is self-sufficient.

Despite its subtitle—*or, On Education*—Rousseau's *Emile*, as he himself hints, concerns more than pedagogy in the narrow sense. It addresses issues, for example, of human nature and the character of social existence and was considered by Rousseau his "greatest and best work" (OC 1:687). Recent attention to the political nature of the *Emile* is surely justified and long overdue. By emphasizing the common threads in the educations of the two sexes, rather than focusing exclusively on the technical aspects of Rousseau's educational schemes, it is easier to place the *Emile* in its proper political context.

What, then, do Rousseau's sexually differentiated educations tell us about his politics, and especially about his conception of freedom? In arguing that Emile is not as free, nor Sophie as enslaved, as is frequently held, one raises the question of whether anyone is really free in Rousseau's scheme. That is, if we are now to understand Emile as being as manipulated, controlled, and directed as Sophie, do we rescue Rousseau, egalitarian, at the expense of Rousseau, advocate of freedom?[20]

Perhaps a good place to start is with an understanding of what Rousseau's freedom is *not*, as evinced in the educations of Sophie and Emile. First, it is not the independence of the natural savage. For Rousseau, the possibility of self-sufficient survival has been irretrievably lost. Thus, the social freedom of Emile and Sophie, who are taught to be dependent upon and accountable to others, does not consist of such things as the independent determination and satisfaction of one's desires or of the absence of sustained ties and moral obligations to others.

Second, Rousseau's freedom is not found in the natural unfolding of individual potential. Despite his persistent association with "negative education," viewing Rousseau as a wholehearted adherent of a "follow nature" philosophy is erroneous. A negative education *is* endorsed, but only for certain ages and lessons. Rousseau assumes that it is both possible (because human nature is perfectible and malleable) and necessary (because of original asociality and indolence) to mold human nature through dialectical interaction with various environmental forces, in order to adapt it to the unnatural though legitimate demands of social life. While nature is not exactly silent, it does not equip us exclusively or sufficiently with skills and inclinations that teach us how to live well together: "[F]rom the little care taken by nature to bring men together through mutual needs and to facilitate their use of speech, one at least sees how little it prepared their sociability, and how little it contributed to everything men have done to establish social bonds" (SD, 126). Thus, the social freedom of Emile and Sophie, who are carefully socialized, is not equated with freedom from restraint or the absence of external direction.

Third, interpretations of Rousseau as a liberal notwithstanding, his freedom is not the autonomy of "bourgeois" individuals. It is not how to survive independently that people need so much to be taught, but how to cooperate, to sacrifice, to go beyond the self to a community with a common good. The pursuit of self-interest, Rousseau adamantly argues, fails to provide a solid basis for community and inevitably leads to everything from fragmented families and false friendships to exploitative politics and dishonest business dealings. Such costs, Rousseau would maintain, are the ones we can least afford; they would, according to his logic, actually render us unfree.

What *is* left of freedom as it existed in the state of nature is twofold. First, that slavery which was impossible and useless in the state of nature is also to be consciously avoided in society as morally unjustifiable, and this applies, among other things, to enslavement based on sex. Freedom thus requires that the social structure not leave some at the mercy of self-interested others, or dependent on a particular, selfish, prideful will. None can be impoverished or systematically exploited. Sophie is not a helpless slave, and Emile is not a tyrant, benevolent or otherwise. Both are to see themselves as parts of larger wholes, to which they contribute and from which they receive necessary and desirable benefits, and both women's and men's educations can be seen as furthering this viewpoint.

Second, freedom as a balance between needs and desires is central to both the state of nature and the civil state, as has been explored above. It is still possible, for both sexes, to talk of a freedom won by simultaneous self-restraint and self-development, possible to work for that equilibrium that came effortlessly to natural savages. The failure to recognize this possibility in the schema of the *Emile* may arise from a tendency to apply the understanding and values of our time too quickly to Rousseau. For example, the fact that certain of Sophie's faculties remain undeveloped does not allow us automatically to conclude that she is stunted and unhappy, while Emile is free and satisfied. By Rousseau's standards, one's closeness to the state of nature, manifested in part by undeveloped faculties, may be an asset: "the closer to his natural condition man has stayed, the smaller is the difference between his faculties and his desires, and consequently the less removed he is from being happy" (*Emile*, 81). Also, the author of the *First Discourse* by no means thinks so highly of intellectual development as we often do today and does not believe that fulfillment can only be found in the so-called public world. He does not exclusively or always value what is considered traditional male work, priorities, or skills. There is no appeal by Rousseau to any hierarchy of values that would lead us to conclude that he sees the roles of the sexes as differing in the extent to which they require both development and restraint, or in the compatibility of each role with a balance between desires and powers.

If freedom is defined as a balance between powers and desires, then the extent of one's powers is irrelevant as long as they are proportionate to one's desires, which, as we have seen, are themselves the objects of socialization. To the extent that freedom is associated with this equilibrium, and not with any substantive state (other than that which is not slavery), it seems that what is important is *feeling* free. Feeling free consists at least in not wanting that which is outside one's power to get and "in never doing what [one] does not want to do."[21] Education must not only restrain our desires but teach us to want to do what we can and must do, so that we may feel free.

Outside of this subjective feeling, whatever exists of freedom in Rousseau must be compatible with community. This limits freedom at the outset, as Rousseau tells us by insisting that his enterprise is to legitimize the chains of society, not to "lose" them. Rousseau sees this circumscription of freedom as painful; it is no insignificant or light matter to give up natural liberty. William Bluhm thus argues that for Rousseau, "the artificial state of society is incompatible with any version of the concept of freedom."[22]

Despite his pessimism, Rousseau may have believed that there was more than myth to social freedom, Bluhm notwithstanding. Looking at the educations of Emile and Sophie, with some light from other works, freedom in community can be seen as involving interdependence, participation, and limited sovereignty.

Interdependence is a sticky issue. Because independence is so strongly associated with freedom and happiness in the state of nature, interdependence in civil society looks, by contrast, simply like unfreedom and unhappiness. But Rousseau also views it as a gain, a "power," not unlike other powers—a feature of his thought generally unappreciated in the secondary literature.

In discussing the cause of departure from the state of nature, Rousseau speaks of how individual resources become inadequate to guarantee survival, while the union of individual resources makes survival possible. Our interdependence is a source of strength. It not only gives us access to the skills, ideas, and products of others but opens up all the possibilities of social life, including moral relations, bonds of affection, and development of our individual and human potentials. Obviously this does not come without inevitable costs and possible dangers. Rousseau's intent, as we will see, is to structure social life so as to render the good consequences more probable and the bad less so, and to have the good and bad balance out in such a way that, overall, interdependence is a benefit. While no person of either sex can any longer think only of, rely only upon, or work only for themselves, none is to be selfless or subjugated either. Social freedom in Rousseau is to be compensated for and moderated by the rewards and demands of community and equality.

Participation is another component of Rousseau's social freedom. His view seems to be that subjection to the community differs formally and substantively from subjection to a self-interested master, which he deplores. Subjection to the common good, in the family and the state, is freedom limited by fairness and concern for others, and is perhaps not so small or mythical in groups where all are trained and constrained to abide by its demands. And having some say in the determination of the general will is reminiscent of classic understandings of freedom, where participation and the possibility of affecting politics is essential to being free. Women, of course, do not participate in Rousseau's sovereign assembly, but he claims that they are still central political actors, a claim I return to later.

Lastly, Rousseau does not endorse creation of a sovereign will that rules on every matter, though where that will speaks it is authoritative. He never attempts what he sees as the impossible task of obliterating private will. It is also worth remembering that he advocated, against the customs of his day, that decisions such as those regarding vocations and marriage be less under the control of class systems and parental authority and more under the control of the individual.

From studying the similarities in the training of Sophie and Emile, however, a certain pessimism about the compromises and insecurity of social life surfaces. Rousseau emphasizes the need for both sexes to be accustomed to suffering, whether from physical discomfort or from injustice, and he repeatedly mentions the flux and uncertainty of modern life that both sexes will encounter. Of course, if one is prepared to face the given reality of "the world of social things," one may, as Rousseau urges, be more resigned, have more attainable desires, and thus may be, as he would say, at least less unhappy.

The author of the *Emile* knew his work to be full of puzzles but did not think it internally inconsistent. Focusing on its oft-neglected program of women's education reveals that while Rousseau's educational programs for women and men are often substantively different, they consistently appeal to identical understandings of the human condition and human development, freedom and dependence, and happiness and suffering.[23] Interpretations of both Emile's and Sophie's educations must be corrected in terms of this political and philosophical framework.

The reading offered here of Rousseau's programs for male and female education is supported by its ability to bring internal coherence to the *Emile* and to bring the principles of the *Emile* into agreement with those of Rousseau's other works. But what has been reconciled almost exclusively concerns theories and principles rather than practice. And I will argue later,

Producing Gender   **35**

especially in chapter 6, that Rousseau's scheme cannot realize in practice the commitments it makes in theory.

For example, while the evidence is quite convincing that in theory Rousseau sees both women's and men's educations as committed to avoiding the twin evils of self-absorption and enslavement, I will argue later that in practice the attainment of this ideal middle ground is hindered rather than promoted by the dynamics of various gendered relationships. Similarly, while Rousseau moves away from a male-biased hierarchy of values in theory, and therefore appreciates the traditional contributions of women to families and societies, in practice his preferred gender arrangement will resurrect and reinforce that male hierarchy. Other issues raised here, to be evaluated later, include the dangers of using "feeling free" as a standard, the calculations involved in Rousseau's cost-benefit analysis of sex roles, the consequences of an all-male assembly, and the precautions taken to keep gendered relations from degenerating into male-dominated ones.

There is good reason to be suspicious of the creation and enforcement of systematic differences. "Difference" is often nothing more than a more palatable name for inequality. Justified skepticism, however, is not the same thing as proof that all avoidable differences are damnable. Some differences, such as cultural ones, can be enriching. Assimilation and uniformity are clearly not always to be preferred.

To see whether Rousseau's sexual politics are defensible or not, we need to explore more deeply the question of why he endorses sexual differentiation, and with what effects. His educational programs may be theoretically consistent, but are they necessary, desirable, and workable? I look next at the claim that Rousseau educates the sexes differently simply because he believes there are "natural" sex differences that leave him no choice, and argue that such a claim overlooks the political ends of sex roles through its overemphasis on the biological.

THREE

ANATOMY AND DESTINY: ROUSSEAU, ANTIFEMINISM, AND WOMAN'S NATURE

The educations of women and men endorsed by Rousseau are not based on incompatible philosophies of education or politics. The two schemes are, however, different. Theoretical consistency does not diminish the fact that in Rousseau's thought no characteristic other than sex so completely determines the education and, consequently, the life of an individual. Women are confined to the private sphere, consumed with the duties of wife and mother and limited to indirect access to power. Men have the duties of husband and father, but also participate fully in public life as tradespersons and citizens and are taught and allowed to express their thoughts and desires openly. Rousseau is clearly an advocate of sex roles, given that "a role is . . . an institutionalized sex role only if it is performed exclusively by persons of a particular sex *and* societal factors tend to encourage this correlation."[1]

While one can assert without controversy that Rousseau advocates a "traditional," radically sex-roled society, dispute remains about why he does so.[2] It has been said that Rousseau's sexual division of labor reflects an attempt to establish sexual equality, but also that it is an attempt to establish male freedom at woman's expense. His position has variously been attributed to his disposition, to his belief in women's inferiority, and to his concerns, separately, about war, citizenship, paternity, and sexuality.

Interestingly, however, despite the generally irreconcilable interpretations offered, all seem to agree that Rousseau sees the sexes as different by nature, and diverge primarily in their accounts of what sex differences he posits as central—whether women are seen as more or less sexual, intelligent, self-sufficient, or physically strong, for example, than men. Perhaps the difficulty in locating what differences are decisive for Rousseau arises because the question being asked is the wrong one.

The most promising strand in the literature that has blossomed with the contemporary feminist movement has emphasized the part that Rousseau's views on the sexes plays in his general politics. This perspective has received its most thorough treatment in Joel Schwartz's *The Sexual Politics of Jean-Jacques Rousseau*, where it is argued that Rousseau advocates sexual differentiation in part because of the effects on politics that he perceives to arise from various relationships between the sexes. Schwartz's book, however, retains the basic assumption that Rousseau believes the sexes have radically different natures. Yet if Rousseau's advocacy of separate spheres for women and men is justified in his thought by its political consequences, then it is necessary to question the extent to which, if at all, Rousseau believes that the sexes are different by nature in any politically relevant sense.

Rousseau is an advocate of sex roles, and most people tend to assume that at the basis of every socially prescribed sexual division of labor lies a belief in natural sexual differentiation. Alison Jaggar, for example, characterizes arguments used by proponents of sex roles as follows:

All claim that men and women should fulfill different social functions, that these differences should be enforced by law where opinion and custom are insufficient, and that such action may be justified by reference to innate differences between men and women. Thus all sexual conservatives presuppose that men and women are inherently unequal in abilities, that the alleged difference in ability implies a difference in social function, and that one of the main tasks of the state is to ensure that the individual perform his or her proper social function.[3]

While Jaggar's model is certainly an accurate representation of many defenses of sex roles, and accords with some intuitive understandings of anti-feminism, it is simply incapable of explaining Rousseau's advocacy of sex roles. For Rousseau can be most clearly understood as saying that the sexes are *not* relevantly differentiated by nature, but that sex differences can and should be created, encouraged, and enforced because of their social consequences, which he considers to be both necessary and beneficial. The claim that Rousseau's sexual scheme is political in nature is greatly strengthened by recognition of the fact that he sees the natures of the sexes as essentially alike but extremely malleable. Further, because Rousseau's sexual scheme is wholly normative and not based upon a deterministic view of sex differences, it offers a valuable perspective from which to reassess his political priorities and concerns, including his advocacy of sex roles themselves.

Feminist literature has carefully defended the view that advocacy of feminist goals is not dependent on the belief that there are no natural differences between the sexes.[4] For example, because nature cannot be taken to be prescriptive in every sense without further argument, it is not possible simply to move from the "is" of sex differences—whatever they might be—to the "ought" of different social roles. The reverse can also be true, and is true for Rousseau; that is, a belief in natural, politically relevant sex differences is not necessarily at the foundation of every endorsed sexual division of labor. The general understanding of antifeminist thought needs to be broadened to encompass thinkers who, like Rousseau, advocate sex roles because of their perceived social utility rather than because such roles are thought to be biologically determined. Too much antifeminist argument is left unanswered without this enlargement.

In the following four sections I examine Rousseau's views on possible sex differences in physical strength, mental abilities, reproductive capacities, and interests. While these are not the only sex differences antifeminists cite, they are among the most common, and exploring them is sufficient to show that Rousseau does not believe that natural sex differences are at the root of his sexually differentiated educational programs. My argument is primarily a negative one, consisting of refutations of claims frequently made about Rousseau. In each section I allude to Rousseau's positive argument—that is, to why he advocates sex roles despite his lack of belief in natural sexual differentiation—but detailed discussion of his actual stance is reserved for later chapters.

My aim in this chapter is to show that while Rousseau clearly endorses what is often called the privatization of women, he does not do so because he believes that woman's nature somehow limits her to domestic tasks while man's nature does not so restrict him. A system of strongly differentiated sex roles need not rest on assumptions about the inferiority or even the essential "otherness" of woman's nature. Rousseau encourages sexual differentiation for specific political ends, and by refuting the claim that he believes in natural sexual differentiation we can in fact arrive at a clearer understanding of those ends.

PHYSICAL STRENGTH

For Rousseau the physical strength of the human male . . . indicates that nature intended he should dominate, and the female should submit in sexual encounters. This is, in fact, the first and most basic supposition on which the argument of *Emile* book V will rest.[5]

The claim that men are physically stronger than women is commonly used both as an explanation of how males have attained and maintained dominance and as a justification for that dominance. The superiority of male force is seen as rendering men fit for certain tasks that women are unable to perform, as making women dependent on men, or as making women more vulnerable to exploitation than are men. Despite the citation above, however, such arguments are not at the root of Rousseau's advocacy of sex roles.

First, some minor points. To argue that Rousseau relegates women to the private sphere because of their relative physical weakness implies that he is hopelessly inconsistent and oblivious to some very simple facts. It seems fair to assume that just as it is obvious to casual observers today, it was also obvious to Rousseau that even if most men are stronger than most women, many men and women are of roughly equal physical ability, and some women are stronger than some men. Only if Rousseau's highest priority is efficiency would it make some sense for him to exclude women from certain activities based on average sexual differences in physical strength, for concern with efficiency might dictate that since men are generally stronger, an unbiased search for the fittest is not worth the trouble. But efficiency is not an overriding or even an especially important consideration in Rousseau's thought. Also, Rousseau does not make distinctions among males on the basis of strength (very old and very small men are still full citizens, for example), and he does not weigh other physical attributes which might be construed as relevant to an assessment of general fitness, attributes which in fact might indicate that the female is the fitter sex.[6] Rousseau is up to something more subtle than incorrectly assuming a perfect correlation between the male sex and physical strength.

Theoretically, Rousseau is committed to the principle that might does not make right.

Force is a physical power. I do not see what morality can result from its effects. Yielding to force is an act of necessity, not of will. At most, it is an act of prudence

40 Anatomy and Destiny

> . . . . [A]s soon as one can disobey without punishment, one can do so legitimately. . . . Let us agree, therefore, that might does not make right, and that one is only obligated to obey legitimate powers. (SC, 48–49)

According to Rousseau, even men's average superior strength constitutes no more legitimate claim to rule over women than the gun of a thief grants a right to someone's goods. Furthermore, his assertion that the social contract "substitutes a moral and legitimate equality for whatever physical inequality nature may have placed between men" (SC, 58) means that any preexisting physical inequalities are not to be a basis for social inequality—that Rousseau's polity is committed to making politically irrelevant whatever differences in strength, including sex-based ones, might exist.

Thus, even if Rousseau assumes that women in general are physically weaker than men, by his own principles no social or political inequality necessarily or legitimately results. But there is an even stronger argument to make: Rousseau does not find women to be naturally weak at all; rather, he intentionally makes them weak. That is, women's weakness is not the necessary *cause* of their social role but rather is the intentional *result* of it. Rousseau believes that it is useful to differentiate the sexes on the basis of physical strength and that he can do so without creating great imbalance in the relations between them.

For example, in discussing women's (in)ability to be soldiers Rousseau does not say that women are inherently too weak for the task. Rather, he claims that a person cannot "suddenly go from shade, enclosure, and domestic cares to the harshness of the open air, the labors, the fatigues, and the perils of war" (*Emile*, 362). He is doing nothing more than making the commonsense observation that those who are accustomed to a relatively "soft" way of life cannot "suddenly" adapt (but presumably could gradually adapt) to the quite different life of a soldier. In saying this he is not attributing to women's nature the fact that they "never endured the sun and hardly know how to walk" (*Emile*, 362). Instead, this lack of fitness for soldiering is part of Rousseau's prescription for women's lives. Rousseau devises a life for women which *renders* them weaker, and his own description of savage woman's ability to preserve herself and her children against beasts and the elements without assistance is evidence that he knows things can be otherwise (SD, 108–9, 112). More generally, it is impossible to understand Rousseau's educational program for females without reference to the forms of physical strength he believes women should have and the forms he considers unnecessary and undesirable. The same Rousseau who claims that children's supposed incapacities to perform certain games is due only to want of practice (*Emile*, 147), the Rousseau who dedicates so much of Emile's early education to training in physical endurance and strength, cannot and does not claim that women are naturally and inherently weak when, as he knows, his educational program deprives them of all training unrelated to the abilities to be graceful and to bear healthy children (*Emile*, 365–66). What Rousseau stresses is not that male and female bodies start out with very different capacities for strength, but that "the *aim [l'objet]* of this cultivation [of the body] is different" for the two sexes (*Emile*, 365, emphasis added), a theme explored in the previous chapter. Rousseau acknowledges that the degree of strength people possess is largely determined by the circumstances with which they are confronted and the extent to which they receive physical training (SD, 106–7, 127–28, 138, 189–91n.). Women's weakness, then, is truly the result, rather than the cause, of their Rousseauean social role.

Schwartz argues that Rousseau considered the sexes to be different by nature because they have different bodies. This is a related argument, since one difference in those bodies concerns physical strength, and is worth considering. According to Schwartz, Rousseau "believes that the nature of our bodies decisively influences our experiences in the world and our reactions to the world."[7] Schwartz maintains that "the vital premise underlying the whole of Rousseau's discussion of the relation between the sexes" is Rousseau's "materialism."[8] But what Schwartz is identifying as Rousseau's materialism is no more than Rousseau's claim that things which affect the body also (consequently) affect the mind. This belief is probably better understood as a facet of Rousseau's environmentalism and is certainly distinct from and broader than the claim Schwartz attributes to Rousseau: that "bodily differences between males and females lead them to differ from one another in certain moral and emotional respects."[9] Further, Rousseau speaks of numerous influences on the body besides gender (climate, food, noise, etc.) and also points to the possibility of manipulating such forces to free ourselves and to encourage virtue.

The possibility that there is nothing natural or inevitable about sexual differences in physical strength is an idea shared by Rousseau and many feminists, for both understand that strength is affected by environmental factors and can be manipulated for social ends. They also agree that the existence of differences in physical strength need not lead to any social or political inequality. The two depart, however, when Rousseau urges that women's weakness be artificially cultivated, and used by women as a tool in their relations with men.

Rousseau's argument, to which I will respond later, is that although the development of male strength could potentially create an imbalance of power between the sexes, women's weakness rightly used can prevent that, can itself actually help reestablish balance while creating a useful attraction between the sexes. Women's apparent weakness, according to Rousseau, draws men to them and allows women to have male strength at their disposal, thereby canceling out any negative consequences of female weakness.

> Far from blushing at their weakness, they make it their glory. Their tender muscles are without resistance. They *pretend [affectent]* to be unable to lift the lightest burdens. They would be ashamed to be strong. Why is that? It is not only to *appear [paroitre]* delicate; it is due to a shrewder precaution. They prepare in advance excuses and the right to be weak in case of need. (*Emile*, 360, emphasis added)

It is not *necessary* for women to be strong because in Rousseau's scheme the male population is adequate for carrying out any social tasks for which strength is a prerequisite and because women can make use of men's strength. More important for understanding Rousseau, it is not *desirable* for women to be strong because men will be "more effective providers and defenders" if women are perceived by them as weak and dependent.[10] Just as children are helped by their weakness in that it motivates others to aid them (*Emile*, 38), so women's weakness properly employed will evoke male assistance rather than exploitation and will motivate men to undertake certain responsibilities.

Rousseau does not believe that women are weak by nature, but he cultivates weakness in them because it motivates men to perform necessary social tasks which, given the asociality and indolence of human nature, might otherwise remain undone or require less acceptable forms of motivation.[11] An effective scheme of sexual differentiation and interdependence may require that women be purposefully made, or at least made to seem, weak, but does not necessarily presuppose that woman's weakness is an unalterable facet of her nature, or a source of danger to her.

MENTAL CAPACITIES

Since men have the natural potential to reason independently of prejudice and to identify with the public good, they are citizens. Lacking such potential, women are meant to be man's helpmates and subjects.[12]

Regarding the actual mental capacity of women, Rousseau does what is rare for him: he confuses a social artifact with a natural quality, a lack of education and opportunity for development, with an actual deficiency.[13]

Supposed differences in mental capacities between the sexes have often been used to justify their different social roles. Aristotle, for example, thought women by nature belonged to the group who are ruled because the deliberative faculty is possessed by them "in a form which remains inconclusive."[14] Despite the citations above, however, Rousseau does not subscribe to such a view.

In Rousseau's state of nature human rationality is hardly distinguishable from that of other animals: rationality is instrumental and exercised only in the service of immediate needs. In this sense, any development of intellectual capacities is unnatural and must be accounted for in both sexes primarily by environmental (including educational) influences. More importantly, like many other capacities that evolve only under certain contingent circumstances, Rousseau considers the awakening of rationality to be a mixed blessing that offers no guarantee of personal or social well-being. His famous discourse concerning the negative effects of popularized science and art on morals and politics is evidence of this. Because both a return to the innocent ignorance of the savage state and unguided development of the intellect are undesirable, Rousseau urges that intellectual growth be steered in directions conducive to public and private goods. Education of the intellect is understood by Rousseau as something that can and should be manipulated and constrained because of concerns unrelated to any supposedly innate sex differences.

Theoretically, Rousseau does not make a distinction between the sexes on the basis of either how they can learn or what they can know. He claims that in society there are only two true classes of people: those who think and those who do not. He sees both of these classes as composed of men *and* women (*Emile*, 408). Rousseau also notes, in accord with his general non-teleological stance,[15] that it is impossible to know with certainty the heights to which the human intellect can soar. "I know of no philosopher who has yet been so bold as to say: this is the limit of what man can attain and beyond which he cannot go. We do not know what our nature permits us to be" (*Emile*, 62). There is no evidence that Rousseau takes this statement, or his remarks about perfectibility in general, to apply only to males and not also to females. Thus far there is every indication that Rousseau thinks that woman's rationality can be developed along the same lines, to the same degree, and for the same ends as man's.

On the more practical level, Rousseau readily concedes that women have rational abilities. Descriptions in his *Confessions* show him to be well acquainted with women who are intelligent, talented, well-read, cultured, and eager and able to learn. The *Emile* itself is dedicated to "a good mother who knows how to think" (33). He acknowledges that young girls are full of curiosity and wit, possess good sense, and are insightful and observant. Further, Rousseau does not write as if woman's domestic duties did not demand the exercise of reason.

It is true that Rousseau sometimes appears to think that the "higher" rational functions are beyond the grasp of women. As an aside, it is interesting to note that even if that was his assumption, one could not conclude that he thinks women are therefore unhappy, inferior, or appropriately relegated to second-class status. Rousseau does not unequivocally extol the virtues of cold, objective reasoning, especially with regard to the "common" people, who constitute the vast majority of humanity. In fact, reason abstracted from the senses is the object of much Rousseauean concern; for neither sex is the philosopher the model of the good person.[16] In addition, to the extent that Rousseau's ideal is the noble savage, one can argue that if Rousseau's woman is limited to the "lower" rational functions she is in some sense closer to this ideal: she is less denatured to the extent that her rationality is less developed. In the state of nature and in civil society Rousseau values the sentiments and contextual reasoning in a way rationalists do not, making the argument against him about gendered rationalities at least more complicated than some assume.

But it is truly not the case that Rousseau thinks women are intellectually limited by nature, for his most consistent position is not that women *cannot* perform certain rational operations but that they *should not*—and the same is true for men. Those who characterize Rousseau's approach on this issue as "functionalist" are correct. "Rousseau does not . . . first assert that woman is mentally inferior to man and then draw conclusions from this about her proper function and position in society. Rather, his method is to begin by making assumptions about . . . woman's role . . . and then to draw conclusions as to what her intellectual capacities *should* be like, in order to fit her for her proper function."[17] Quotes such as the following support an interpretation which says that in deciding upon woman's educational program

Rousseau does not appeal to the natural limits of her rational abilities, but rather, to that which is "useful" or "suitable" for her to know.

If it is important for men to limit their studies to *useful [d'usage]* knowledge, it is even more important for women.

They ought to learn many things but only those that are *suitable [convient]* for them to know.

Wit alone is the true resource of the fair sex . . . the wit which *suits their position [l'esprit de son état]*.

She *must* . . . make a profound study of the mind of man—not an abstraction of the mind of man in general, but the minds of the men around her, the minds of the men to whom she is *subjected by either law or opinion*.

The art of thinking is not foreign to women, but they *ought* only to skim the sciences of reasoning. (*Emile*, 368, 364, 371, 387, 426; all emphasis added)

Rousseau clearly distinguishes between what women *can* learn and what they *ought* to learn. He is endorsing a particular pattern of relations between the sexes, one for which he prepares both sexes, and in which intellectual development plays an important role. This scheme, furthermore, is backed "by either law or opinion" and is not simply mandated by nature. Women's education, like men's, is guided by what is "useful" to them in their prescribed role and what is "useful" to society. If women are to be overtly subjected to the men around them, it is useful that they know the minds of those men well in order to please and manipulate them and to achieve their own ends. Most important, Rousseau considers it useful to educate the sexes differently because women and men are made interdependent if the knowledge of one sex complements the knowledge of the other. Because of his view of natural asociality, Rousseau goes to great lengths to ensure that the sexes will need, as well as desire, each other.

The social relationship of the sexes is an admirable thing. This partnership *[société]* produces a moral person of which the woman is the eye and the man is the arm, but they have such a dependence on one another that the woman learns from the man what must be seen and the man learns from the woman what must be done. If woman could ascend to general principles as well as man can, and if man had as good a mind for details as woman does, they would always be independent of one another, they would live in eternal discord, and their partnership could not exist. (*Emile*, 377)

Thus, Rousseau advocates intellectual sexual differentiation in the name of mutual dependence.

It is easy to see that Rousseau directs the education of women toward certain ends and does not endorse the free and complete development of women's rational capacities. But it is often overlooked that Rousseau also restricts Emile's intellectual development.[18] Emile's training is different from Sophie's because his social role is different from hers and must complement it, but Rousseau would guide and limit the intellectual growth of men fully as much as that of women.

No one will vaunt Emile's intelligence. . . . His intelligence will be sharp and limited. . . . [T]he sphere of his knowledge does not extend farther than what is profitable. . . . Emile is a man of good sense [*bon sens*], and he does not want to be anything else. (*Emile*, 339)

In order to be decent human beings and good citizens, both sexes must have common sense, sensitivity, and the ability to reflect upon and evaluate an argument or a given situation. In addition, women must have the practical intelligence necessary to educate children and manage a household, men to pursue a trade and participate in household and political decisions. The education of both sexes is constrained by social concerns and not by any supposedly natural limitations on the rational capacities of either one. Further, Rousseau does not feel that such constraint is destructive of happiness for either sex for, as we have seen, all that is necessary for happiness in his account is a balance between what one is able to do and what one desires to do. In this context, their sex-specific educations provide each with the rational capacities to perform the duties toward which their socialized desires point them.

REPRODUCTION

Most attempts to justify different roles for the sexes appeal at some point to differences in their reproductive capacities. Whether the claim is that women need special care and protection during pregnancy or that there is a maternal instinct which uniquely binds women to their children, it is held that woman is both fitted for and limited to the roles of wife and mother. It is impossible, however, to see Rousseau's argument in this light.

In Rousseau's thought, women have no "maternal instinct," as that concept is usually understood, for with regard to their young, women feel no bond and possess no insight not also potentially available to men. In the state of nature women nurse children to relieve themselves of milk (self-interest), and perhaps respond to a child's cries out of pity, a sentiment common to both sexes. Beyond that, any attachment to children arises from the habit of living with them, and to this kind of attachment men are equally susceptible. Feminine or maternal instinct is no part of Rousseau's justification for assigning to women the primary care of children.

Further, Rousseau's condemnation of women devoting themselves to tasks other than childrearing is not based on a belief that when they do so they somehow fail to fulfill their nature, for such a teleological concept is truly alien to Rousseau's thought. There is for him no predetermined human end, and no sex-based destiny either. Nor does he believe that women necessarily require constant care during pregnancy or that childrearing precludes the possibility of engaging in other kinds of labor. "There are countries where women give birth almost without pain and nurse their children almost without effort. I admit it" (*Emile*, 362). In the state of nature women carry their children everywhere with ease, even while they seek food or flee from danger (*SD*, 108, 112). There is nothing then, inherent in the nature of women, of pregnancy, or of childrearing that directs all or only women to the care of their mates and children.

Further, the patriarchal family did not exist in the savage state. In refuting Locke's claims Rousseau states that

> [A]lthough it may be advantageous to the human species for the union between man and woman to be permanent, it does not follow that it was thus established by nature; otherwise it would be necessary to say that nature also instituted civil society, the arts, commerce, and all that is claimed to be useful to men.[19]

At a certain stage in human and social evolution, however, the family becomes useful. And it is because of the ability of the family to serve vital social functions that Rousseau then urges the domestication of women, and not because women are naturally drawn to or destined for such a role.

Rousseau constantly emphasizes the beneficial consequences of women's privatization and devotion to the family, a theme more fully explored in the next chapter. Briefly, he believes domesticated women can potentially be a positive moral force. They can help attach men to their children, can educate children in loyalty to the state, and, via an attractive domestic life, can aid in preserving male fidelity, which in turn plays a part in making men citizens.

Rousseau clearly acknowledges that women's lives need not be limited to or wholly dominated by domestic cares, but he urges women to find their happiness in the family. Rousseau does not believe that "anatomy is destiny," that women have no choice but to confine themselves to the private sphere, but he thinks that women *ought* to do so, and he educates them accordingly.

INTERESTS AND DISPOSITIONS

Lastly, it is impossible to see Rousseau as arguing that woman's natural interests or disposition point her toward domestic life. Sophie's education is dominated by the attempt to *teach* her to accept and love "the duties of her sex." "What Sophie knows best and has been most carefully *made to learn* are the labors of her own sex. . . . She has been *taught* from her childhood nothing so much as to adjust herself to the people with whom she had to live" (*Emile*, 394, 404; emphasis added).

Once again, however, Rousseau sometimes seems to write as if he believes that the sexes "have particular tastes which distinguish them" by nature (*Emile*, 367). One example he discusses of a "very definite primary taste" is girls' interest in adornment. But this talk of natural interests is a case of Rousseau's using the language of nature to make his normative political position seem merely descriptive, and hence more palatable.

Rousseau speaks of girls' early love of adornment as evidence of how they are naturally disposed to care about what other people think of them and how they can therefore be governed with the weapons of approval and disapproval. His wording can easily leave one with the impression that the nature of boys is such that they are without a similar disposition and, therefore, these weapons would be without effect on them.

Little girls love adornment almost from birth. Not satisfied with being pretty, they want people to think that they are pretty. One sees in their airs that this concern preoccupies them already; and when they are hardly in a condition to understand what is said to them, they can already be governed by speaking to them of what will be thought of them. When the same motive is—very inappropriately—suggested to little boys, it by no means has a similar empire over them. Provided that they are independent and that they have pleasure, they care little what might be thought of them. It is only by dint of time and effort that they are subjected to the same law. (*Emile*, 365)

Rousseau's appeal to different sexual natures here seems to contradict my argument that his sexual scheme is purely normative. But, for any of the following reasons, we cannot but conclude that Rousseau *wants* women to be more vulnerable to public opinion, despite the fact that they are naturally neither more nor less sensitive to it than are boys.

First, in the opening sentence of the paragraph that follows the one just cited, Rousseau says that "[f]rom *whatever source [De quelque part]* this first lesson comes to girls, it is a very good one." That is, Rousseau is at the very least ambiguous regarding the source of women's sensitivity to others. It could arise from some innate female nature, or it could result from careful training. Thus, Rousseau does not unqualifiedly assert that woman's susceptibility to opinion is natural, in the sense of spontaneously arising from within.

Second, what Rousseau actually says is not simply that boys, unlike girls, are innately immune to approval or disapproval. Rather, he says boys are immune "*provided that* they are independent *and* that they have pleasure." But is it not a truism to say that if one is independent and happy then one is neither dependent nor likely to desire to become so? Further, Rousseau has just admitted that boys are impervious to opinion only under certain conditions, and therefore such a state is certainly not natural in the sense of it being inevitable. The same would have to be said of girls' dependence as well.

Third, Rousseau says that "[i]t is only by dint of time and effort that they [boys] are subjected to the same law" of caring what others think of them. Implicit in this statement is the assumption that *with* "time and effort" boys can be "subjected to the same law" as girls. And he only calls such efforts "inappropriate," not impossible. Again, nature is at best malleable. And we need only consider the "time and effort" invested in fostering female sensitivity and care for appearance to conclude that girls have been subjected to an external "law" just as boys could be. As Wollstonecraft puts it, "I will venture to affirm, that a girl, whose spirits have not been damped by inactivity, or innocence tainted by false shame, will always be a romp, and the doll will never excite attention unless confinement allows her no alternative."[20]

Lastly, it would be utterly incomprehensible for Rousseau to consider love of adornment as natural. It is impossible to imagine his noble female savages bedecked with jewels and paints and flowers. All people lack vanity in the state of nature, being moved only by true needs, and thus adornment is also not natural in the sense of having existed in the primitive state of nature.

Thus, in his discussion of "natural" sex interests and dispositions, Rousseau's use of "natural" means something like "that which is useful in a given context." Only such a meaning, combined with Rousseau's belief in the malleability and adaptability of human nature, can make sense of the passage about adornment cited earlier, and of much of the *Emile*. This sense of "natural" is completely compatible with my interpretation of Rousseau's sexual politics. Rousseau's language of nature is a socially useful rhetorical device, not mandated by theoretical or empirical considerations regarding the natures of the sexes. His own premises tell us that neither interests nor dispositions naturally differentiate the sexes, but that it is possible to create such differences.

CONCLUSION

Based on his views of possible sex differences in strength, mental abilities, reproductive capacities, and interests, I have argued that Rousseau does not believe natural differences are necessarily either great, inevitable, immutable, or politically relevant. However, he finds sex roles to have beneficial social consequences and therefore strongly endorses differential treatment of the sexes.

That Rousseau can envision the creation of sex differences, and a mythology or ideology to support them, is consistent with principles and assumptions fundamental to his thought. As a philosopher who believes that there is no unchanging and distinctive human nature, Rousseau is left with the possibility of encouraging people to develop in ways that are conducive to the general well-being at a given moment in the history of the race. In addition, given his understanding of freedom, as explored in chapter 2, there is no basis in his thought for repugnance to the idea or practice of manipulation. Further, as a philosopher who believes that people are naturally asocial and easily prey to egoism in society, Rousseau must find ways to make people need and desire each other without succumbing to the temptation to exploit each other, and it seems that he finds sex roles to be part of the solution.

There are three ways in which Rousseau is commonly misunderstood in his statements regarding the sexes. The first and most fatal error is taking Rousseau to be merely descriptive when in fact he is taking a strong normative stance. Thus, it has been supposed that Rousseau limits woman's education because he underestimates her intelligence and powers or believes "women are inferior and subordinate beings."[21] Yet how frequently is the word "ought" used in Rousseau's discussion of woman's role. He thinks the faculties of both sexes ought to be developed in certain directions for specific reasons, as I have indicated. To prescribe particular roles for the sexes and not to educate people for them would be ineffective. To prescribe such roles and to educate people beyond them would be wasteful at best and unwise at worst. Rousseau begins his discussion of Sophie's education by saying she must have the attributes which will allow her "to fill her place [*remplir sa place*] in the physical and moral order" (*Emile*, 357). He admits that the extent of sex differences is unknown; his discussion can proceed, nonetheless, because such knowledge is unnecessary for one who is basing the sexual division on social utility.

A related error concerns Rousseau's use of rhetoric. While Rousseau does not believe women are inherently limited to the role he advocates for them, he uses all of the themes and language common to such a view.[22] Book 5 of the *Emile* may be unique among Rousseau's works for its numerous references to the laws and decrees of nature. While such language may be relatively rare in the body of Rousseau's works, it is quite common to philosophy.

For the same author may generally use language which exhausts itself in prolemogena to any discourse and wears itself out in caveats, while elsewhere devoting a chapter, paragraph or just a phrase to sexual difference, excuse me, to women, where all of a sudden there is a shift from the height of sophistication to a mode which has been somehow squared off and is at the same time so dogmatic that there is no place for mediation or dialectics.[23]

Rousseau is attempting to persuade the sexes to adopt certain ways of life, and his rhetoric is consistently undercut by his theoretical argument. Just as the legislator in the *Social Contract* uses the language of religion to persuade the people to adopt his laws, so does Rousseau use the always-respectable and always-nebulous language of nature to appeal to the sexes to fulfill particular social functions. Just as the tutor's will must seem to be, like disease, the "necessity of things," so must sex roles be made to seem, not arbitrarily willed, but natural, necessary, and inevitable. Thus, people do not become rebellious (*Emile*, 33). Natural sex roles are, perhaps, what Rousseau might consider a noble lie.[24]

The failure to recognize the normative and rhetorical character of Rousseau's statements about the sexes is causally connected with a third and more substantial error in interpretation, explored in the previous chapter— that of supposing that the principles which guide Rousseau's programs of male and female education are totally dissimilar. A careful reading of the *Emile* shows that *both* sexes are being prepared for certain roles in life and are being taught to accept the limitations these roles entail. In his discourse on women's education, Rousseau does not abandon all the principles underlying the education of males. Because their tasks differ, the education of the sexes differs. Yet both sexes are educated in accord with specific ends, and each is made to rely on the other for the "wholeness" Rousseau has ensured that neither will possess alone. The sexes are intended by Rousseau, rather than by nature, to be perfect complements.

Rousseau presents feminists with a challenge. Feminist literature has thoroughly refuted the view that sex differences necessarily mandate the establishment of sex roles. But, as Rousseau shows, the argument must go farther. A feminist critique of Rousseau's thought must demonstrate either that the benefits thought by him to be consequences of separate sexual spheres can be attained without a rigid sexual division of labor, or that these supposed benefits are in fact unwise or unnecessary objectives. It is fair to judge a critique of Rousseau's sexual scheme by the extent to which it answers his political concerns. It is also fair to judge his general politics on the basis of the sexual politics that serve as their necessary foundation.

Many important issues, of course, are not settled with the argument that Rousseau's pedagogical scheme is not grounded in biological determinism. What assurances are there that men's now much superior physical strength will not be used against women? If the rationality and interests of the sexes are trained so differently, how can we be certain that they are capable of fully communicating with each other, that there is enough common ground to build community? Finally, can we really condone the rhetorical use of the concept of biological destiny, knowing to what abuses this concept almost invariably leads? Dworkin, for one, holds that biological determinism, "the most pernicious ideology on the face of the earth," once unleashed cannot be contained.

It was this very ideology of biological determinism that had licensed the slaughter and/or enslavement of virtually any group one could name, including women by men. . . . Anywhere one looked, it was this philosophy that justified atrocity. This was one faith that destroyed life *with a momentum of its own*. [25]

What grounds exist for thinking that Rousseau's rhetoric of innate sexual differences will not develop a similar momentum? In order to prepare the ground fully for these inquiries, in the next chapter I take a deeper look at the political concerns that lead Rousseau to endorse the sex-roled family.

FOUR

FAMILIES AND POLITICS: SEX ROLES AND COMMUNITY

Thus far two major theses have been defended. First, that Rousseau's sexually differentiated educational programs both have as their goal the production of a particular kind of social person and appeal to similar understandings of the human condition, child development, and politics. While females and males are molded by education to be different from each other, for each there exists a model touching on every important aspect of their life. Second, Rousseau's rationale for these substantively distinct programs is not to be found in an appeal to the different natures of the sexes. When he seems to make such appeals, he is attempting to persuade, for by his own account no natural sex differences in strength, intellect, reproductive capacities, or interests mandate the establishment of a strict sexual division of roles and traits in society.

Recent feminist critiques of Rousseau's sexual politics have generally been severe. Perhaps more was reasonably expected of someone with such high praise for liberty and equality, one actually familiar with feminist ideas, an individual with painful personal experience of second-class treatment, and a thinker convinced of how fatal oppressive power is to a community. When, in spite of these experiences and principles, Rousseau sends women to the home and men to the assembly, there is some cause for thinking he was in a position to know better and want more. For feminists studying the history of political thought Rousseau's advocacy of sexual differentiation seems to be yet another poignant reminder of how major figures in the history of political theory, regardless of their commitment to equality and freedom, continually (and inconsistently) direct women to the domestic and men to the public arena.

It is still possible, however, that Rousseau does not precisely follow the usual pattern. The question we need to explore is this: "If Rousseau does not resort to claims about the different natures of the sexes, and if his scheme reflects more than the misogyny or blindness of its author, then how is it possible to explain his system of sexual differentiation?" Rousseau offers a hint as to how to proceed.

While frequently making rhetorical reference to the different natures of men and women in defending his proposals, Rousseau ultimately appeals to claims quite unrelated to sexual natures. For instance, in discussing female chastity he speaks on the one hand of how the "Supreme Being . . . while abandoning woman to unlimited desires . . . joins modesty to these desires in order to constrain them" (*Emile*, 359). On the other hand, however, despite the apparent reliance here on the (divine) given of woman's nature, his more consistent and convincing position emerges when he writes, "Even if it could be denied that a special sentiment of chasteness was natural to women . . . it is in society's interest that women acquire these qualities" (*d' Alembert*, 87). Quotes such as this do not merely bolster arguments about woman's nature. Instead, by referring to the traits women should *acquire* "in society's interest," Rousseau introduces a completely independent, and more internally consistent, justification for his rigidly sex-differentiated society. Instead of focusing on the supposed *causes* of sexual differentiation, as found in nature, Rousseau directs us instead to an examination of the *effects* of sexual differentiation on various social relations. This chapter sets out to discover Rousseau's grounds for thinking that sexual differentiation is "in society's interest."

Rousseau's strategy of evaluating and justifying sexual differentiation by its consequences, especially after comparing them to the effects of the alternatives, is not so surprising. It is not the question "Is X good in itself?" that preoccupies the citizen of Geneva but, instead, "Is X beneficial and useful?" For example, the *Letter to d' Alembert* inquires into the effects on different peoples of establishing a theater. In that letter he writes, "To ask if the theatre is good or bad in itself is to pose too vague a question. . . . The theatre is made for the people, and it is only by its effects on the people that one can determine its absolute qualities" (17). Similarly, Rousseau's famous opposition to the Enlightenment stems not from a belief that the arts and sciences are unequivocally bad in themselves but from reflection on the consequences of imperfect learning on various groups and relationships. Thus, the suggestion that Rousseau's sexual scheme is devised for its social consequences is not as idiosyncratic as it might at first appear.

Despite the obvious contradictions in and objections to Rousseau's model of the sex-roled family, I hope to offer an interpretation of it that can incorporate, explain, and surpass some of the incompatible interpretations of his work offered by others, and that can demonstrate what Rousseau might have been trying to accomplish in endorsing sexual differentiation.[1] I argue that, at least on the theoretical level, he is in general internally consistent. Rousseau's advocacy of sexual roles is based on his understanding of their ability to bring individuals outside of themselves into interdependent communities, and thus to combat egoism, selfishness, indolence, and narcissism—goals that consistently inform much of his politics. Evidence of this is found in Rousseau's rejection of both aristocratic and bourgeois families, rejection founded upon their inability to accomplish politically what the sex-roled, affectionate family can accomplish.

Defenses of the "traditional" family are often thought to arise from either ignorance of its oppressiveness, disdain for women, or belief that its differentiated roles fulfill the distinct natures of women and men. But the picture these explanations paint of defenses of the sex-roled family is seriously incomplete, and feminist responses to these defenses, consequently, are also incomplete.

In order to figure out why Rousseau sees sexual differentiation as socially beneficial, I consider his sex-roled family in two related contexts. The first context is his general thought, where sexual differentiation can be understood as a response to certain aspects of what he perceives as "the human condition." For example, the bonds created in the sex-roled family, and the interdependence fostered by sex roles in general, motivate us and teach us how to be part of a political community, a community Rousseau holds to be necessary for survival and morality. The second context is the historical forms of the family with which Rousseau was familiar. Rousseau witnessed the decline of the aristocratic family and the emergence of the bourgeois family (both of which may be considered patriarchal), and found both politically unacceptable. A look at the kinds of families Rousseau rejects gives a sense of both what he is trying to accomplish by creating sexual differences and what he is trying to avert.

Rousseau's views on the sexes are thus strongly political, in at least two senses. First, Rousseau is certain that the private and public affect each other in numerous and central ways—that forms of education, the status of women and children, and norms governing sexuality and family life, matter to politics as much as do the actions of men in the assembly. Because the private has political consequences, Rousseau to a great extent constructs the private with an eye to its political repercussions. The private becomes the parent and servant of the public: sex roles serve political ends and teach us lessons that give birth to certain desirable social possibilities. Rousseau's views on the sexes are also political in a second sense, in that they reflect assumptions and choices about what kinds of communities are possible, necessary, and desirable, and offer practical strategies for attaining them.

Rousseau might be considered antifeminist at the outset because he determines what the role of women should be based on more than simply what women want to do or can do. But men are treated no differently, as shown in chapter 2. Moreover, what women want to do or can do is not dismissed as irrelevant. Indeed, some opposition to feminism, including Rousseau's, may arise from viewing feminists as evaluating the role of women abstracted from political considerations. Rousseau's argument is that certain necessary social benefits result from the establishment of sexual differentiation, far-reaching benefits that serve as the cornerstone of its justification. Such a defense of the traditional family presents a different set of questions to feminists than those presented by more familiar defenses based on appeals to biological determinism or the usefulness of a haven separate from the marketplace, and calls for a more thorough understanding by feminists who hope to critique it effectively.

The first two sections of this chapter develop the two contexts in which the ends of Rousseau's sexual politics can be discerned. The succeeding two sections explore the negative personal and social consequences of the aristocratic and bourgeois families he rejects. These "case studies" offer evidence of what Rousseau thinks a family ought to provide for its members and for society and why he finds the sex-roled, affectionate family to be the most personally and politically beneficial. The conclusion will point out some of the questions Rousseau's defense of the sex-roled family raises for feminist theory, and some of the questions feminist theory raises for Rousseau.

ROUSSEAU AND THE HUMAN CONDITION

Rousseau portrays people in the state of nature as free, happy, independent, amoral, innocent, and isolated. They are without need for the services or esteem of others and can generally satisfy their minimal desires independently. While self-absorbed, they do not desire to injure others. These asocial individuals possess numerous faculties in potentiality, but neither internal nor external forces naturally operate to motivate them to do any more than is necessary to survive. Rousseau's primitives are lazy and contented.

All relations in the state of nature are temporary and amoral and provide no precedent or model for the sorts of relations needed between social beings. There may be some infrequent instances of cooperation in the search for food, but such actions are temporary and based entirely on self-interest. Sexual encounters, too, are random and fleeting, motivated by the coincidence of desire and opportunity, and cause no lasting attachment between the partners.

Even the mother-child relation in the state of nature provides a poor model for the interdependent, moral, sustained relations modern social people need. As Rousseau portrays it, mother-child relations in the state of nature do not differ significantly from those of other animals. He sees the demands of children in the state of nature as simple, of short duration, and compatible with satisfaction of the mother's meager needs and desires. A father's assistance is unnecessary, even were he able to grasp his relation to a child, which Rousseau thinks he is not. A mother cares for a child to relieve her own swollen breasts of milk, out of compassion for a crying creature, and finally out of affection born of habit. But Rousseau imagines that in the state of nature children strike out on their own permanently at a very young age—as soon as they have learned to feed and defend themselves—and that this uneventfully marks the end of all relations between mother and child.[2]

However, accidental events and developments alter the easy balance between desires and powers in the state of nature, until interdependence finally becomes necessary for survival. The question now becomes how to teach and motivate asocial, lazy, independent individuals to work with and for each other as well as for themselves. Rousseau considers this change radical and difficult. The fact that people need each other does not automatically mean that they will cooperate for mutual advantage rather than attempt to exploit each other for personal gain. Self-love, once complicated by social relations, can easily lead to selfishness and concern with advantage over others, bringing about the long train of personal and social evils so dramatically described in the *Discourses*.

Rousseau does not take egoism, competitiveness or conflict to be endemic to the human condition. Nor does he assume, however, that by nature we are as concerned with others, including even our own children, as with ourselves. Rousseau's quest is to establish a social framework that can both end the isolation, self-absorption, and independence of natural people and combat the egoism, competitiveness, and conflict among "civilized" people who have become interdependent.

The contrast between childhood in the state of nature and modern social childhood helps clarify Rousseau's "political problem." As society "advances," the period of childhood is extended, and being a parent becomes more demanding. In civil society children are dependent for much longer than in the state of nature, for they must learn to speak, to read, to earn a living, to behave properly—the list is virtually endless, and the specific skills needed can change rapidly.[3] Further, parents are now subject to judgments by others regarding the quality of the care they bestow upon their children, making their task even more burdensome.

Looking at Rousseau's views on sexual differentiation and the family in the context of his general thought, we can surmise the kinds of problems he is trying to address through gender roles: How can we help ensure that women, once sufficiently motivated by pity, full breasts, and a child's modest requests to pay some minimal attention to offspring for a relatively short period of time, will now sacrifice so much more for so much longer? And what will turn a naturally lazy and asocial male, whose participation in childrearing was once unnecessary, into a father? What will help turn both into citizens? These are the questions Rousseau faces; his position on sexual relations provides a large part of his solution to them. Rousseau's rejection of certain family structures arises from their inability to respond to fundamental crises of the human social condition and their tendency to support corrupt political and social relations. His defense of the sex-roled, affectionate family is likewise based on its beneficial social consequences.

THE CHANGING FAMILY

In the aristocratic French family of the sixteenth, seventeenth, and early eighteenth centuries, the male exercised powerful rule over both his children and wife. Arranged marriages were standard, with economic and family rank and reputation the criteria in mate selection. "Within these marriages, relations between husband and wife and between parents and children were cold, distant, and unloving. . . . Noble wives were poorly treated by their husbands" and remote from their children.[4] "The marriage contract seemed to have little meaning in Paris, except in separating a man and woman effectively, so that they were ashamed to seem to care for each other, and in most cases lived apart, slept in separate apartments, and had each other announced when they called."[5]

Needless to say, this family was not a reliable source of emotional satisfaction for any of its members, and illicit relationships regularly filled the vacuum. Even here, it has been said that "[t]he ceremony of taking a lover was momentous; position, family, social attainments, were all weighed."[6] Children were cared for by wet nurses, nursemaids, and tutors, successively. This aristocratic family was thus seldom more than a reproductive and economic entity, with birthing legitimate heirs as its primary function. Rousseau, we shall see, rejects this type of family on a number of grounds. It is to this type of family that his remarks about "unfaithful" wives, "brilliant" wives, and women turning to "entertainments of the city" are directed (*Emile*, 44, 409), as are his comments about tyrannical and neglectful fathers (*Emile*, 38n.).

In addition to analyzing the defects of the family of the ancien régime, Rousseau focuses his attention on its likely successor: the bourgeois family. Actually, in Rousseau's view the self-absorbed bourgeois individual is incapable of really being a member of a family. As Bloom states,

[H]e is the man who, when dealing with others, thinks only of himself, and on the other hand, in his understanding of himself, thinks only of others. . . . The bourgeois distinguishes his own good from the common good. His good requires society, and hence he exploits others while depending on them. . . . The bourgeois comes into being when men no longer believe that there is a common good.[7]

These self-interested bourgeois "role-players" are not part of a greater whole, be it family or community, in any sense but the limited and inadequate one based on self-interest. "I observe," writes Rousseau, "that in the modern age men no longer have a hold on one another except by force or by self-interest" (*Emile*, 321). People are self-centered and view others as means to their own ends. The bourgeois family, accordingly, is without a common interest or firm bond. Each member of the family pursues their own interests, considering the others and fulfilling their obligations when it is useful or convenient, or when they are forced to do so. Such relations are superficial and unreliable and do nothing to teach us the important lessons Rousseau thinks we need to learn about interdependence, loyalty, and community. It is to this emerging family that Rousseau's remarks about families composed of strangers are directed, as are many of his comments about women seeking entry into previously male arenas—about liberal feminism, that is.

Rousseau's general thought and his understanding of the propensities inherent in aristocratic and bourgeois families provide a framework within which his views on sexual differentiation can be understood. Examining specific features of the family models he condemns offers a picture of what Rousseau held to be their negative effects on parent-child and male-female relations, and, consequently, on general social and political arrangements. These families are cast aside on political grounds—because of their inability to mitigate, or their propensity to encourage, undesirable human relations —and the sex-roled, affectionate family is proposed by him as a better alternative.

PARENT-CHILD RELATIONSHIP

As discussed above, parent-child relations in the state of nature are of limited usefulness in helping establish the kinds of human bonds Rousseau asserts we now need. He also considers the families of his own time inadequate. The status quo to which Rousseau was responding was parental neglect of children and the disparaging estimation of the child as uninteresting, useless, or sinful.[8] Until almost the very end of the ancien régime, childcare in most noble and bourgeois households was handled primarily by servants. Even in the latter half of the eighteenth century, when a few notable women began to breast-feed and supervise their own children, household servants played a major role in childrearing.[9]

The role of servants in the lives of children began at birth, when the infant was immediately sent to a wet nurse *(nourrice)*. This custom was deeply rooted by Rousseau's time, having begun as early as the thirteenth century, when Paris had a bureau of *recommanderesses* that made arrangements for hiring nurses. In the eighteenth century the hiring of wet nurses was prevalent among the bourgeoisie and the artisanate as well as the aristocracy. In artisanal families the motives for wet-nursing were primarily economic: the mother's labor was essential to the family economy, and she could not afford the interruption that nursing would entail.[10] There were social reasons for wet-nursing as well: nursing was considered a degrading and vulgar activity which supposedly ruined one's figure and strained one's health. Another reason was sexual: there were folk taboos against resuming sexual intercourse during lactation. Thus wet-nursing was an economic necessity for some women and their families and a response to social pressures and taboos for others. Rousseau's opposition to wet-nursing in particular, and to parental neglect of children in general, is unwavering, and he is given much credit for persuading mothers to breast-feed their babies and for contributing to "what was almost a cult of the mother figure."[11]

Sounding like some twentieth-century antifeminists, Rousseau states that nonparental childcare arrangements entail a greater risk of abuse and neglect, because the caretakers generally have no long-term stake in the child's well-being. Their greatest concern is to minimize the amount of trouble a child causes them while under their charge. (It is interesting to note how often, even today, infants are called "good" who are, more precisely, easy to care for, i.e., who sleep a great deal and cry but a little.) Rousseau refers to wet nurses as "mercenaries," evoking the imagery of professional soldiers who serve any country *merely* for wages (*Emile*, 44). Rousseau thus implies that the nurse really takes no interest in the child's needs but is basically concerned with earning an income and saving herself trouble. This assumption explains the practice of swaddling infants, which Rousseau abhors and which he uses as representative of the poor treatment of children under such arrangements. However, while there is no reason to doubt Rousseau's sincere concern with the health and welfare of children narrowly understood, and while the stories of neglect and abuse of children by nurses in his time were numerous,[12] concern with the quality of care bestowed upon children accounts for but the smallest part of his proposed reconstruction of the family.

That Rousseau's focus is not primarily the quality of care given children outside the nuclear family is supported by his awareness of the need to strengthen family ties beyond what may "naturally" exist; he never takes their strength, safety, or reliability for granted. Rousseau does not believe that nature goes very far in ensuring that children will be cared for; outside of pity, which motivates anyone to help a suffering child, and full breasts, which encourage women to nurse for their own comfort, nature is essentially silent. The point is that even if Rousseau could be shown that children are as well tended by nurses or childcare workers as by parents, he would hesitate to endorse nonparental care. By spelling out some of the numerous negative consequences he perceives in such arrangements, it is possible to understand that the basis of his objection to them is essentially political.

Rousseau first notes the simple fact that when a child is put into the charge of someone other than her or his parents, the family spends less time together. He finds the consequences of this worrisome, for habit is not then allowed the opportunity to strengthen the ties of blood (*Emile*, 46). Given his assumption that such blood ties are fragile and require reinforcement, extrafamilial childcare will not contribute to the development of bonds of affection between family members that Rousseau considers critical. Spending so much time apart, and in different pursuits, family members do not even know each other well. Rousseau's concern is that in the end they will be like residents of a corrupt city, polite strangers who really think first of themselves (*Emile*, 49). The habit of caring for another is vital to the strengthening of blood ties, which alone are easily broken. Rousseau's broad definition of *nature* includes acquired "habits conformable to nature" as expressed in the original condition (*Emile*, 39). Such habits would never be lost once learned, because they would conform to our dispositions as strengthened by our senses, but not yet corrupted by our opinions. Thus habit can strengthen nature, even though it can also stifle it. In this case, the habit of caring for one's own infant can strengthen the rather meager biological bond just as the habit of not caring can destroy it. The failure to spend ample time together, to allow family members to be drawn to one another from affection born of habit, threatens to maintain original human separateness and fails to combat egoism.

From the child's point of view as well, extrafamilial childcare has drawbacks. A child spending long hours away from the family can easily come to love the care-giver rather than the parents (*Emile*, 49), or become prone to making "secret comparisons which always tend to diminish his esteem for those who govern him and consequently have authority over him" (*Emile*, 57). The "losing" party in such comparisons—whether parents, wet nurses, or tutors—may consequently find it difficult to elicit affection and obedience from the child, making their already unnatural duties more distasteful and possibly leading to lack of concern for childrearing responsibilities. Or they may attempt to win back the child's affection by educational practices which are of dubious merit. Even if parents are preferred, their children may resent them for having entrusted them to those whose care is inferior, rather than providing it themselves.

Rousseau also fears that a child cared for by "mercenaries" may "bring back the habit of having no attachments" (*Emile*, 49). It is especially this politically dangerous possibility that disturbs him. While not uninterested in nutrition and the high rate of infant mortality, the alienation of affection between mother and child was what most worried Rousseau about a practice like wet-nursing. Once wet-nursing was finished, at about two years of age, the child was usually brought back into its family of origin and taught to regard its former nurse as a servant. Sometimes children were no longer allowed to see their nurses. Rousseau thinks this attempt to make children forget or disdain their first caretakers instills in them a general contempt and ingratitude (*Emile*, 45). He fears the child will in the end despise both the biological parents, who did not offer much care during infancy, and the substitute parents, whose class or status now makes them an unacceptable object of affection. In addition, the failure of the mother to nurse and rear her child robs her of an opportunity to learn to care for someone other than herself.

Thus, Rousseau's argument for breast-feeding is not a biological one. His main concern is not infant health and the quality of milk—its vitamins, antibodies, or other nutritional benefits, as emphasized by some twentieth-century advocates—but the quality of human relationships formed from the beginning of life. If one allows a young child to be completely cared for by a servant for whom one then teaches the child to feel contempt, one creates a monstrous person who does not know how to treat anyone else properly.[13]

Rousseau's arguments are not directed only to "neglectful mothers." His injunction to fathers to take responsibility for their children is less well known than his pleas to mothers but is of no less importance and is based on similar considerations.

Rousseau first tries to counter the notions that fathers are either inept parents or rightly consumed with more "important" tasks than caring for their children.

He will be better raised by a judicious and limited father than the cleverest master in the world; for zeal will make up for talent better than talent for zeal. . . . But business, offices, duties . . . Ah, duties! Doubtless the least is that of father? (*Emile*, 48–49)

It is possible and important that men actively father their children, for Rousseau regards "surrogate fathers," or tutors, in the same light as wet nurses—as mercenaries who corrupt the family just as mercenary soldiers do the state. Rich men who claim that they do not have time to care for their children purchase the time of others to perform their parental duties.[14] As Rousseau well knew, preceptors were often picked from among the male domestics in the household and were treated as family servants. He chastises fathers for subjecting their children to a master-servant relationship that ultimately produces a servile mentality: "Venal soul! Do you believe that you are with money giving your son another father? Make no mistake about it; what you are giving him is not even a master but a valet. This first valet will soon make a second one out of your son" (*Emile*, 49).

Hiring tutors may leave children and fathers unattached and thereby also fail to develop a common interest in their children between parents. Use of "mercenaries" also teaches children that money buys servants and that people only "care" out of self-interest, and fails to allow any true attachment even between child and tutor to develop, for it is in fact a relationship based on money.

The family in the ancien régime was an institution primarily organized for the transmission of property and rank from one generation to the next. Rousseau's new definition of fatherhood is rooted in the antipatriarchalism of Locke's political theory and expands Locke's view of the father as friend of his children to include the notion of father as educator or governor of his sons.[15] Like Locke, Rousseau emphasizes that the legacy or "portion" that a father bestows on his children should be a personal involvement in their education. While Locke still places high value on the transmission of property along with the "good breeding" of a gentleman, Rousseau is occupied with the transmission of a set of values that will enable children to be *independent* of wealth and rank.

Rousseau wants fathers to give their children something of themselves, rather than only their money. He wants them to provide an example of citizenship that rests on love and benevolence for others rather than on wealth. At the outset of *Emile*, he complains about "[f]athers' ambition, avarice, tyranny, and false foresight, their negligence, their harsh insensitivity" (*Emile*, 38n.). Fathers are rather like the laws, which Rousseau finds "always so occupied with property and so little with persons, because their object is peace, not virtue" (*Emile*, 37n.).

66 Families and Politics

Another negative political consequence of having two sets of care-givers is the risk of presenting conflicting guidelines to children. He writes:

A child ought to know no other superiors than his father and his mother or, in default of them, his nurse and his governor; even one of the two is already too many. But this division is inevitable, and all that one can do to remedy it is to make sure that the persons of the two sexes who govern him are in such perfect agreement concerning him that the two are only one as far as he is concerned. (*Emile*, 57)

Certainly, if Rousseau expresses doubts about two people sharing care of a child, he will be extremely hesitant to involve more parties, who might introduce additional principles into education. But why is this seen as so problematic?

If different "authorities" espouse conflicting guidelines, children may conclude that such guidelines are merely reflections of individual wills. It then becomes more difficult to persuade children that any beliefs about what is useful, truthful, moral, etc. are anything but purely subjective. Yet, as we know, members of both sexes must eventually be counted on, in separate ways, to participate in a community beyond the self. Thus, the difficult project of moving self-absorbed individuals into a greater whole could be made even more complicated by the consequences of inconsistent authorities. Further, recall how thorough is Rousseau's effort in the *Emile* to make the tutor's will seem to be part of the "nature of things." People will, he fears, rebel against having to submit to another's will if it is seen as such. Similarly, if children are presented with different guidelines, they may come to see all authority as merely an obstacle, a set of arbitrary rules that one may be able to evade or "get around" if one puts one's mind to it. Not only does this make parenting less attractive but, more importantly, fosters an attitude toward rules and authority that is dangerous, from the point of view of political stability, for future citizens of a regime largely operating under the rule of law.[16]

According to Rousseau, aristocratic and bourgeois families pose grave problems both for the bonds between parents and children and for general social relations. First, these families fail to reinforce natural ties with habitual ones, leaving people separate and self-absorbed. Second, these arrangements present children with torn loyalties, leading to any of three negative consequences: childcare, already "unnatural" and a sacrifice, is made more onerous by weak bonds; education, essential for making us responsible social creatures, may be compromised for the sake of children's affection; or, most important, children cared for by "mercenaries" may learn that people only minister to the needs of others when it is profitable or convenient for them to do so. The ultimate danger is that respect for persons and for law is not learned. Rousseau's firm belief in the insufficiency of self-interest as a basis for community and in the necessity and difficulty of combatting natural human isolation and egoism lead him to reject aristocratic and bourgeois families as personally and politically useless or dangerous. Similar problems are presented by the relationships between spouses in these families.

MARITAL RELATIONS

Rousseau advocates that women and men be not only good parents but good spouses as well. His sense of the negative repercussions of an aristocratic or bourgeois family structure on relations between spouses, and the consequences of these "inadequate" male-female relations on general social arrangements, are central to his argument for the sentimental, sex-roled alternative.

Rousseau's words on sex education are often remarkable for the sense of danger they convey. "How many precautions must be taken!" he exclaims (*Emile*, 335). The relations one will have with other people in general will, Rousseau believes, be affected by how one deals with the desire for a partner. Human sexuality has political implications.

In the contemporary discussions of marriage there was a debate about *mésalliances*, "bad matches," which meant marriages between members of the aristocracy and the bourgeoisie. Rousseau changes the meaning of the term: for him a bad match is one where the characters of the partners, rather than their ranks, are not compatible. Rousseau draws a further inference:

[T]he farther we are removed from equality, the more our natural sentiments are corrupted; the more the gap between noble and commoner widens, the more the conjugal bond is relaxed; and the more there are rich and poor, the less there are fathers and husbands. Neither master nor slave any longer has a family; each of the two sees only his status. (*Emile*, 405)

Rousseau is saying that the greater the inequalities in society, the less husbands and wives are bound to each other. Apparently this is because people marry for reasons of social rank and not for compatibility of character, thus making it unlikely that they will love each other and be sexually faithful. The "family" is destroyed by the inequality of the social structure, or, more accurately, the family is never truly established in the first place. In turn, the quality of married life affects the morality of the citizens. Rousseau witnesses individuals who by and large seem incapable of establishing meaningful relationships as family members or as fellow citizens.

In contrast to eighteenth-century French law and practice, Rousseau emphasizes that a woman should have a voice in determining whom she will marry and that marriage should be understood as a social institution requiring mutual respect and fidelity from both partners. He opposes the authoritarian model of relations between parent and child that entitled parents to choose a husband for a daughter based on wealth and rank. Aristocratic families, characterized by arranged marriages based on economics, do not establish an arena of love and affection between the spouses. Rousseau seems to see this as encouraging adultery. In fact, it can be said that adultery was institutionalized at the highest level of French society, for the married Louis XV had a publicly acknowledged relationship with Madame de Pompadour, herself a married bourgeoise who played a powerful role in France as advisor to the king and patron of the arts.

Rousseau directs great wrath at the adulterer, who inevitably "destroys the family" (*Emile*, 324). His argument here is quite different from many offered today, for Rousseau does not consider that only one model of male-female relations is somehow ordained and that any straying from it is sinful. One need only consider relations in his state of nature, where sexual encounters occurred when and with whom the desire arose and established no moral or lasting bond.

Infidelity is condemned because of its undesirable personal and political effects. First, there is the possibility of a woman bearing children which biologically are not her husband's. A man unsure of his biological relation to his wife's children may see less of himself in them, identify with them less strongly, and be less motivated to work and sacrifice for them; this injures both his relationship with his children and his partnership with his wife. Given Rousseau's assumption that motivation to sacrifice for others is already in short supply, the loss could be a significant one for the family unit. Second, an unfaithful partner, male or female, causes one to distrust others outside the family, who are seen as threats or potential competitors. This creates strained social relations in general, precisely what Rousseau wishes to avoid. Third, with suspicions of infidelity in the air, spouses do not trust one another and only feign love. "Under such circumstances the family is little more than a group of secret enemies" (*Emile*, 325).

The worrisome political consequence here is that without love for those nearest, it is difficult to develop love for the larger community. There appear to be two connections for Rousseau between familial love and patriotism. First, the "unnatural" lessons of cooperation and obligation are more easily learned on the micro level of the family—where habit breeds affection and the objects of one's affection are known well—and then extended to larger groups. Second, one is motivated to sacrifice for the state in large part by the protection the state offers one's family. In either case, Rousseau's opposition to aristocratic spousal relations is rooted in their failure to move people beyond the self, to foster those responsible, reliable bonds within the family that help establish the habits and motives for political community.

Rousseau also rails against the aristocratic wife "seeking entertainment" in the city and the bourgeois wife demanding entry into previously male educational and social institutions. In both cases, according to Rousseau, women are not fulfilling their domestic duties. This seems to be both a symptom and a cause of political problems.

Women engaged in activities outside the household may come to see motherhood as a burden. They are apt to try to avoid pregnancy through birth control, to which Rousseau objects vehemently (*Emile*, 44). The basis of his objection is at least in part concern with population increase, a familiar concern in eighteenth-century France, where one-quarter of the babies born died before their first birthday. But Rousseau also sees reproduction as a barometer of parental sacrifice, of the degree to which adults have moved beyond self-absorption and self-interest.[17] In this sense, neglect of domestic duties is a symptom of political problems.

Rousseau in several places focuses on the negative consequences of women's refusal to dedicate themselves to their mates. To women's demand for education he gives short shrift: "They have no colleges. What a great misfortune! Would God that there were none for boys; they would be more sensibly and decently raised!" (*Emile*, 363). This may be taken as an example of Rousseau's general response to the desire of some women to engage in heretofore male activities, rather than devoting themselves to their families. That is, he questions the worth of the (male) enterprise.

All the evils of modern civil society, according to Rousseau, are derived ultimately from the fact that personal or particular interest is the dominant rationale for action.

. . . Rousseau thought that the idea that the sexes might *both* operate on these principles and that women should not be denied the right to advance their particular interests as men do was one of the most absurd and lamentable consequences of this modern philosophy.[18]

To the extent that women's participation in certain arenas expands the mentality of self-interested individualism, it is a cause of continued political decline. In this light, Rousseau's opposition to liberal feminism, with which he was familiar, can be understood as rooted more in an opposition to liberalism than to women's equality. And, it must be noted, Rousseau, unlike his most famous liberal predecessors, does not desire men to be self-interested individuals either.

Rousseau also says that if women do not dedicate themselves to the home it will not be a refuge for men, who will then be less devoted to the family (*Emile*, 46), will seek their pleasure elsewhere, and will not fulfill their duties to their wives and children. Her concentration on her husband, however, causes him to respect and support her—to be a good husband. Once again Rousseau's assumption is that these domestic relationships are not "natural," and that without certain "enticements" to draw people to them, isolation and egoism are likely to prevail. The arrangement he envisions is at least intended to "entice" both sexes and to promote a sharing of the burdens and benefits of social life.

In the bourgeois and aristocratic families Rousseau portrays, the family is of little importance to any of its members. The children are burdensome strangers to the parents, who find their principal pleasures separately and outside of the family. None are firmly attached to the others, and each remains self-interested and essentially alone.

Rousseau's vision of the family, however sentimental, is an attempt to control the Hobbesian individual. In a world in which the individual is posited as a self-interested actor whose only legitimate obligations are those she or he contracts, Rousseau proposes that the marriage contract should be akin to the social contract: an irrevocable commitment freely undertaken, a set of legitimate chains that makes true community possible.

CONCLUSION

Rousseau's advocacy of sexual differentiation is rooted in his understanding of the human condition. He is concerned with establishing a family that can lead people to be better social creatures, capable of attachments to others that go beyond limited and destructive self-interested liaisons. His argument is that natural independence, self-absorption, and asociality, as well as social competitiveness and egoism, must be countered and that a politically effective means to this end is found in the relations of the sexes.

Rousseau's political advocacy of the sex-roled family differs from much antifeminist argument today. For example, contemporary opponents of extrafamilial childcare tend to emphasize the "enormous care" demanded by children, "the nurture and support" only a mother can offer, or how "vitally important" to women mothering is.[19] Rousseau, as we have seen, does not think a natural nurturing ability or desire exists in either sex and does not assume that only parents can possibly tend to the health and welfare of a child. Rousseau's general defense of specialized sex roles thus also diverges from more familiar ones, which frequently appeal to different sexual natures finding fulfillment in different social roles. In fact, Rousseau provides a potent critique of biological determinism that feminists can make use of.

He should also be distinguished from antifeminists who make harmful or derogatory assumptions about women's potential or character; for example, he does not portray women as inherently more immoral or moral, more selfish or selfless than men. While it is tempting to condemn Rousseau for advocating sexual differentiation at all, for whatever reason, it is worth at least pausing to consider his reasons, and the questions they raise for feminists.

Rousseau assumes that humans are originally asocial and self-interested, that survival requires the overcoming of both of these conditions, and that human malleability allows them to be overcome, though such a task is as difficult as it is important. It is these assumptions that lead Rousseau to endorse sexual differentiation. Its consequences are a major part of the solution to what he sees as the fundamental human dilemma. It is a solution that purports to bring woman and man together in a common enterprise, and to unite both with children in a situation in which they are bound by love and duty, not just self-interest. Feminists often charge that sexual differentiation and its vast resulting social arrangements make each sex "incomplete" — but this result is precisely what Rousseau wants, for it creates a reliable need for others, for interdependence, a configuration which nature does not provide and which is essential to survival and nonexploitative relations. Rousseau is concerned that in the quest for equality, for all to have the right to live as they choose as individuals, liberals, including liberal feminists, fail to address the instrumental and inherent goods of interdependence and community. While women in his scheme are in a sense treated as means to greater ends, so are men, and the ends are held to be legitimate and advantageous to both. Each must play a part in the whole, which Rousseau has in view, a part that directs each toward certain things and away from others, developing some potentialities in each and leaving others dormant. And it is important to remember that Rousseau often challenges the supposed superiority of the public over the private, abstract over practical reason, and reason over affection. Thus, that each sex is excluded from certain activities may not result in inequality according to his standards.

For Rousseau, the sentiment of attachment and the lessons of legitimate obligation are best learned in a loving family and are necessary developmental predecessors of unselfish dedication to the common good of the state.[20] He comes to endorse what feminism challenges—the sex-roled family—through pursuit of certain questions that feminists need to show can be answered or even posed differently. What devices, institutions, and practices can feminists suggest both to overcome exploitation and egoism and to develop community? Do the diverse forms of the family feminism supports nourish community? Can any supercede Rousseau's, by both alleviating the tension between self-development and care for others and constructively contributing to politics? It is not enough to say that competitiveness and conflict are not "natural" —indeed, Rousseau would agree! Instead, we need to work out educational, political, and familial arrangements that combat the egoistic, privatistic status quo without the sexual differentiation Rousseau's remedy relies upon. Rousseau's sense of the dangers of forsaking the affectionate, sex-roled family needs to be addressed thoroughly, and determining whether his means are unnecessary to or even destructive of his own ends are avenues I will pursue later.

In turn, feminist theory raises questions for Rousseau. The motive behind Rousseau's advocacy of the sex-roled, affectionate family is its ability to develop communal bonds, an ability he finds other family structures lacking; thus, his preferred form of the family is turned to as a means to other ends, ends which are both necessary and desirable. Rousseau is not so crude, however, as to argue that the ends justify any means: a family which oppresses any of its members would be both unjustifiable and ineffective; that is, it would not teach us to treat others decently and to make sacrifices for them. Thus, like the larger political community, in order to be legitimate the family must share fairly the benefits and burdens of social life among its members; it must, in fact, establish the equality Rousseau deems essential to community.

Since Rousseau's family and society are based on sexual differentiation, the tasks of each sex are different. For feminists, Rousseau must show that these differences, in the family and in politics, really are compatible with equality, and thus with community. Too often antifeminists simply claim the sexes are different but equal. Schwartz seems to follow this trend, for he tends to assume that the fact that women have *some* power is an argument that the sexes are *equally* empowered.[21] While he is right to assert that Rousseau's women are not powerless, the burden is on Rousseau to show that different kinds of empowerment really can be compatible with equality, with equal voice and respect for all, and Schwartz does not make that case for him convincingly.

In his understanding of the family Rousseau displays an awareness of the political consequences of private relationships. There is, however, less focus on the private consequences of political arrangements, commonly the result of an unjustified and unjustifiable belief that the private can pretty much take care of itself, at least once women assume their domestic duties. I will argue later that this failure to see the family itself as constrained by certain patriarchal political practices undermines community and disproportionately harms women.

Questions also arise over the need for sex role socialization as a means of making people social. To what extent, for example, is Rousseau's portrayal of the state of nature accurate for each sex, or even relevant to either sex today? Are self-absorption, indolence, and egoism among our most pressing problems, thus warranting activation of a far-reaching scheme to trick and lure people into sociality? Even if these problems are urgent and severe, are sex roles the only solution or even a solution at all? Might some of these problems be the *result* of sexism?

How safe is Rousseau's solution? What precautions are (or even could be) taken to assure that his generally familiar plan of sexual differentiation does not evolve into an all-too-familiar reality of the exploitation of women? Are we as indifferent to connection as Rousseau indicates? Do feminist analyses of the oppressiveness of current family and work structures, for example, get us closer to the source of asociality and alienation than do visions of a golden age of family life? Finally, given that Rousseau's directing desire is to move away from bourgeois liberalism, including liberal feminism, what other alternatives—including the numerous varieties of nonliberal feminism

74 *Families and Politics*

—might exist that would require fewer social resources for maintenance and would exact less damaging sacrifices from individuals?

While antifeminists are too quick to assert that sexual differentiation poses no problem for equality, feminists should not be too quick to point to any role differences as proof of inequality. The differences have to be evaluated in terms of their personal and political consequences. A closer analysis of Rousseau's balance sheet will help to resolve questions of consistency in his thought. It will also contribute to answering the question of when different can and cannot be equal, a matter of great importance in feminist political theory. The next two chapters look at Rousseau's balance sheet from two quite distinct angles.

FIVE

THE JUSTICE OF SEX ROLES: "ROUSSEAU, JUDGE OF JEAN-JACQUES"

Rousseau's political theory acknowledges that social differentiation of the sexes is not a given but something that can be created in varying degrees and forms; he argues that it should be created for social and political purposes and recognizes the care and thoroughness with which a scheme of differentiation must be implemented and reinforced if it is to be successful. His arrangement indirectly supports a central thesis of radical feminism: that sex roles infiltrate every aspect of public and private worlds and are not an excisable feature of the social structure, as some "reformists" seem to believe. This means, too, that it would be a mistake to think that Rousseau's sexual scheme could be altered without consequence to the entirety of his politics. In his plan, the lives of females and males differ profoundly and for the sake of achieving certain political ends. Without sex roles his politics would have to be rethought, perhaps radically. Yet like feminists, Rousseau is well aware that both individual lives and political communities can and do depart from his model, potentially for worse or for better.[1]

The previous chapter offered a functional account of sexual differentiation in Rousseau's politics. Sexual differentiation can help both sexes become contributing members of a community, enabling them to overcome their original self-absorption, isolation, and indolence by channeling males into particular models of "husband" and "father" and females into corresponding ones of "wife" and "mother." But in Rousseau's thought the usefulness of this scheme is not enough to justify its implementation. First, almost any institution or practice can be justified as useful within some given political framework. Rousseau wants to question *what* ends are being served, not merely the efficacy of the means. For example, social structures and policies which indiscriminately foster development of all the arts or which devote massive resources to the development of commerce would obviously pose problems for the author of the *First and Second Discourses*, however effective they might be. What earlier chapters have shown is that Rousseau does see sex roles as serving legitimate and important societal functions. But utility is still an incomplete standard for Rousseau, because he acknowledges that the means employed even toward legitimate ends can themselves be unacceptable. For example, enslaving some so that others are freed to attend to other—even essential—social tasks is always illegitimate, regardless of efficacy. On what basis does Rousseau sees sex roles as a legitimate means, a means by which "justice and utility are not at variance" (SC, 46)?

The literature on Rousseau has generally not concentrated on the social utility argument laid out in the previous chapters. Therefore, when judgments have been offered regarding the justifiability of his sexual politics, factors indispensable to a fair and complete appraisal have been omitted. Nonetheless, the literature on sexual differentiation in Rousseau's philosophy has offered important objections to his scheme. These arguments focus on the incompatibility between his general principles of political justice and legitimacy and his politics of sexual differentiation, and they often challenge the internal consistency of Rousseau's sexual politics on grounds other than those considered heretofore.

While the utility of sex roles is a necessary but insufficient basis for their justifiability, the other relevant criteria are not always clear. Neither the usefulness nor the justifiability of sex roles in general finally rests, of course, upon Rousseau's standards of utility or justice. But judgments about his internal consistency do depend entirely upon them. In the final chapters larger issues about the justice and efficacy of sex roles will be raised, but more needs to be said about the internal coherence of his thought first.

Numerous objections have been made to Rousseau's recommendations about gender roles and relations. I am interested in what commentators have established, either explicitly or implicitly, as the criteria for justifiability that Rousseau's scheme must meet and their evaluation of why he has failed to meet them. I find room to disagree with what some have said Rousseau's principles are, and with what others have said about the social practices compatible with these principles. To establish and explore that room, I offer a series of Rousseauean responses to objections that are most commonly raised and that present the best opportunity for grappling with Rousseau's standards of justice. Laying out alternate interpretations in order to find fault with them is a disagreeable task, especially when one is deeply indebted to those interpretations for many important insights. But responding to them is a necessary part of offering a new interpretation, and I undertake such a response in the belief that the most convincing feminist critique of Rousseau's sexual politics will emerge after he is heard and defended on his own ground. A Rousseauean defense of Rousseau's sexual politics is what I present below. In the next chapter I will give my own responses to this defense.

JUSTICE AND DEPENDENCY

It has been held that Rousseau's sexual scheme is unjustifiable and inconsistent because it establishes a role for women that renders them dependent on men, while men are not made similarly dependent on women. Two quotes will suffice.

With no explanation . . . we have the division of labor between men as breadwinners and women as housewives. This division of labor . . . means that the entire female half of the human race is no longer self-sufficient.[2]

Rousseau designs the education of Emile so that he can recapture his natural inclinations toward independence and free will. . . . Sophie['s] . . . very definition is in terms of others rather than an independent self.[3]

Minimally, the implied principle of Rousseauean justice in these quotes, held to be violated, is a prohibition against buying the independence of some (men) at the expense of the freedom of others. This seems to be a fair reading of Rousseau, for in the *Social Contract* he provides as evidence of the legitimacy of the contract the following characteristic: "since each person gives himself whole and entire, the condition is equal for everyone" (SC, 148). But his sexual scheme does not necessarily violate this principle. A reassessment of what this prohibition against unequal conditions allows, and of the relative freedom enjoyed by each sex in the Rousseauean arrangement, will help to make this clear.

Both citations claim that Rousseau's inconsistency lies in making only women dependent, while leaving men free. This can be responded to fairly easily, relying on discussions in earlier chapters. First, it must be remembered that the state of nature ended because independent self-preservation had become impossible.

> I assume that men have reached the point where obstacles to their self-preservation in the state of nature prevail by their resistance over the forces each individual can use to maintain himself in that state. Then that primitive state can no longer subsist and the human race would perish if it did not change its way of life. Now since men cannot engender new forces, but merely unite and direct existing ones, they have no other means of self-preservation except to form, by aggregation, a sum of forces that can prevail over the resistance; set them to work by a single motivation; and make them act in concert. (SC, 52–53)

The survival of individuals and of the species is dependent on the institution of a division of labor. Its establishment is necessary for all, without regard to gender. The division of labor does do away with women's self-sufficiency, but by its very nature a division of labor means that *none* who partake in it are self-sufficient. Each does only some fraction of the work which has been divided, yet all are interested in access to various fruits of this divided labor.

As Eisenstein herself notes, "Rousseau's [male] citizen is not as free as he likes to present him," because "freedom defined as atomistic individualism" is incompatible with sexual dependence and financial responsibility.[4] The charge against Rousseau does not reckon with the fact that in his scheme men, like women, are supposed to be both dependent upon and responsible to others—members of a community and neither natural savages nor bourgeois individuals. While the particular structures of interdependence are the subjects of political choices, Rousseau argues that the alternative of savage freedom is unattainable and of liberal freedom undesirable.

Further, to say that as "housewives" women are not self-sufficient while men as "breadwinners" are is to take a perspective on social and economic relations foreign to Rousseau's. Individuals of both sexes contribute to their own survival, to the maintenance of their household, to the survival of their offspring, and to the well-being of their community. Too often both those who support and those who condemn the sexual division of labor pay insufficient attention to how dependent men are upon women, whether for personal nurturance, childcare, domestic services, or assistance with labor for which he alone is paid. Even the independent "economic man" of classical liberal theory is a fiction, only able to do what he does because women do certain other things. This must be understood, in Rousseau's thought and elsewhere, as male dependence, and it *is* understood by Rousseau as such.[5] In his scheme the sexes are dependent on each other by design, and the contributions of both are essential to survival and constructive social life.

In addition to incorrectly assessing the independence of men and the dependence of women, a theme more fully explored earlier, the condemnation of female dependency often misses the point that it is precisely Rousseau's goal that neither sex remain self-sufficient and that mutual, nonexploitive dependence be fostered. As he said in the quote above, it is necessary for people to "act in concert." This objective is constantly emphasized in Rousseau's thought, whether he is writing about the arts ("the principle advantage of literary occupations [is] that of making men more sociable by inspiring in them the desire to please one another with works worthy of their mutual approval" [FD, 35–36]) or about education ("good social institutions are those that best know how to denature man, to take his absolute existence from him in order to give him a relative one and transport the I into the common unity" [*Emile*, 40]). Much as Rousseau might crave to restore to the individual absolute freedom and independence, at the root of his work is the realization that such a possibility was forever lost when life in the state of nature became impossible, and now we must do the best we can with the options we possess. While I will raise additional questions later about the extent to which Rousseau's plan results in constructive interdependence, the claim that he is inconsistent because he makes either women or men, or both, dependent is based on a misunderstanding of his objectives and the central problem with which he sees himself faced.

JUSTICE AND SUBJUGATION

A related objection to Rousseau's sexual arrangements is that despite the language of interdependency, the dependence of women upon men is of a sort repugnant to his principles of justice, while male dependence upon females is not. In short, women's dependence amounts to women's subjugation.

> Rousseau alleged that to avoid subjugation, women must be pleasing to men. One sees now that this is actually a disguised formula for subjugating women. . . . [I]n directing effort toward pleasing a man, a woman abdicates autonomy. The most disabling part of Rousseau's program closed to women the development of an independent, autonomous will and the dependency on self as the major source of validation.[6]

80   *The Justice of Sex Roles*

If one part of an intimate union does all the acting and willing, and the other is defined by receptivity and non-resistance, the two parts are related as positive and negative. We cannot then speak of two separate and incommensurate paths for the two sexes; the one defines and dominates the other.[7]

It is certainly true that not all relationships of interdependence are ones of equal dependence. Both the kind and degree of dependence may differ significantly, and parties in personal, professional, and political associations can have mutual dependencies but significantly unequal power. One may, in other words, grant the interdependency of the sexes in Rousseau's society but still hold that women's dependence on men is of a particular kind that is objectionable, while male dependence is not. It is true, given the entire thrust of the *Social Contract*, that the dependence of females on self-interested males would amount to "illegitimate chains" by Rousseau's standards.

The concern here frequently focuses on Rousseau's declaration that women should be pleasing to men, a central and oft-cited notion worth unpacking. The objection can be restated as follows: by being pleasing to men women are supposed to avoid subjugation to them, but precisely by being pleasing to men women in fact become subjugated, because they must become what men want them to be and cannot validate their own existence. Even if Rousseau's intent is for women to avoid subjugation, the argument runs, the dynamics of the male-female relationship he recommends will lead to the opposite outcome. Rousseau's response might be threefold.

Rousseau could argue that in his plan women are not simply supposed to do whatever men want whenever they want it. He is making a more moderate and general claim: that men must be attracted to women. Rousseau does not argue that one person need be a mere creature of another, or a person without an independent will, in order to be attractive to them. To prove attractive, one must only have some goods (skills, traits, etc.) that another desires and cannot provide for him or herself, or not as easily or as well. Rousseau does not believe that women need satisfy men's every whim to be pleasing, perhaps because he sees men as less "power-hungry" than such a view implies, and/or because sex roles help ensure that the sexes will need and desire each other. Thus, for women to be pleasing to men would not seem to require that women give up all self-identity and merely fulfill the wishes of men.

Rousseau could further defend his arrangement by explaining how being pleasing to men actually serves women's interests. Assuming the necessity of a division of labor, his goal is for women to gain power over men through their possession of or access to certain goods and pleasures in which men are interested. If women please men, men will be motivated to do things they otherwise would not do, in order to get certain benefits from women, benefits which could include women's respect, domestic service, or sexual interest. If women do not please or interest men, Rousseau's reasoning proceeds, men will at best be uninterested in women and at worst will misuse their now superior strength against them. Either way, men will not do what women want them to do. Men will remain what they were—isolated, self-interested, and lazy—which is to say that men will be useless or detrimental both to women and to society. But if women can offer men the pleasures of private life, men may be motivated to participate in childrearing and to work not only for their own benefit but also for the benefit of their familial and political communities.

Rousseau's argument is that if women are clever and desirable enough, they can generally have their own way. Through charm and manipulation, he believes that women can not only avoid subjugation to male power, but can get men to carry out women's will. While serious questions remain about the desirability, efficacy, and necessity of using this strategy, questions to which I will turn in succeeding chapters, it is wrong to say that in Rousseau's plan men do all of the willing. Rousseau, who believes that our first desires are all self-interested ones, could never hold that any creature is egoless. Women have legitimate desires and rightfully act to fulfill them. His contention is that once the sexual division of labor is established, it is best if each sex uses different means to achieve its ends, means that are more appropriate to the different roles each is now to play.

It is important to add that in Rousseau's scheme men must please women, as well. He often refers to women as the judges of men. Women also have some say in what pleases men. As was explored in the previous chapter, Rousseau thinks women can be a moral, redemptive force in society because of the kind of power they can exercise over men. Discussing the "ascendancy of women," Rousseau writes, "Men will always be what is pleasing to women; therefore if you want them to become great and virtuous, teach women what greatness of soul and virtue are" (FD, 52–53n.). There is no reason to think that these are vain words. Rousseau believes that in an arrangement in which each sex has power over the other and in which each is made dependent on the other for certain pleasures and necessities, each will find it right, pleasant, and useful to please the other. Thus, the claim that Rousseau's scheme is flawed by the enslaving requirement that women please men is not, at this stage, convincing.

JUSTICE AND POLITICAL PARTICIPATION

A third objection to Rousseau's sexual politics focuses on women's confinement to the domestic sphere, and consequent exclusion from the political: "That 'sacred and imprescriptible' law of nature which mandates participation, or at least representation, for all who can legitimately be obliged to obey the laws, apparently was regarded by Rousseau as having no application to any member of the female sex."[8] This is a twist on the theme that the different activities and traits of the sexes empower them unequally. The argument here is that women neither participate nor have representation in the assembly, an arrangement that contradicts Rousseau's own standard of political legitimacy and unjustifiably diminishes the power and influence of women.

Often the accusation that Rousseau excludes women from politics wrongly assumes that serving in the assembly is the only way of influencing politics. It is probably true, as Okin states, that "Rousseau never envisaged that women should be enfranchised citizens," but definitely false that women's voices should not be "contributed to the formulation of the general will."[9] There are many ways of contributing to politics. Okin notes that "[o]nly through their domestic influence on their husbands . . . women were to have . . . power in Rousseau's ideal republic."[10] But why does she minimize women's contribution by beginning this sentence with the word "only"? In a similar vein, Keohane writes: "The act of marriage marks Emile's entry into society, as head of family, property owner, and citizen. That same event consigns Sophie to the household and excludes her from politics *except* as the guardian of moral values and educational practices."[11] Neither commentator explains why we should dismiss women's contribution to politics in Rousseau's ideal society, when Rousseau emphasizes the critical political importance of mores and education, which women influence more than do men in his scheme (as is in fact acknowledged by both Okin and Keohane). Those who have a hand in the educational system surely have influence over the ideas of those who will serve in the assembly: "Everything we do not have at our birth and which we need when we are grown is given us by education" (*Emile*, 38). Further, as discussed in earlier chapters, women have the greatest influence on mores, which Rousseau sees as at the foundation of society, a force which is stronger than written laws and influences them. If women control mores, they surely also affect politics. As long as women affect the assembly, through their general influence on mores and education and their particular influence on individual men, they are considered by Rousseau to be political actors. His definition of "politics" is a broad one, not unlike the feminist definition.

Ultimately, to be justifiable, it must be "safe" for women to participate only indirectly in the assembly, while men participate directly. Rousseau is noted for the opinion that because people are more interested in themselves than others, it is unwise to allow another to judge what is in one's own best interest. Further, for the sovereign general will to be general, deliberations cannot systematically exclude any interests. Is it possible for the interests of women to be represented and protected in the assembly despite their physical absence? As discussed above, the influence of women is felt in the assembly because of their influence over mores. But it is also possible to argue that women's interests are protected, because those interests are identical to those of men and therefore can be represented by men. In order for this to be true, the interests of men and women must be so deeply intertwined that they are for all practical purposes inseparable. We must, moreover, be able to demonstrate that Rousseau is not absolutely opposed to the notion of one individual's representing the will of another.

Is it likely that males, as the brothers, husbands, fathers, sons, etc. of women, will represent women fairly in the assembly? For Rousseau, the sexual division of labor he prescribes means that men need women and are engaged in a cooperative venture with them. If Rousseau's family scheme is successful, one of its primary beneficial consequences is that egoism and narcissism are discouraged, and the interests of each member are blended, as far as possible, with those of the others and of the familial unit as a whole. It is true that people are so self-regarding as to make it risky to subject some to the general will as determined by others. But the sexes rule each other, and each influences what the other wills. Rousseau would claim that in his scheme men could not hurt women without hurting themselves. This is an argument for the scheme's safety and justice, for it resembles a central justification of the social compact: "since the condition is equal for everyone, *no one has an interest in making it burdensome for the others*" (SC, 53, emphasis added).

Granted, there is no guarantee that men will always see and act upon that shared interest, but Rousseau endorses the assembly even while noting that it may not always recognize the general will. He can only claim that the errors that occur will not be caused by systematic injustice. And of course, much of male education (like female) is concerned with giving men the abilities and inclination to regard not just their particular will but also the general will. Lastly, it is interesting to note that what is true of the sexes does not necessarily hold true for economic classes. Rousseau believes it is more probable that the interests of different classes will be opposed to one another than will the interests of the sexes, which helps explain why he deprecates distinctions of class, all the while favoring exaggerated sexual differentiation.

Richard Fralins's work on representation adds evidence to the view that Rousseau was not totally opposed to the notion of one individual representing another in the assembly. "Representative government is illegitimate because it violates the principle of generality by granting a particular group of citizens the right to impose their will on the whole body of citizens. But . . . assuming the accountability of representatives, it is just as consistent with Rousseau's insistence on generality to determine the general will indirectly through the use of representatives as it is to determine it by a direct vote of all citizens."[12] Thus, Rousseau's exclusion of women from direct participation in the assembly could be considered consistent with his principles. According to him, with sex roles male interests can be intertwined with those of females, women can hold men as representatives accountable to women, men can be led in the assembly to attend not to their private interest but to the common good, and women can have some influence in politics, indirect though it may be.

Lynda Lange makes an additional, interesting point: "[T]he nature of Rousseau's ideal state makes the refuge of the home a virtual necessity for the citizen. Because the demands of citizenship are so stringent and impersonal, it would be appalling to imagine everyone called to that status."[13] In the overall scheme of things, that is, it is undesirable for everyone to participate in the assembly, because it requires transcendence of personal, particular interests and independence of judgment. Some must be left to care about emotions, sentiments, and personal relationships, which Rousseau considers of equal social importance. The sexual division of labor ensures that both "tasks" are attended to. So "unnatural" is the political task that one part of the population, men, might not be willing to undertake it if another part, women, did not maintain the private family as a refuge to retreat to. Thus, women's participation in the assembly can be seen as both unnecessary and undesirable, but not because of any inherent limit on the capabilities of women nor because of any desire to establish male authority over a silenced female population. Under certain circumstances, it appears that representation might be able consistently to replace direct participation.

JUSTICE AND ADVANTAGE

Rousseau's scheme of sexual differentiation is unjustifiable, it is held, because by it women lose more than they gain, and/or gain less than do men: "Whatever one may think of the fate of savage man, savage woman got the short end of the deal."[14]

Rousseau stresses that "since all are born equal and free, they only alienate their freedom for their utility" (SC, 47). The change from the freedom both sexes enjoyed in the state of nature to the chains both know in civil society *can* be made legitimate, but only under certain conditions.

The move into civil society must be fair to all and in everyone's self-interest to be legitimate. What men and women gain and lose in moving to long-term, monogamous, heterosexual, sex-roled relationships are factors to be considered in calculating the overall plusses and minuses of social existence. The arrangement must be in the interest of both parties, and must fairly distribute the social and personal benefits and burdens of social existence. If it does not, Rousseau's plan is fatally flawed by its own inconsistency. It will help to look at what both sexes gain and lose in both the move to civil society and the move to sex-roled relationships, trying again to establish how Rousseau might have thought his arrangement just.

As soon as one tries to weigh the gains and losses of women and men in the transition to civil society, a difficulty arises. Because the sexes are to be differentiated in society, their relative gains and losses frequently cannot be seen as involving different "amounts" of the same thing. For example, standard lists of what the transition entails include a development of rationality and morality. But if we ask the question "Do the sexes gain in development of their rational capacities equally?" we are forced to compare the more practical thinking which women are encouraged to acquire with the more impersonal kind of thought men are taught. We should remember, however, that Rousseau does not distinguish between them as superior and inferior. Certainly Aristotle would say that women's gain in the area of rationality is inferior to man's, because man alone is taught to understand generalities, ends, and systems, and such thinking is superior to that which concerns particulars, means, and the personal. But in Rousseau there is no such hierarchy. One truth is as good as another; whether it be particular or general, women's or men's, makes no difference. So here the gain is equal, because both sexes, in entering civil society, have developed rationality. Only if one sex did not would there be an issue here.

The same is true for many other items on non–gender-specific lists of what the transition to civil society entails. As another example, consider morality. While in the state of nature individuals were "naturally good," in civil society the sexes are often bound to differing moral codes. For instance, virtue demands of women that they tend to the community through direct caring for others and of men that they tend to the community by such means as participating in the assembly. But from Rousseau's perspective the crucial point of these gendered moral codes is not their difference but their similarity: through them both sexes are limited by public opinion, which censures certain acts and approves others; both have models of virtuous behavior to which they must conform; and both have rules to follow regarding their sexual, marital, and work lives. Each sex is governed by distinctive rules, but the rules in both cases involve sacrifices and the imposition of unnatural duties as well as rewards and possibilities for goodness. And both sets of rules are essential to the well-being of the community. Rousseau truly does not seem to have any hierarchy of virtuous acts operating here that would cause one gender's socially beneficial morality to be praised or desired more than the other's.

Surveying the costs and gains of social life, without reference to gender, leads back to the conclusion of chapter 2: the sexes are to lead different lives but guided by the same formal principles of happiness, virtue, and sociability. But can the same be said of the costs and gains incident to that particular facet of social life, the sexual division of labor? Is that move advantageous to both, or does one receive more of the burdens or benefits of social life than the other?

If anything, woman's life was at greater risk than man's in the state of nature, because while both had to feed and defend themselves, many women had the additional burdens of (1) pregnancy and childbirth, both of which are potentially life-threatening, and (2) defending and training an infant, which could distract or slow women, making them more vulnerable. In civil society, women have men to defend them in war and to assist in childrearing. However, such women also have more children, which means that they risk their lives more often and must dedicate more of their lives to childrearing.

Put this way, the burden that men assume in being soldiers and defending others is not disproportionate to that assumed by women in increased pregnancies and childbirths. If each woman is to bear approximately four children, as Rousseau recommends in light of eighteenth-century infant mortality rates, this would require a risk of life not incomparable to men's in war. The burdens here can be considered to be reasonably distributed. Overall, the exchange seems an equal one for women, who gain assistance in defense but risk life more often through pregnancy. Similarly, woman loses the relative ease and shortness of primitive motherhood but gains the assistance of the male in childrearing. It also seems reasonably fair that woman's loss of capacity for independent self-preservation through the intentional diminution of her physical strength and prowess is compensated by having the male share the fruits of his labor with her and aid in her defense.

In the state of nature only women and children had regular interaction with each other, though for a short time and apparently without attaching much emotional or moral significance to the relationship. Still, men by comparison were even more isolated, the main exception to their solitude being the chance, fleeting, and seemingly unimportant sexual encounters they had. In the move from the state of nature to the state of society, men gain the chance to have stable, affectionate relations. They can no longer be sexually promiscuous and must contribute to the care and education of offspring, but this limitation is offset by (1) the inherent pleasures of stable union, (2) having a wife who runs one's household and is attentive to one's pleasure and well-being, and (3) the reasonable assurance that the children one is working for are one's biological heirs. Men must share the fruits of their labor with their families, but their partners do the same; and women must, like men, forgo sexual promiscuity so that men will identify with and be more inclined to care for their children.

Men do gain opportunities in public life which women do not. But again, it is important to note that Rousseau does not assume, as we often do today, that the public world holds more pleasures and possibilities than the private. Each allows for development or perfection of some capacities. Most importantly, though, woman's life in the household is less remote from the state of nature than is man's in the public realm: this advantage could offset some of the positive features of public action.

Given the framework of values and the assumptions about the human condition that inform Rousseau's thought, it is possible to conclude that his distribution between the sexes of the benefits and burdens of social life is not blatantly unjust. Both suffer limitations they did not confront in the state of nature, but this is inevitable to the extent that social existence is "unnatural"; and while the burdens they bear are different, it is not patently obvious—at least in theory—that one suffers more or benefits less, as Rousseau understands suffering and benefit. Both have the opportunity to be happy as well, for in Rousseau's thought, as we have seen, happiness is not the attainment of a particular way of life but a balance between what one wants and what one can attain, and this balance can be reached by both women and men. Thus, the "public man/private woman" division in Rousseau cannot be discredited by the feminist rejoinders normally so effective against such schemas, because, first, in his thought the division is not complete—women influence politics and thus are not totally private, while men also have private roles to fulfill—and second, neither the public nor the private sphere contains all the rewards or sacrifices of social life.

CONCLUSION

The fact that "Rousseauean" defenses of his sexual politics can be marshaled is evidence that his position is more than an unreflective or reactionary endorsement of the status quo and that sex roles play an integral part in his political thought. While in stating his political goals he says nothing about sexual differentiation, it enters his thought as an effective and permissible means to those ends.

One way to challenge Rousseau's sexual politics is by offering a liberal defense of individual choice, fulfillment, and freedom. That challenge will not be made here, for two reasons. First, a wealth of literature exists on both liberalism and liberal feminism, from classic sources such as John Stuart Mill, Mary Astell, and Mary Wollstonecraft to contemporary sources such as Betty Friedan and Carole Pateman. Second, one of the limits of some of the literature advocating liberal feminism is that it is more a call to liberals to endorse feminism, which is certainly important, than part of a conversation with nonliberal antifeminists. A challenge to Rousseau's system of sexual differentiation should talk to rather than past him—should assume the desirability and necessity of human interdependency, and the necessity for arranging the social structure in such a way as to foster a nonexploitative, mutual dependence that benefits all.

Rousseau's defense of sex roles is based upon seeing them as an effective and permissible means to community, a goal shared by many feminists. A feminist challenge to it should focus on the ineffectiveness and illegitimacy of that means. The defects of Rousseau's communitarian defense of sex roles can be challenged not only by liberals but also by communitarians. I will now show that, despite all that can be said in defense of Rousseau's program of sexual differentiation, as a means to community, sex roles in fact are self-defeating and illegitimate.

SIX

ROUSSEAU AND FEMINIST REVOLUTION: THE IMPOSSIBILITY OF GENDERED COMMUNITY

Rousseau created and institutionalized gender roles as part of his plan for attaining genuine political community. There are some plausible arguments supporting the view that the sexual division of labor is consistent with his principles of justice. His sexual politics are less mysterious and inconsistent, and more integral and intentional, than many have maintained. If I have played the part of Rousseau's "apologist," this is because I believe a feminist critique of him would be more effective if it gave him the benefit of the doubt wherever it was not blatantly unreasonable to do so. This accomplished, I leave the task of textual exegesis and move to a feminist evaluation and critique of Rousseau, much of which builds on questions raised earlier.

I have taken issue with some feminist commentaries condemning Rousseau's sexual politics because of the general interpretations of his thought on which they are based. Too often, for example, they have called him an inconsistent liberal when he is not a liberal at all, consistent or otherwise. I most wholeheartedly agree, however, that his theory is not informed by a feminist consciousness and that in practice his scheme will contribute sizably to the subordination of women, as such schemes have done and continue to do today. My reasons for coming to this conclusion differ from those usually offered because they issue from a different general reading of Rousseau as a communitarian. His communitarian defense of gender roles now needs a feminist appraisal.

A certain impatient dismissal of and disregard for Rousseau, as for others whose thought is limited and tainted by its patriarchal framework, is understandable and warranted. But in this chapter I discuss how Rousseau can be of interest and use to feminists in two important ways. First, I show that several of Rousseau's fundamental arguments are in accord with those of feminists. Too often the history of philosophy, like the histories of many disciplines (biology, psychology, etc.) and institutions (religious, familial, etc.), is falsely universalized, said to present a uniform and thus an authoritative voice that "proves" the naturalness and inevitability of social sexual differentiation. A display of Rousseau's failure to sing along in complete harmony allows the reclaiming of an instance of diversity regarding gender even among the lionized in the history of philosophy, thus rebutting a popular argument used by antifeminists and adding support to and precedent for some feminist positions.

Second, despite the absence of familiar antifeminist assumptions and despite his best efforts, Rousseau fails to make a system of sexual differentiation function also as a system of sexual equality and community. This failure is due to the practical workings of a socially enforced sexual division of labor. Rousseau's failure is indicative of the inherent limitations of any such system, even those defended on the basis of the "social welfare" or the "common good." His work thus inadvertently supports the feminist contention that equality requires abolishing the political categories of "woman" and "man."[1]

A "FEMINIST" ROUSSEAU

The idea that Rousseau says anything that not only agrees with but sometimes even adds support to feminist arguments may surprise many.[2] But, drawing on the arguments of earlier chapters, we will find at least five important issues where Rousseau and revolutionary feminists agree. Because some of these issues continue to be the subjects of heated debate today, Rousseau's contributions are worth noting.

First, he consistently questions the notion of a fixed human nature, male or female. Antifeminists who base their defense of sex roles on biology thus find a foe in Rousseau. He goes to great lengths to show how human nature is affected by a wide range of environmental forces. There is, for Rousseau, no fixed "woman's nature" that mandates a particular social role for her as either fulfilling her inborn desires or matching her supposed biologically limited abilities, just as there is no fixed "male nature."[3] He offers much evidence that what are often taken as unchanging male and female natures, biological and psychological, have in fact evolved radically throughout history and will no doubt continue to do so. He discusses the deep impact of nutritional, economic, social, political, educational, and geographical factors on our ways of seeing the world, on our ways of relating to each other, and on the development of our intellectual and physical capacities. Rousseau, like most feminists, finds it more meaningful to speak of human conditions than of human nature and realizes that we continue to have the power to make political choices that can lead to qualitatively different conditions. Feminists could make more use of Rousseau's evidence and arguments in debates about the malleability of sexual natures, as we often make use of Marx's ideas about human nature, despite the fact that neither is essentially feminist.[4]

Second, Rousseau treats the family as a social construct, not a natural one, in both its origin and function. Given the extent to which "the" supposedly natural family, like "woman's nature," has been used to justify virtually every conceivable limitation on women's freedom—dictating the jobs and hours we could work within and outside the home, the civic responsibilities we could fulfill, and the rights we could possess—this is no small concession.[5]

With respect to origins, Rousseau does not posit the patriarchal family as a feature of the early state of nature, as he explicitly criticizes Locke for doing, or as a configuration to which we are naturally drawn, as his work implicitly criticizes antifeminists from Aristotle to Phyllis Schlafly for doing. Rousseau views the family as arising from particular historical needs and as originally involving no sexual inequality. This means that for Rousseau woman does not naturally require or desire man or the family headed by him. He knows the family to be a pliable social institution with many possible forms and uses, depending on the needs, abilities, and desires of both individuals and communities. In public policy debates today, effects upon "the family" are cited as a sort of trump card; a Rousseauean (and, better, a more thoroughly feminist) sense of families as variables that interact dialectically with a number of other variables is, unfortunately, absent.

Rousseau understands that in practice the family both affects and reflects the social and political life beyond its doors. His endorsement of the nuclear, sentimental family is based on political considerations—its ability to teach us the lessons of obligation, loyalty, and attachment that make true political community possible—just as, conversely, his condemnation of aristocracy is based in part on its negative personal consequences. The radical feminist slogan "The personal is political" would make good sense to Rousseau, and we see precedent in him for reconceiving the private with an eye to the political, and vice versa.[6]

Third, and related, feminists can find in Rousseau a theorist who does not disparage the private. He views private life as morally relevant, socially important, and personally fulfilling. He does not assume, as both antifeminists and nonrevolutionary feminists often do, that traditional woman contributes less to her own welfare, or that of her family or community, than does traditional man, or that the skills and morality women gain by virtue of their traditional role are any less real, useful, or laudable. Portions of Rousseau's writings resonate with Carol Gilligan's descriptions of the equally developed and praiseworthy, but different, modes of moral reasoning that correlate with the two genders. Although his presentation is incomplete, he says more about both the sources and the political consequences of these differences than does Gilligan.

Fourth, Rousseau's critique of bourgeois individualism bears some similarity to feminist critiques of it, as the next chapter will show more fully. Rousseau lays bare the myth of the naturally selfish, competitive, independent, autonomous man, a pervasive figure in antifeminist ideology from Thomas Hobbes to Steven Goldberg, and elegantly notes both the personal and social costs of pursuing self-interest and neglecting community. His biting account of the dangers of this ideology could be useful to feminists.

Lastly, like most feminists, Rousseau ardently wishes to establish the basis for true community, which he sees as necessary for survival, personal happiness, and moral relations. Community entails, for Rousseau, arrangements in which all explicitly recognize their mutual dependence. None should pretend to be above or outside of the need for others, or attempt to make such autonomy a goal. Combined with the absence of any teleological perspective in Rousseau, such recognition of interdependence can lead to respect for others, acknowledging the small and large debts one incurs to others every day, visibly and invisibly. Community also entails, for Rousseau, arrangements in which all fulfill their obligations to others, not reluctantly or from mere self-interest, but because they see themselves embedded in a community which they view as legitimate and whose fate is their own.

Rousseau also asserts that equality is a precondition of community, for great inequalities destroy social bonds, replacing them with fear, envy, and distrust.

These areas of agreement between Rousseau and feminism show that we cannot account for or argue against his advocacy of sexual differentiation in the usual ways. Rousseau does not read nature, history, biology, or culture as automatically rendering patriarchy inevitable or legitimate. Instead, with an antifeminism in many ways less obviously flawed in its logic and reprehensible in its morality than most, Rousseau endorses sex roles as a path to community. The creation of "complementary" males and females is meant to help establish an interdependence between people. Based on need, this interdependence moves us out of our original isolation and asociality, and moderated by affection, it turns us away from exploitation. The sex-roled family is where we learn about community and loyalty; where, in a small group bound by ties of familiarity and affection as well as obligation, we step outside of the self and self-interest into a larger whole. That's the theory.

THE "ANTIFEMINIST" ROUSSEAU

Do Rousseau's sex roles successfully establish community, or do they come complete with burdens that in fact destroy community? Grant that Rousseau was a careful thinker, deeply committed to freedom, community, and equality. His consistent opposition to slavery, bourgeois individualism, and economic inequality (at least some of which positions set him off as distinct from other social contract thinkers)[7] makes this characterization reasonable. Grant as well that he imagined and endorsed sex roles as both compatible with and a means to these goals. The arguments of the earlier chapters make such a reading plausible.

Granting this much, we can use Rousseau to test the coherence in theory and the equality in practice of radically gendered community. Based on the explication I have offered of his sexual politics and on the fact that his sex-roled society is structurally a fairly typical one, Rousseau provides a good study by which to test what I call a communitarian defense of enforced gender identity. That defense states that a sexual division of labor can not only coexist with but can even contribute to the creation, nurturance, and sustenance of freedom, equality, and community.

If Rousseau's scheme successfully combines sex roles with these personal and social goods, there are important ramifications for feminist theory. It would certainly raise questions about precisely what the "enemy" of sexual equality is; if a system of socially exaggerated and enforced sex differences itself does not necessarily lead to the subordination of women, under what circumstances does it do so? It would have practical implications for deciding where feminists ought to direct our analyses and action.

If, on the other hand, Rousseau's scheme is one in which sex roles are shown to be incompatible with freedom, community, and equality, then we have grounds for thinking that communitarian defenses of traditional, enforced gender differentiation can be discarded with other defenses—sociobiological and liberal ones, for example—that have been exposed as inconsistent in theory and unjust in practice. If Rousseau's reasoning—which we have ceded is careful and well intentioned—proves unsound, we can raise questions about the coherence of any communitarian defense of sex roles and lend even more credence (and many are still quite unconvinced) to the view that sex roles must go if we care about making freedom, community, and equality available to all people.

I evaluate Rousseau's sexual scheme by its ability to produce the benefits for which it is instituted. Thus, social sexual differentiation will be problematic for him if it renders women more exploitable by, vulnerable to, or devalued by men or by society than men are by women or by society. For if that happens, difference has become inequality, which is unjustifiable and politically self-defeating. In addition, his socially induced and enforced gender roles will be useless or counterproductive if they contribute to the maintenance or growth of individualism, an attitude of self-interestedness, or a desire to dominate—the enemies of community discussed by Rousseau himself in a number of contexts.

In looking at Rousseau's sex differences for their compatibility with freedom, equality, and community, I have chosen as a framework one systematic difference central to his politics, useful for the range of issues it raises, and familiar to readers of our time as well as his. In *The Sexual Politics of Jean-Jacques Rousseau*, Schwartz claims that Rousseau intends the sexes to be equal and empowers them equally, though differently. Rousseau's scheme, Schwartz's argument runs, endows women with indirect power which, like the indirect power of the *Social Contract*'s founding legislator, Emile's tutor, and social mores, is not only real but often more effective than direct power, precisely because of its invisibility and secrecy.

Schwartz is right regarding both Rousseau's intent to empower women and the character of that empowerment; in fact, the present study supplies new evidence for some elements of Schwartz's thesis.[8] I think, however, that we need to stop and ask questions that the supporters of Schwartz's thesis do not pose: "Since both women and men are to be social actors, people who influence mores and laws, what assurances do we have that women's indirect power is as heard and heeded as men's direct power—that as externally directed forces, they are similarly effective?" Second, and related, "Since sexual differentiation is a means to community, exactly what effects on interpersonal, and especially familial, communities follow from female and male access to different forms of power?" Last, and also related, "What consequences for an individual's sense of themselves and of others arise from association with indirect versus direct power? What sorts of (gendered) individuals does this system produce?" These questions are distinguished by their focus, respectively, on the political, social, and personal consequences of a division of people into sex-based groups distinguished by, among other things, the forms of power to which they have access. But while the questions point to issues that differ in important ways, they are also utterly inseparable. One's self-image, for example, will influence and be influenced by the treatment received from one's partner and by the fate of one's political efforts. The questions are also united by an underlying, and overriding, concern: "Might the sorts of power women and men have in Rousseau's scheme, as in most other traditional systems of sexual differentiation, have costs that outweigh or negate their benefits, or lead to ends quite opposed to those which are intended?" The arguments I present below answer this with a "yes." In what follows I briefly recall what indirect versus direct power entails for Rousseau and comment on the lack of attention by political theorists to this sexual distribution of the forms and locales of influence. I then explore some ramifications of sexually differentiated power that either undermine or endanger, rather than create or sustain, community.

INDIRECT POWER

In discussing the indirect power Rousseau allots to women, most commentators refer to his endorsement of such devices and tactics as wiles, craftiness, coquetry, flattery, disguise, and gentleness as means to accomplish their ends, rather than such direct means as assertions, requests, demands, and reasoned arguments.

It may be useful briefly to reconstruct here why Rousseau restricts women to indirect power in the first place. Since, as has been established, sex roles are unconnected to assumptions about female and male natures in Rousseau's thought, it is again necessary to ask what social ends they serve. Schwartz in fact offers a social defense for these contrivances. In Rousseau's thought, he argues, women's protecting, indulging, and appealing to male ego—via flattery, insinuation, etc.—motivates men to do certain work they would not otherwise desire to perform, given natural indolence and asociality, but which is socially indispensable. To use an example of Schwartz's cited earlier, one who has been taught to think of himself as the "great provider and protector" will be motivated to earn and retain that title, and the personal and political rewards that accompany it, by much exertion: he will ply a trade and, if necessary, risk his life in war. Rather paradoxically (of course), the rule of women, according to Schwartz's interpretation of Rousseau, is legitimate and praiseworthy only if it preserves men's masculinity and the appearance of male rule, which it does by being indirect. The contention, however, is that appearances notwithstanding, women really do govern. Arthur Melzer sees an analogy in this regard between Rousseau's ideal state and his ideal marriage:

Rousseau states as clearly as one could wish [!] how the seeming contradictions are to be resolved, how the family and also the state will really function. The man (or the people) will possess the legal sovereign power, the "right to command," and on this official level the woman (or the executive) is subordinate and must simply obey. But formal sovereign power is not everything, and in vehemently insisting that this power must belong exclusively to the man (the people), Rousseau by no means intends to exclude the woman (Government) from every form of dominion. Unofficially and indirectly, the latter will "reign" by dint of "governing him who commands." While publicly affirming the man's right to command and her duty to obey, she will use her various feminine wiles to manipulate him into commanding what she desires.[9]

To speak directly is something of a privilege. To be effective, it entails being aware of and able to express what one wants, living with others who are willing to listen,[10] and having a social and political environment that does not penalize speaking. Some sort of an indirect voice is useful to all of us when there is a possible negative consequence attached to speaking directly. Whether in a university, a corporation, or a family, those of us in relatively vulnerable positions often choose our words, strategies, and battles carefully, knowing there are egos to stroke and power relationships to heed if we wish to protect ourselves and our projects. But women, according to

Rousseau, should always and as a matter of course express themselves indirectly, and this must raise the somewhat obvious question of whether women in his society are always working from a position of vulnerability, bolstering male egos in a system designed to serve someone and something other than women's interests or the common good. Yet substantive, well-defended responses to questions like this are almost nonexistent.

IGNORING THE SEXUAL DIVISION OF LABOR

Perhaps the costs of indirect power are less obvious than its benefits, judging from the lack of consideration such costs get from Rousseau, Schwartz, and many antifeminists. Of course, limitation to indirect power may not be conclusive evidence of inequality in itself, for if all roads lead to Rome, then indirect access may not be inherently better or worse than direct: it could, in fact, get one there through lighter traffic and more attractive scenery. But the limitations and flaws of the feminine backroads and byways need more attention. It is at least curious (and at most unconscionable) that the differentiated powers of the sexes never receive the same careful scrutiny for "balance" in political theory as do, for example, the powers allocated to the various branches of government. Yet the balance of power in sexual relationships is in no less need of defense, for certainly no less is at stake.

For Rousseau, Schwartz claims, sexual relationships resemble political ones, in that they involve each partner ruling and being ruled by the other. "Sexual differentiation gives men power over women, but it also gives women power over men. Rousseau believes that this power has historically been exercised by women both for better and for worse, and that it could be so exercised again. He is in short quite ambivalent about the power of women over men."[11] Perhaps, given the history of political theory, Rousseau is "progressive" for allowing that women's power *can* be exercised for good. But it is striking that Schwartz, perhaps following Rousseau, focuses almost entirely on the troublesome nature of women's power over men. He seems to take it on (patriarchal) faith that men's power over women is relatively innocuous and unproblematic, while women's power over men is fraught with dangers. A more feminist analysis, grounded in the realities of women's lives, might start with precisely the opposite assumption. In fact, Rousseau's own analysis—and Schwartz's—should arguably have begun with the opposite assumption.

Rousseau often bases his political recommendations not on an abstract ideal but on the real character of a particular situation. He even makes a principle of it: "Just as an architect, before putting up a big building, observes and tests the ground to see whether it can bear the weight, so the wise founder does not start by drafting laws that are good in themselves, but first examines whether the people for whom he intends them is suited to bear them" (SC, 70). Patriarchy was well entrenched in Rousseau's culture. Given that particular situation, and following his own principle, he should have invested less in continued restriction of, and justification for restriction of, women's power, and turned instead to checking the ambition, the violence, the power of men. The power of men, then as now, was often as unrestrained in extent and form as women's was restrained, and already as supported by arguments of nature, God, and politics as women's was unsupported. To transfer Publius's concerns about legislative usurpation to concerns about male usurpation of power, we might conclude, "[I]t is against the enterprising ambition of men that the people ought to indulge all their jealousy and exhaust all their precautions."[12] Instead, however, Rousseau concerns himself primarily with women's abuses of power, as have so many men before and after him.

Claims that women have great power in their traditional roles but that fail to acknowledge or even consider the possibility of any overriding costs are numerous. I cite just one more. In a letter to Abigail Adams, John Adams responds to her call to "Remember the Ladies" in writing the Constitution of the United States and not to "put such unlimited power into the hands of the Husbands." He answers:

We know better than to repeal our Masculine systems. Altho they are in full Force, you know they are little more than Theory. We dare not exert our Power in its full Latitude. We are obliged to go fair, and softly, and in Practice you know We are the subjects. We have only the Name of Masters, and rather than give up this, which would compleatly subject Us to the Despotism of the Peticoat, I hope General Washington, and all our brave Heroes would fight.[13]

The patronizing and sarcastic tone of John Adams's response is as noteworthy as the absence of substantive argument: he declares that he is the subjected and she the master, and thus protests about women's unjust subordination are dismissed. Such is the usual form and extent of concern over the sexual balance of power.

To challenge the allocation of indirect power to women and direct power to men is not necessarily to assume that men at present possess *all* the power. True, "[t]he accumulation of all powers . . . in the same hands . . . may justly be pronounced the very definition of tyranny."[14] But power can rarely, if ever, be so fully monopolized. Tyranny is a concern even within distributions of power, for not every distribution of power protects either freedom or equality; nor does every distribution of power promote community.

The best defense to date of Rousseau's sexual politics—Schwartz's—has been made in terms of the sexes' having power over each other, an arrangement of central relevance in assessing Rousseau's scheme's (in)effective role in establishing community. Schwartz claims that Rousseau intends each sex to have power over the other; the image of a balance of powers is evoked. But whether the powers of the sexes are balanced or unbalanced, whether "power over" the other is rotated successfully or unsuccessfully, sexism informs the very questions Rousseau asks and the answers he offers, and that same sexism contributes to the failure of his scheme to sustain community. First, as just discussed, he cavalierly assumes that a balance of power exists without proving it and without seeming to sense any need to prove it, and without carefully elaborating safeguards against abuse. More importantly, it is unclear whether community is compatible with such a system of differentiated roles and powers, of checks and balances. What Rousseau sets up between the sexes seems to presuppose a conflict of interests and the desire of both parties to transgress, just as the separation of powers and the provision of checks and balances in the government of the United States presupposes such a conflict and such a desire to usurp power. Further, the solutions of separation and checking are the solutions most appropriate to an adversarial relationship, not one of friendship or affection—or of true community.[15] Finally, solving problems by granting people "power over" one another may not be compatible with a feminist ethics. As Wollstonecraft noted, "'Educate women like men,' says Rousseau, 'and the more they resemble our sex the less power will they have over us.' This is the very point I aim at. I do not wish them to have power over men; but over themselves."[16] Thus viewed, Rousseau's very means for attaining community and maintaining equality are incompatible with both feminism and communal structures.

The remaining arguments against Rousseau's scheme also grant the legitimacy of his end—community—and the sincerity of his intention to attain it, but they question and oppose the injustice, unimaginativeness, and inefficacy of the means—sexual differentiation. While the issues I raise overlap to some degree with points made by others, the twist will come, given my interpretation of Rousseau, in my emphasis on the incompatibility of gender differences with community. The dangers and pitfalls I discuss are inherent in the personal and political dynamics of enforced sexual differentiation. These dynamics undermine the ends they are established to serve and inflict a kind of systematic injustice upon women that is intolerable even by Rousseau's usual standards. I discuss five related, troubling aspects of sexually differentiated forms of power: the acceptance of and need for manipulation, the preservation of male ego, the objectification of women's sexuality, the relative overvaluing of the masculine, and the silencing of women.

THE RESORT TO MANIPULATION

The protector and massager of egos is often in a peculiar position. She picks her words carefully, trying to allow the listener to see things as he wants to see them rather than as they really are, or to get him to do what she wants without directly requesting him to and without him perceiving her decisive influence. What follows is one detailed account of the workings of manipulation:

Imagine that I want [you] to behave in a particular way but don't think that you will. If I wanted to manipulate you into acting in this way, my reasoning would take the following form: If you believed that your situation was of Type Q, you would behave as I want you to behave as a matter of course; moreover, if the situation appeared to you as being of Type Q—if, for example, there is present to you a body of evidence that normally suffices for you to judge that your situation is of Type Q, you would think that your situation is of Type Q. I therefore set out to manufacture this body of evidence. . . . Needless to say, if I am to succeed in my efforts, it will be critical not only that I am correct about your dispositions to belief and to action, but also that you are not aware of what I have done to influence you. . . . It is thus not surprising that trying to manipulate someone involves such activities as misrepresentation, staging, lying, dissembling, and the like.[17]

I leave aside for the moment the risks, when one resorts to manipulation, of misjudging another's disposition or level of awareness, and of being misunderstood or not heard at all. A separate charge is that this Rousseauean arrangement seems to involve precisely the sort of game playing he condemns elsewhere, and which he condemns because of the interpersonal barriers it creates. In fact, if one has ever read contemporary "how to" books on sex roles, such as Marabel Morgan's *Total Woman* or Helen Andelin's *Fascinating Womanhood*, one is struck by the artificiality of it all, and women's consciousness of the artificiality.

In *Fascinating Womanhood*, the tactics Andelin endorses for women range from practicing voice modulation ("The main thing to avoid is loudness, firmness, or any of the qualities that men have") and monitoring one's stride ("Avoid a heavy gait or long steps such as men take") to acquiring an "attitude of frail dependence upon men to take care of you" ("You must first dispense with any air of strength and ability, of competence and fearlessness") and expressing "anger with the innocence of a child" ("Stomp your foot, lift your chin high, . . . make childlike threats").[18] The reasoning behind all of this is that such behavior will "cause a man to protect you, and offer you his true devotion . . . [and allow you] to obtain those things in life which mean so much . . . and for which you are dependent upon your husband."[19]

Andelin's practical advice bears much similarity to Rousseau's, and the end is similar as well: getting men to give women, children, and the community what the latter want or need, and which men are somehow uninclined to offer. In these "how to" texts women are made conscious of the artificiality of the scheme, encouraged to *learn* to *act* the part in the play of heterosexual relationships, and told it is in the interest of all to do so. If women are as conscious of being manipulative in Rousseau's scheme as in Andelin's (and how could they use their wiles effectively without doing so consciously, at least at times?), it creates a situation quite contrary to that for which Rousseau is striving. Rousseau's scheme forces women into role playing, conniving, and deceit. Whether or not one agrees with Starobinski that the existence of "deceit was *the* driving force behind all [Rousseau's] theorizing,"[20] women's manipulation reintroduces the detested "veil" between people that leads to social mistrust. Women are placed in a position where, like the despised bourgeois individualist in general, they look at men as means to be manipulated. As a consequence, and most importantly, women are really not fully transformed into social beings by sexual differentiation, into members of a true community. Sex roles themselves force women to act in ways that Rousseau acknowledged in other contexts to be destructive of community and authenticity and wished to avoid; women's forced resort to manipulation via sexual differentiation is not an avenue to community but a roadblock. He is right about the general effects of manipulation: "No more sincere friendships, no more real esteem; no more well-based confidence" (SD, 38). He offers no reasons for thinking those effects will be any different in the recurring case of female manipulation of men.

Finally, how much sense of community will women feel when they see men behave well toward them when manipulated into doing so, or when gratuitous indulgence by men takes the place of real appreciation and cooperation? Why is such constant manipulation required in the first place? Why invest such vast personal, educational, and social resources in establishing this contrived situation, in creating men who will be somewhat blind and therefore susceptible to feminine craftiness and women who will disguise their abilities as helplessness, express their anger with a pout, etc.?

The very necessity for appealing to men's amour-propre as a way of enticing them to perform necessary and desirable social tasks is not proven by Rousseau. Rousseau's women do without similar pampering and obsequiousness, yet their work is as socially indispensable as men's and as foreign to the work of savage woman as social man's work is to that of the savage male. At the least Rousseau's scheme thus either fails to provide the motivation for women to be good citizen wives and mothers or leaves open the possibility that alternate sources of motivation are also possible for men.

Schwartz answers this by claiming that Rousseau believes women are necessarily more social than men and thus less in need of motivation to perform their social tasks, a belief quite common in antifeminist theories. But Schwartz claims, inconsistently, both that Rousseau's women are more social than men and the cause of men's sociality and that in Rousseau "men do not become husbands because mothers require their assistance as fathers. . . . Instead, mothers require men's assistance as fathers because men become husbands."[21] Neither is Schwartz's position saved by claiming as the source of women's easier sociality her "more immediate ties" to her children. That may be an interesting historical fact, but Schwartz himself notes that in Rousseau's thought "paternal love for children follows no less automatically than does maternal love from the experience of living with children."[22] Thus Schwartz leaves unanswered the question of why men require such personal, lifelong manipulation and flattery to bring about sociality and community, whereas women do not.

Though nothing in the state of nature, as Rousseau conceives it, supports the idea that men need disproportionately intense coaxing to leave it, Rousseau does resort to reliance on "feminine" indulgence and accommodation to motivate men to be responsible social actors. Is this a consequence of seeing the world through a biased patriarchal lens that magnifies problems most incident to men while ignoring the surrounding field? Or is it a result of relying upon the familiar antifeminist ideas of natural male independence and female dependence for his own ends? Either way, the consequences are destructive. In the first case, problems more common to men are not even fully remedied, for the solution of female indulgence is one to which women have always expressed some opposition and resistance. And adding unfairness to inefficiency, Rousseau's solution consistently and systematically marginalizes or ignores problems most incident to women. In the second case, Rousseau's calculated use of ideas about natural female dependence/sociality and male independence/asociality have an impact on social reality. It makes people "understanding" of and "lenient" toward male social irresponsibility. It justifies intolerance toward a woman's assertion of a demanding "I," yet fails to cultivate her sense of community to a point where this "I" is not a source of conflict for her.

PRESERVING MALE EGO

The woman who searches for the right words to say is doing so in order to appeal to something in the male to which he is likely to respond. That something is male ego. Women are explicitly told to be (or to feign being) fearful, weak, incapable, and dependent. This makes men feel fearless, strong, competent, and independent. These "masculine" feelings are intended to motivate men to care for and protect those who need (or seem to need) him. However, in leaving male ego intact, Rousseau is allowing for all of its inherent dangers, is supporting an arrangement that can give rise to very large problems. First, his plan does not acknowledge the possibility that women will actually believe themselves to be inferior—a loss of self with grave consequences even for performance of their Rousseauean tasks. When both her own life's energy and her society's institutions and practices are directed toward maintaining (the appearance of) male rule and male strength, little remains to develop or maintain a woman's belief in (the reality of) her own strength, intelligence, and worth. "In time, subordinate behavior, whether real or contrived, eventually produces a habitual sense of internal vulnerability. . . . What starts as posturing and pretense soon feels automatic and authentic."[23] Likewise, the same feelings that can cause men to protect women can cause them to think themselves really superior. He who is always stroked sometimes strikes and exploits others, from a false sense of his relative importance. Rousseau's advice to women to restrain brutal husbands with gentleness reveals an ignorance of the causes (including, most centrally, male ego), consequences, forms, and severity of domestic abuse. It places responsibility for male behavior on women (despite the fact that it limits the means at her disposal for meeting that responsibility)[24] and implicitly feeds the dangerous mentality of "boys will be boys, and they can't help themselves."

To treat such "manliness" as compatible with familial community, or any other kind, is to look at community from the perspective of the male. It seems easy enough to understand why a man might be drawn to those who give him all "official" power and who never directly challenge him. It is also easy enough to see why a man might even do some things for these others in order to preserve the set-up. But when we turn to an evaluation of such "manliness" from the perspective of a woman, different issues arise. It is, at best, tiresome constantly to work around the ego needs of another. It is, at worst, a constant reminder of whose feelings and needs are more important, a repeated reinforcement of secondary status. That Rousseau puts virtually no limits on what women must endure only strengthens what is already a convincing argument against his plan. It is terribly difficult to see how repeated "feminine" accommodations of men could draw independent women to men, could deepen the connection between them, or even allow it to arise or to survive. As a device that reinforces and maintains women's subordinate status, appeal to male ego is a destroyer of the equality and friendship essential to heterosexual familial community. Community feeling, like friendship and love, can develop only where there is an experience of mutuality. Whatever distorted form of community is established between overconfident men and accommodating women, it will please and benefit the men more than it does the women.

Further, the need for constant use of manipulation, wiles, and indirect speaking by women raises important questions about whether Rousseau's men are in fact ever transformed into social persons. When what he responds to is her weakness, what he is feeling is his own power. When she successfully manipulates him into thinking that he wants to do what she wishes him to do or that an idea which originated with her is really his own, what moves him is his self-interest, his inflated view of himself, his ego. These are not attitudes reflective of or conducive to the development of sociality and concern for others. Rousseau's man may be manipulated or fooled into acting as a social person should act, but he does not in fact become a social person. This is precisely the sort of individual condemned by the man who penned the *First Discourse:* one who has "the semblance of all the virtues without the possession of any" (FD, 36).

This is a fairly damning criticism of Rousseau, as is the similar one made earlier with regard to women. It is not clear, that is, whether women are ever really socialized in Rousseau's world, because through their confinement to manipulation they are using others as means. Nor are men really socialized, because through manipulation neither their inflated views of themselves nor their deflated and instrumental views of others (women and children) are challenged. And since, according to Rousseau, the lessons we learn in the family are what we bring to our political lives, the privately nurtured male ego and delegitimized female voice will also haunt political deliberations.

If the best Rousseau can offer us is people who can be manipulated into acting socially out of pride or self-interest, it is not clear that his scheme is superior to those liberal ones he so despised or that his wish for community comes anywhere close to being realized. Further, the ones most victimized by this relapse into individualism are women, for it is they who are left with the least access to individualistic resources and skills and who are made most dependent on the will of a self-interested other. It is in the context of this individualism that arguments about the negative consequences of women's pleasing men are most relevant and incisive. Having to please under these circumstances is a sign of women's oppression and of an inequality utterly incompatible with community. As Charlotte Gilman wrote:

The dependence of women on the personal favor of men has produced an exceeding cleverness in the adaption of the dependent one to the source of her supplies. Under the necessity of pleasing, whether she wished or no, of interceding for a child's pardon or of suing for new pleasures for herself, *"the vices of the slave"* have been forever maintained in this handmaid of the world.[25]

Within the context of induced and enforced sexual differentiation and limitation to indirect power, pleasing is a survival skill of the subordinated rather than an expression of affection by a respected equal.

THE OBJECTIFICATION OF WOMEN'S SEXUALITY

One who is denied use of her direct, open voice, risks losing her voice altogether. The woman who is not allowed to say "No!" or "I want that" can lose touch with the legitimacy of her own desires, as is shown by Rousseau's advice to women about sexuality. He champions something with which we are all too familiar. Sex for women is a weapon, something with which they are to manipulate men. They must be neither too eager nor too reluctant to engage in sexual activities, lest they cease to be the attainable but hard-to-get rewards which, supposedly, men find so irresistible. In this scheme a woman's own sexual desires are not merely restrained, as perhaps men's also are, but are irrelevant, transformed into a means of getting, keeping, and motivating a man. The legitimacy of her own sexual desires, or lack thereof, is lost. Schwartz is therefore off the mark when he implies that Rousseau has a positive understanding of women's sexuality: "Rousseau is not a Victorian; as he portrays women, they are not insensible to sexual pleasure, they are in no way 'above' sexual pleasure. . . . [He] realizes that women have bodies and desires."[26] Yes, he realizes that women have bodies and desires, but he only speaks of women's bodies as they are items of interest to men, and he only considers women's desires as they can be manipulated and restrained for personal and social advantage. This may not be Victorian, but neither is it liberating. For women, sexual interludes and encounters are based on calculation and manipulation, not their sexual inclinations.

The organization of sexuality is rightly seen by Rousseau as influencing and reflecting political arrangements. But in discussing the contortions of sexuality he sees political life as justifying, Rousseau omits mention of the costs of women's sexual self-alienation and utterly fails to grapple with what it means for women to be transformed into sexual rewards for socially desired "masculinity." Women's sexuality becomes a service to the state, and when the state requires making males into "real men," women are sexually objectified by and subordinated to men. As Virginia Woolf wrote:

If such is the real nature of our influence . . . it is either beyond our reach, for many of us are plain, poor and old; or beneath our contempt, for many of us would prefer to call ourselves prostitutes simply and to take our stand openly under the lamps of Piccadilly Circus rather than use it. If such is the real nature, the indirect nature, of this celebrated weapon, we must do without it.[27]

Wollstonecraft also questioned the long-term effectiveness of women's indirect influence: "The woman who has only been taught to please will soon find that her charms are oblique sunbeams, and that they cannot have much effect on her husband's heart when they are seen every day, when the summer is passed and gone."[28]

Rousseau seems to treat women as always willing and able to engage in sexual intercourse. Perhaps this is because, unlike men, women do not need an erection for intercourse to occur. But this male perspective on women's sexuality is clearly self-serving. When it is challenged, when women's desires are honestly reckoned with, it makes good sense only to a rapist and in a rape culture to talk of women's desire and consent wholly in terms of men's and society's needs and desires. True community cannot be built on such a foundation. The sexual games and ploys Rousseau suggests make light of the reality to which he condemns women. Yet Rousseau here is taking part in an antifeminist tradition, one that equates male victory with social harmony.[29] While both sexes must accept some loss as the inevitable cost of social existence, even Rousseau's own assumptions and criteria of legitimacy mean that requiring women to pay this unacknowledged price is neither inevitable, workable, nor justifiable. "Our sexuality is such a deep, spontaneous, and powerful part of our core identity, that the conscious or unconscious need to falsify it is a little death."[30]

The Rousseauean understanding of differentiated power simply does not comport with women's experiences and evaluations of it. It may well be that a man feels himself "subjected to," unable to resist, the allures of women. But what are we to think the consequences of this are for women? "In truth woman has not been socially emancipated through man's need—sexual desire and the desire for offspring—which makes the male dependent for satisfaction upon the female."[31] There exists no necessary connection between men feeling sexually or reproductively awed by or dependent upon women and men feeling obligated, or even at all moved, to treat their female partners as equals or to support sexual equality in general. In fact, it may be that men are overwhelmed by women because woman is made an "exotic," mysterious Other, and this same Otherness also prevents men from taking women's demands for equality seriously. Women's charms are thus inherently limited as a source of potential power for women.

Man's powers are extensive. He has a voice in the family, the market, and the assembly. He picks the religion of his wife and, based on his preferences, picks the arts with which she will entertain him. He enacts the laws to which both are subject. The limits of his power are unclear. They are marked neither by a "separate sphere" nor by a set of skills. They are marked only by his susceptibility to feminine wiles in the home, by his marketability as a laborer, and by his identification with his fellows in the assembly. The limits of women's power, Rousseau might say, are equally unclear. While physically bound in a separate domestic sphere, while restricted in style to indirectness, while uneducated about the public sphere from which she is excluded, still, Rousseau says, her influence is as great as are her charms. The extent to which this is false—and women's indirect power can now be seen as both limited and limiting—is also the extent to which Rousseau's communitarian defense of sex roles breaks down.

OVERVALUING THE MASCULINE

Rousseau believes that if people are carefully educated and socialized to believe that sex differences are inevitable, each sex will see the other as equally valuable and will search out in the other sex that which is beyond their own. However, the sex roles he creates are most unlikely to be socially interpreted as equal. In the family men receive bolstering, accommodation, and flattery; they also get the rewards of public activity, among which are money, reputation, public affirmation, honor, and the intrinsic benefits of direct political participation. As woman's power is secret and invisible, so too are her rewards. It then seems an unjustifiable leap of (patriarchal) faith to hope that while all that is openly lauded is male, the female will really be deemed equally important, by herself or by others, and will be treated equally well.

This situation is complicated by the fact that "masculinity" and "femininity" are gained and proved by distance from each other. Men are taught to fear or despise the "feminine" in themselves, women to loathe the "masculine." But one who is wary of the "masculine" or "feminine" in themself can easily despise or fail to appreciate it in others. Thus sexual differentiation may help ensure that women and men *need* each other but may fail simultaneously to develop, and may even undermine, the bonds of *affection* between them that Rousseau asserts is part of what makes community possible, what turns us away from exploitation. Gender differences are so much the objects of attention that the common humanity of the sexes gets lost.

In fact the "masculine" and "feminine" are not described or evaluated similarly in Rousseau's or today's politics or culture, which contributes further to women's subordination through differentiation. Rousseau's own writings are an example of this. He purports to advocate sexual equality, and would protest that what appears inegalitarian in his system is justified by a more fundamental and less obvious parity. But the power of unequal appearances, and of the structures and practices necessary to maintain them, are in fact inseparable from real inequality.

In ridiculing "reasoners, strong-minded men, philosophers, [and] soldiers" who fear the dark, Rousseau says that they "tremble like women" (*Emile*, 134). He fails here to acknowledge that some of women's tasks also require courage and, more importantly, assumes that to compare a male with a female is automatically and obviously insulting. He never does the reverse; in fact, when commenting on women who act like men he always speaks of how women cannot reach male standards or will be harmed (by "manlier men") if they do. That is, for a woman to imitate a male is to risk failure, while for a man to resemble a woman is to be demeaned. Granted, both strategies may effectively drive the sexes to act in what Rousseau thinks are socially desirable ways not part of their natural bent. But they also have the effect of making one sex seem not just different from but better than the other. If it is imperative to use such devices to get the sexes to act in accord with gendered social roles, and if these devices also necessarily have the negative effect of marking women as inferior, then Rousseau's scheme of "different but equal" is fatally flawed in practice.

Rousseau's scheme, like those prevailing in so many historical periods, religions, and cultures, hopes and claims to be one of sexual complementarity. Rousseau is somewhat unusual, as argued in chapter 3, because he "no longer trusted nature to make men and women complementary."[32] But Rousseau is quite typical in that for him, as "during the last three millennia in which patriarchal societies have flourished, the logic of opposites has often been translated into a logic of exclusion,"[33] of female subordination destructive of community. Given the historical record, which shows that "complementarity" exists in words only, while in practice it degenerates into inequality, we are justified in demanding from Rousseau far more protection for women's status than he can offer.

THE SILENCING OF WOMEN

A final risk inherent in Rousseau's system is the silencing of women's voices. Rousseau has created genders with different and frequently incompatible, even if supposedly complementary, traits and concerns. In their personal relationships they may end up bewildered by each other's perspectives, especially if one perspective—woman's—is indirectly voiced and publicly unacknowledged. The possibility of each sex's both hearing and respectfully responding to the other is reduced. This minimizes the chances that people will learn to identify with others, to see them as engaged in common causes, and therefore to treat them well. Politically, this difference raises a new question about the all-male assembly. Despite the general will, the different training and functions of the sexes destroys men's ability to represent women's voices. Precisely what led many twentieth-century U.S. feminists to demand the vote was the felt need for representation of women's *different* voices in politics, different voices that would seem to arise in Rousseau's scheme, as well. The argument, for example, of Jane Addams was that if women are responsible for the moral and physical welfare of the family, then it is illogical to give men control of the conditions under which women's tasks are carried out. For men have never "attempted to care for children, to clean houses, to prepare foods, to isolate the family from moral dangers," and the perspectives from which men are trained to solve problems (she cites the military and industrial points of view) are inappropriate in women's sphere.[34] One cannot have it both ways. If the sexes are to be truly different, one of them cannot be counted on always to know, understand, and advocate the point of view of the other, despite the common interest that supposedly unites them. Again, the difficulty is exacerbated when women can only speak indirectly and when male concerns receive more public attention and reward. Even understood as representatives of the family unit or the common good, an all-male assembly seems, ironically, to be particularly dangerous, more capable of systematic injustice, in a society built on strict sex roles than in one where such roles are more flexibly defined or not defined at all. A system of sexual differentiation combined with the practice of all-male representation practically guarantees that one particular understanding of ends and means (male) is heard, and the other (female) is silenced.

From the perspective of a communitarian, exclusion through silencing should be extremely troubling. First, it signals the degeneration of difference into domination: "The sacrificing of women requires the silencing of women, which takes place in myriad ways, in a maze of ways."[35] Male domination is anathema to community between the sexes and even compromises the potential community between the dominators. Second, women's exclusion from public deliberations is a missed opportunity for socialization, an especially unwise choice from Rousseau's perspective, for he argues that community needs all the support that can be mustered. Look at what is passed up, according to Nagel's study of the intrinsic benefits of participation:

> Paradoxically, the chief among them—often experienced simultaneously—are an enhanced sense of one's own individual worth and an intensified identification with one's community. . . . For most participants, perhaps the deepest gratification comes from the sense of having a purpose, of being part of a community or movement greater than oneself, identifying with a group or nation in which all may assert themselves, in which all have a share of power.[36]

Without doubt the sexes today continue to reason and speak in what, following Gilligan, are often called "different voices." While the correlation between voice and gender is imperfect, it is strong and easily observable. Rousseau's predictions of how gender-differentiated training will affect the individual roughly agree with the outcomes Gilligan observes. One extremely important consequence of research done or inspired by Gilligan is that many have been reminded of the worth, dignity, and morality of women's indirect, connection-oriented, situationally constrained voice. There is much to applaud in Rousseau's women, who speak gently, nonconfrontationally, and with consideration for others. Such is a voice, such are the skills, that *can* in fact nurture connections, and that have done so, while a demanding, inconsiderate, competitive, confrontational, and overconfident voice can destroy community.

Men do less to sustain community even while they receive more benefits from it. Their political contribution in Rousseau's system as full citizens is akin to that of the abstract, universal rule-oriented voice described by Gilligan. Such contribution need not be minimized. But there is a problem. In Rousseau's planned society woman's role, power, and voice have the grave defect of not attending adequately to woman's own well-being, and man's role, power, and voice do not attend adequately to woman's well-being, either. Fighting wars and financially supporting relatives, for example, have a weak connection to nurturing or becoming one with others. Rousseau saw this truth politically—recall his strong opposition to mercenary soldiers and tax-paying citizens—but he lost sight of it interpersonally.

Woman in Rousseau's system as in too many others helps create a community in which she herself is not always fully a part and from which she does not receive due benefits. A community nurtures all of its members, rather than sacrificing one group by assigning it the task of nurturing the rest. When to be "feminine" is to be self-sacrificing, accommodating, flattering, serving, and undemanding, community will both depend upon and exclude women. Thus, while Rousseau is absolutely right that the role he assigns women is utterly crucial to politics, he gives the sexes different ways of being "constructive" social creatures and defines "constructive" social relations in ways that systematically and predictably slight women's well-being.

CONCLUSION

In Rousseau, as in scheme after scheme of sexual differentiation before and since, we have a division of traits and tasks that is riddled with dangers, harms, and losses, a *division* of people into gender groups that does in fact *divide* people and that diverts attention and energy away from practices and tasks that really could establish and enhance community. Rousseau is right about the importance of traditional women's work, its decisive contribution to both individual and social well-being. And this is certainly no trivial improvement over theories that insult women and downplay or ridicule the traditional work women do. But Rousseau is wrong, finally, about the conditions under which that work is best carried out. The sexes are not halves of an entity completed through heterosexual union. The world is not divided into tasks or traits or skills that are best covered by dividing people into two gender groups. Male power is not adequately controlled by sex roles, and charms that "empower" women can simultaneously disempower them. And it is certainly not enough simply to be told it will all work out —why "worry our pretty little heads" about all of this, anyhow? Nor is it enough to be told that such is the tragic nature of life or of politics. The tragedies here have sources we can locate and solutions well within the realm of possibility.

Is sex-role socialization worth all that is demanded to sustain it? Even if we could train people to accept their Rousseauean lot, maintaining the myths means channeling tremendous resources into the project: economic, religious, educational, political, and familial. Perhaps Rousseau has underestimated what such a system demands; in any case, he has not convincingly shown that such an investment is warranted. It might, for example, be simpler, safer, "cheaper," and more effective to concentrate our resources on directly imparting the social skills we need and, for whatever reasons, currently lack: to teach, for example, conflict-resolution skills, parenting skills, and the art of discussion; to encourage creative action in forming communities; and to educate people quite explicitly about the numerous forms and benefits of cooperation and the costs and injustices of untempered individualism. Given the lack of evidence for thinking that sex roles contribute significantly to the development of any of these socially desirable skills and traits, a more direct approach is certainly worth a try. Similarly, if the work we are made to do is so onerous, so unattractive, that we have to bribe and manipulate people to do it, maybe we should turn instead to creating forms of the family that decrease the heavy and often isolating work of childrearing and forms of production that share or eliminate degrading labor. Rousseau's plan is based on a deep pessimism that I would suggest may actually be a reaction to, rather than an improvement upon, the many failures of traditional sex roles. Why are suggestions like those mentioned here so quickly dismissed as naive or utopian? Such a dismissal ceases to be even superficially plausible once we see that "those elaborate, oppressive systems are just as difficult to create as their supposedly unrealistic alternatives—perhaps more so, since no uniform system, no matter how repressive, has ever completely succeeded in producing uniform people."[37]

That Rousseau is not a biological determinist, as I demonstrated in chapter 3, is ultimately of no comfort. Patriarchal rationalizations come in a number of forms. While Rousseau provides evidence that we need to expand our models of antifeminist theory, he also provides support for the suspicion that biological arguments are generally a mask, a way of making sexual (or racial) inequality seem inevitable and desirable when it is neither. He consciously, and at least somewhat overtly, uses biological arguments for just that purpose.

As discussed in chapter 2, Rousseau's educational plans for women and men are informed by the same political framework, the same concept of the labor, both physical and psychological, involved in creating a viable society. Nonetheless, the role that each sex plays in solving the problems of political life is distinctive, and the formal similarities tell only part of the story. To say that women and men are both social actors, or that both experience restraint, is to say too little. There are mountains of evidence that the support and service roles assigned to women have different consequences for them than do the roles assigned to men. To be so oriented toward satisfying others can over time easily mean to lose one's self, and one's awareness of the existence and legitimacy of one's own needs, wants, interests, and talents. While on the theoretical level Rousseau does not deny or attempt to obliterate the socially acceptable ego he calls "amour-de-soi," on the practical level it is in fact delegitimized for women.

Rousseau's formula for happiness offers no comfort either. To say that both sexes have equal chances of attaining happiness (as defined by Rousseau) is finally to offer too little to the advocate of sexual equality. Given the almost unlimited power ceded to education and socialization, a Rousseauean perspective could lead one to conclude that people can be trained to accept almost anything—any condition in which they find themselves, any portrayal of their nature, any explanation of social relations. This makes happiness a rather dubious measure of freedom, of equality, of anything except successful socialization. In the end, "if happiness was all that mattered, there would be nothing intrinsically wrong with forcing women to swallow tranquilizers instead of doing something about their problems."[38]

There is another problem connected with using access to Rousseauean happiness as a gauge for women's real well-being. The fact of the matter is that Rousseau offers no convincing account of the unhappiness of women who are fully immersed in traditional gender roles and family structures. According to him such women are either unsatisfactorily socialized or are unaware of what costs accompany relinquishment of their powerful feminine charms, their charming feminine power. This explanation is simply and grossly inadequate. It neither acknowledges that women have been thoroughly socialized for roles they have nonetheless challenged nor listens to women's own assessments of their conditions. It is condescending in its arrogance, its masculine dismissal of the need to listen to women, and its "You don't know how good you have it" moralizing.

If Rousseau's division of powers provides no safeguards against abuses of power, against artificiality in personal relationships, with its concomitant deceit, distrust, and pessimism, against the loss of one's own voice, against the perpetuation of unequal power relationships, then he has truly failed. He has failed to meet his own goals, and this failure raises serious questions about the ability of differentiated forms of power to be equal and compatible with community at all. With decent motives and no small amount of intellectual and imaginative resources at his disposal, Rousseau, unwittingly and against his own design, teaches us that community and sexual equality require a feminist revolution: personal, social, and institutional transformation.

Rousseau is on shaky ground in the *First Discourse* when he applauds military virtue for its ability to instill the values of community. An emphasis on military virtue is inseparable from militarism, and the community experienced within the military is exclusionary, closed-minded, and violent. As a model of community its casualties cancel out its supposed benefits. In a similar and quite related manner, Rousseau's male "virtue" is inseparable from male dominance, and community is one of its casualties.

As the literature has amply demonstrated, a liberal defense of sex roles is impossible, because enforced sex differences unjustifiably drive particular individuals into roles which mute or betray their abilities and inclinations, at least damning the exceptions in a system based on group characteristics. But save for a very few, notably John Stuart Mill, the "great" (male) historical thinkers have consistently sacrificed their liberalism on the altar of male supremacy. What Rousseau teaches us is that there are also fatal flaws in a communitarian defense of sex roles. As the study of indirect versus direct power shows, sex differences enforced in the name of the community and the common good perpetuate both incidental and systematic injustices against women and the interests assigned them, injustices which tear apart the community that would benefit both sexes. Equality *is*, as Rousseau saw, necessary for the existence of true community. Differences exist today, including but not limited to biological sex differences. Those who desire community need to endorse political arrangements that consciously, consistently, and equally applaud the different virtues of individuals and groups and the very richness such diversity brings to our social existence. Communitarian thinkers must acknowledge differences when ignoring them creates inequality, and ignore, transform, or minimize them when they are irrelevant or destructive. Community requires that we advocate practices that diminish rather than add to the chasms already separating us and that we expend extra resources battling divisions which, like those based on gender, have the longest and most offensive history of causing exploitation.

The lessons that Rousseau would have us learn via sex roles can be gained without them. While families may present one of the most likely arenas for combining affection, interest, and obligation, there is no reason for thinking that the sex-roled, heterosexual, nuclear family has a monopoly on this combination of features. Not only do alternate models of the family present similar possibilities, but so do cooperative, participatory models of education, politics, and paid labor. Furthermore, employment of these alternatives adds to and enhances communal feelings. Acceptance of diverse families makes all feel an acknowledged and respected part of the whole, regardless of the "minority" status of one's arrangement. Such a stamp of acceptance and worthiness bestowed by the community upon their family structures, inclinations, abilities, or contributions increases the likelihood that individuals will, in return, see the community as legitimate and valuable and worthy of the sacrifices required to maintain it. And the extension of models of cooperation beyond the walls of the private household both reinforces and supplements the lessons of community learned within them. If we agree with Rousseau that community is essential to human welfare, we should both alter and expand the means he suggests for attaining it.

One remaining question is how someone like Rousseau, who starts out with commitments and concerns quite similar to those of many feminists, ends up with a political structure so abhorrent to them. That is to say, why, despite his hearty condemnation of liberalism's approval of, indeed obsession with, self-interest, his sincere desire for community, and his understanding of the effects of (in)equality on political legitimacy, stability, and attachment, is Rousseau not more of a feminist? The question only arises in this form because so many feminists also oppose liberalism's obsession with self-interest, sincerely desire community, and see the issue of equality as inextricably linked with issues of political legitimacy and commitment.

In the next chapter I leave my focus on Rousseau and turn to contemporary communitarian thought in general. Like Rousseau, the other communitarian thinkers I cite are not feminist. I am interested in answering the question "Why is there so much interest in community among feminists, and so little interest in feminism among communitarians, past and present?" To address this question, I compare the cases feminists and communitarians make against liberalism.

PART TWO

SEVEN

FEMINISM AND COMMUNITARIANISM: EXPLORING THE RELATIONSHIP

And what of the paths that Rousseau's thought does not take? Rousseau endorses sexual differentiation not because he is convinced of the inevitability of "natural" sex differences or of the inferiority of the female sex but because he believes that such differentiation can help originally asocial individuals to overcome or avoid self-interest and egoism and to learn to be members of familial and political communities. Nonetheless, his scheme is incapable in practice of serving the ends for which it is established, because sexual differentiation in fact undermines community. Analysis of Rousseau as a communitarian defender of gender roles opens up the possibility of considering his work in another theoretical framework: communitarian thinking about gender. To repeat, the question I want to explore is "Why, when feminists are so interested in community, are communitarians (including, but not limited to, Rousseau) so uninterested in feminism?"

Rousseau shares with many feminists a condemnation of central features of liberalism and an endorsement of community. That this does not lead him to feminism is clearly not unusual in the history of political theory; communitarian thinkers have generally had little commitment to gender equality, for its own sake or for the sake of community, and indeed have often had a hostility toward it. Dating back at least to ancient Athens, communitarian thought and practice both excluded women as members of communities and was used to justify that exclusion. "Community" was a union of men that sacrificed women, that normalized and depended for its existence upon women's being self-sacrificing. Men united in the name of masculine values,[1] which allowed, if it did not require, the degradation of people and things associated with the female. Plato's city, for example, worships the masculine gods of efficiency, obedience, abstract reason, and order, all for the sake of social unity, itself understood in a hierarchical, exclusionary, and sacrificial manner. In another variety of male community, Aristotle's free men only have the leisure deemed essential to their citizenship because of the labor performed by certain noncitizens: "free" women and slaves and manual workers of both sexes. Inclusion of the latter groups as citizens, as more than "necessary conditions" for the state, would, according to Aristotle, corrupt the city; their inferior rationality fits them for a life of obedience and service, supposedly for their own good but especially for the good of the whole.

Not only does Rousseau have many highly regarded predecessors but, most troubling of all, many contemporary followers. Communitarian thought today also seems to be decidedly nonfeminist at best and antifeminist at worst. The gains made by contemporary feminist politics and the findings of feminist research appear to be making virtually no dent on communitarians. Despite feminism's very strong interest in community, nonfeminist communitarians remain oblivious to, or at least aloof from, the issues that inform feminism. It is therefore doubtful that the communal structures and principles they endorse have the capacity or motivation seriously to address feminist concerns. There are grounds for thinking that contemporary communitarianism is headed toward repeating its misogynist past.

Whatever the extent to which communitarian theorists might be said to be egalitarian, inegalitarian threads also connect them—threads that define women out of certain communities, that downplay the negative effects of women's domestication, that exclude women in conceptions and calculations of the "common" good, that refuse to address sexual differentiation and inequality as obstacles to personal and political bonds, and that advocate patriarchal principles, values, and structures as guides to community. Rousseau's community belongs to this long tradition inasmuch as it includes women exclusively in their capacities as wives and mothers, assumes rather than proves the existence of women's private power, and fails to address the obstacles to community gender differentiation creates. While, according to Rousseau, this arrangement serves the general interest, that general interest is determined by a process that mutes women's voices by design.

We are in the midst of what Michael Walzer calls "a recurrent [communitarian] critique" of liberalism.[2] The disciplines at least of philosophy and political theory are awash in communitarian attacks upon liberals and responding defenses of liberalism. Walzer sees such debate as useful even if, as is likely, never-ending. A constant feature of the recurring debate that Walzer neglects to note, however, is the absence of concern by both sides about sexual equality. To the extent that the communitarian-liberal debate continues to command so much attention from social and political theorists, feminism continues to be relatively ignored.

When debates about feminism and community do take place, feminists are chided by some for being too communitarian,[3] and by others—including Rousseau—for being too liberal.[4] In both instances feminists are being judged by conformity to standards that are not of women's making, not in women's interests, and not the only options available. These criticisms are really ways of warning feminists to declare allegiance, to choose one side of an old battle in which women's interests, at best, are secondary. While Rousseau does stand apart from contemporary communitarians in some ways, ultimately neither he nor they move the debate between liberals and communitarians to ground that incorporates or even addresses the central concerns of feminists. Feminism challenges both liberalism and communitarianism in ways that neither challenges the other. Rousseau is of little help in reconfiguring the two-sided exchange into one that can include what, for purposes here, might be called communitarian feminism, or the communitarian strain of numerous feminisms.

In terms of their philosophical assumptions and political ideals, one would expect some overlap and fruitful cooperation between feminism and communitarianism; the adversarial relationship between them, now and in the past, is somewhat curious. At best, each continues to be somewhat isolationist, or to resemble young children engaged in parallel play;[5] at worst, they attack one another's principles and practices. Some feminists have explicitly warned *against* alliances with communitarians, despite such acknowledged commonalities as emphasis on context, care, and community. Feminists certainly have good reason to be wary of too quick and uncritical an attachment, given their experience with models in which "two become one" by one's devouring the other. Yet precisely because it does initially seem that feminists and communitarians ought to be more consistent allies than they are, I think it important to explore why they have not been, are not, and perhaps cannot or should not be. After comparing feminist and communitarian critiques of liberalism, I conclude that neither Rousseau nor contemporary communitarians offer a critique of liberalism that gives voice to concerns heard in feminist critiques of liberalism, even when those feminist critiques are informed by a commitment to community.

While both communitarianism and feminism are almost astonishingly diverse in theory and practice, focusing only on their critiques of liberalism allows me to talk about each in something resembling a generic form. I treat writings by a number of feminist and communitarian thinkers without attempting systematically to analyze any particular individual, since my aim is more general.

Not all feminists are strong communitarians. Feminist opposition to community exists, for example, among liberal feminists wary of politicizing the private due to fear of government power, among postmodern feminists wary of the fate and status of differences in a unified community, and among those feminists dissatisfied with facile glorification of "the feminine" as a model of community.

The warnings issued by feminists about community are valid and important to address. But all feminisms, including liberal feminism, challenge aspects of classic liberalism from a position that is less individualistic and more communitarian than classical liberalism, and what really matters here is the ground on which feminism *does* challenge liberalism. Despite the fact that there are feminist visions very much more and less informed by communitarianism, generic feminism still opposes central ideas and practices of classic liberalism. So too does Rousseau. Yet the critiques of liberalism by Rousseau, contemporary communitarians, and feminists are not based upon and do not lead to similar understandings of various political processes or similar visions of ideal political arrangements.

I compare the feminist and communitarian critiques of liberalism on three issues: conceptions of the self, conceptions of social relations, and conceptions of political community. Regarding each of these, I consider central aspects of (1) how communitarians and feminists understand the liberal point of view, (2) what each finds problematic in it, and, at least briefly, (3) what alternative views each endorses. My emphasis here is on contemporary communitarianism. However, the differences between feminism, liberalism, and communitarianism are similar in other eras, and I weave Rousseau into the dialogue as some evidence of that.

1. CONCEPTIONS OF THE SELF

1a. Understanding Liberalism

Communitarianism

The dispute between communitarians and liberals hinges on opposing conceptions of the self. Where liberals conceive of the self as essentially unencumbered and free to choose among a wide range of alternatives, communitarians insist that the self is situated in and constituted by tradition, membership in a historically rooted community.[6]

[For liberals] Individuals . . . are primary and society secondary, and the identification of individual interests is prior to, and independent of, the construction of any moral or social bonds between them.[7]

[Liberalism's] atomism posits that as physical beings, humans are separate, integral, self-contained, unitary particles or atoms.[8]

Feminism

Abstract individualism considers individual human beings as social atoms, abstracted from their social contexts, and disregards the role of social relationships and human community in constituting the very identity and nature of individual human beings.[9]

Although it would be mistaken to suggest that all liberal theorists conceive of human nature as being egoistic, most do argue that people tend naturally in this direction and must work to develop moral capacities to counter their basic selfish, acquisitive inclinations.[10]

[Abstract individualism is] the assumption that the essential human characteristics are properties of individuals and are given independently of any particular social context. . . . [It] takes human nature as a presocial system.[11]

Both feminists and communitarians find in liberalism the notion of a presocial, solitary subject with natural rights. Both see as a central feature of liberalism its belief that individual interests exist before or independent of social relationships, moral bonds, a social context, and/or the human community. Liberalism, it is said, views the individual as having an identity apart from their ends. That liberal self is also one who can and should be free—an individual whose relations, attachments, and goals are chosen from a wide range of alternatives and are detachable, independent of the self.[12]

To the extent that the independent self of liberalism is given content, the substance is in terms of tendencies, motivations, and capacities. The individual of liberal theory is thought, for example, to tend to be self-interested, to be motivated by profit, pleasure, and pride, and to be capable of rationality, usually equated with prudential reasoning. That toward which one moves is undetermined: what gives pleasure, what profits, and what inspires one to reason instrumentally are individual variables and not essential or social features.

Rousseau's understanding of liberalism's view of the self, because drawn from many of the same sources of classical liberal theory as used above, also sees it as starting with the individual outside of society, fully developed, in possession of "natural" rights and duties, and unable to live very well with other basically self-concerned individuals, even with the guidance of "natural law." It is a view from which Rousseau departs, against which his own philosophy is often directed.

While contemporary feminist and communitarian understandings of liberalism's view of the self have much in common with each other and with Rousseau, and while it may be "a commonplace amongst communitarians, socialists and feminists that liberalism is to be rejected for its excessive 'individualism' or 'atomism,' " [13] their grounds for rejecting it are not identical. And this is true despite the fact that each understands the implications of their critique to undercut everything from the liberal conception of freedom as noninterference to the liberal justification of the state as fulfilling the interests of its citizens.

1b. Critiques of the Liberal View

Communitarianism

[For the] right to exist prior to the good it would be necessary for the subject to exist independently of his/her intentions and his/her ends. Such a conception requires therefore a subject who can have an identity defined prior to the values and objectives that he/she chooses. It is, in effect, the capacity to choose, not the choices that he makes, that defines such a subject. He can never have ends which are constitutive of his identity and this denies him the possibility of participation in a community where it is the very definition of who he is that is in question.[14]

Feminism

Feminist theorists argue that the vision of the atomic, "unencumbered self," criticized by communitarians, is a male one, since the degree of separateness and independence it postulates among individuals has never been the case for women.... Indeed, her individuality has been sacrificed to the "constitutive definitions" of her identity.... If unencumbered males have difficulties in recognizing those social relations constitutive of their ego identity, situated females often find it impossible to recognize their true selves amidst the constitutive roles that attach to their persons.[16]

[T]he peculiarly modern self, the emotivist self, in acquiring sovereignty in its own realm lost its traditional boundaries provided by a social identity and a view of human life as ordered to a given end.[15]

[A]t each moment of our lives our every thought, value, and act—from the most mundane to the most lofty—takes its meaning and purpose from the wider political and social reality that constitutes and conditions us.[17]

Communitarians and feminists both reject the liberal notion of an isolated self with rights, interests, values, and ends independent of a social context. They do so, however, for different reasons. I discuss three differences in the communitarian and feminist critiques of liberalism's conception of the self, looking both to describe the differences and to give some account of their origins and implications. The three differences concern the sources of identity, the extent of socialization, and the evaluation of traditional societies. Rousseau's criticism of liberalism's vision of the self distinguishes him from liberalism as well as, on different points, from communitarianism and feminism.

First, in discussing the range of social forces that influence the formation of the self, Sandel talks of the "family or community or nation or people,"[18] and MacIntyre includes families, neighborhoods, cities, guilds, professions, clans, tribes, and nations.[19] The factors left out of such accounts are often precisely the ones with which feminists are critically concerned. From a feminist perspective, most centrally affecting the formation of the self are factors such as sex, age, race, sexuality, and class. Yet about such things most nonfeminist communitarians are peculiarly silent. Despite communitarian interest in "traditions" and "practices," the notion of social context seems to be somewhat narrowly conceived by them. While including certain well-defined groups and communities, it omits such traditions and practices as sexism and racism, practices that may have a larger role in forming the self and determining one's social place than do cities or neighborhoods, not least because the former are more pervasive, constant, intimate, and unconscious. Such forces as sexism and homophobia, for example, not only often create distinct communities ("the lesbian community," Boy Scouts, etc.) but also establish relations which pervade and structure all communities, including ones which seem to have nothing to do with gender, race, sexuality, or class.

According to feminists, communitarian language and theory are falsely universalized; communitarians challenge liberalism's pronouncements without noting how their accuracy varies according to the race, class, gender, or sexuality of individuals and groups. Without attention to such factors it is difficult to assess the accuracy of liberalism's descriptions. For example, communitarians fail to note that the separated self of liberalism reflects the reality of men more than women. Liberalism's portrait may also be more reflective in many western cultures of those who are white and/or heterosexual than of those who are black and/or homosexual, for as oppressed minorities the latter have bonded together in "subcultures." In the communitarian critique there is some wavering about whether the picture of the self drawn by liberalism is descriptively accurate but normatively undesirable, or both inaccurate and undesirable.[20] Such wavering may be a consequence of a misguided attempt to universalize what sexism and other social forces render incapable of universalization. Liberalism's descriptions of social identity are more apt in some areas than in others, and in most areas vary according to factors ignored by communitarians.

In their critiques of liberalism's view of the self feminists not only recognize a broader range of social forces that influence identities than do communitarians, but they also find that these forces have a deeper impact than is generally acknowledged by communitarians. For example, while communitarians are most likely to consider the social nature of individual interests and ends, feminists stress how social context affects everything from individual characteristics, emotions, beliefs, capacities, and motives to human nature itself.[21] This difference may be attributed to the fact that feminists have always had to engage in debate over whether women and men have different natures. Feminists from Christine de Pizan and Mary Wollstonecraft to Harriet Taylor and Simone de Beauvoir have understood the differences between the sexes to be caused at least in large part by the different social experiences of the sexes, their different social contexts. It would seem that one of the earliest and most consistent sources of feminist rejection of abstract individualism is the understanding of how strongly desires, physiques, interests, values, emotions, and other traits, are dependent on a social context, and how rejection of this truth historically led to lies about the natures of the sexes, lies which were claimed to provide evidence for the naturalness and inevitability of male supremacy. Perhaps, then, the absence of this political history is what permits communitarians to see the impact of social context as both narrower and shallower than it is seen by feminists.

A third difference in the feminist and communitarian critiques of liberalism's view of the self is the standpoint from which they are leveled. As the earlier quotes show, the contrast can sometimes be stark: communitarians are concerned with the *loss* of "traditional boundaries," while feminists are concerned with the *costs* of those boundaries, especially for women. Nostalgia for communities of the past almost forces nonfeminist communitarians to gloss over or ignore those social forces and structures that have allowed and justified exclusion, oppression, and hierarchy. Feminism's defining commitment to ending oppression directs it at precisely those structures and practices communitarianism so often denies or marginalizes.

The difference in standpoints does not mean that the communitarian critique is apolitical, as evidenced by MacIntyre's concern, for example, with social decay and dislocation. But communitarian criticism often remains politically vague and abstract. It is not clear, for example, who feels dislocated and why, and who, perhaps, does not. It could be the case, for example, that the women's movement and the black civil rights movement have raised uncomfortable questions about "place" for white men, and that the emergence of such questions contributes positively to society. The vagueness of the communitarian critique tends in practice to reinforce conservative, inegalitarian politics.

Although Rousseau resembles liberals in positing a condition—a state of nature—in which people are self-contained and separate, his belief that *each* distinctive environment—various stages of the state of nature as well as varieties of civil society—shapes us and aligns him with feminists and communitarians. Rousseau sides more with feminists than communitarians in his attention to the range of forces that affect our identity, as discussed earlier. His attention to slavery and class privilege makes it impossible for him to overlook or downplay the impact of oppression on individual identity, and his emphasis on mores also attunes him to the often unconscious and yet pervasive social factors contributing to identity formation. Still, Rousseau does not extend these insights to the question of gender roles. The costs of sexual differentiation disappear in the stream of rhetoric applauding its ability to restore morality. Like communitarians, he is more concerned with criticizing individualistic societies than with questioning the ways of life of those which are more communitarian, as his evaluations of Sparta and Geneva show.

1c. Alternatives to the Liberal View

Communitarianism

[I]t is through his or her membership in a variety of social groups that the individual identifies himself or herself and is identified by others. I am brother, cousin and grandson, member of this household, that village, this tribe. These are not characteristics that belong to human beings accidentally, to be stripped away in order to discover "the real me." They are part of my substance, defining partially at least and sometimes wholly my obligations and my duties. Individuals inherit a particular space within an interlocking set of social relationships; lacking that space, they are nobody, or at best a stranger or an outcast.[22]

Feminism

[W]hereas communitarians emphasize the situatedness of the disembedded self in a network of relations and narratives, feminists also begin with the situated self but view the *renegotiation* of our psychosexual identities, and their *autonomous reconstitution* by individuals as essential to women's and human liberation. . . . The simple identification of the subject with its social roles reinstates the very logic of identity that feminists have sought to critique in their examinations of the psychosexual constitution of gender.[23]

As may already be clear, what communitarians prefer to liberalism is an Aristotelian understanding of the self as fundamentally political, realizing itself only in a given historical setting, a particular social context. The Aristotelian understanding views the self as embedded in and constituted by particular communal commitments and values. It sees participation in a value-defining community as giving the self a conception of right and justice. It understands that by and large the forces that constitute one's self—family, nation, etc.—are outside of one's free choosing. Finally, this view is preferred by communitarianism because of its ability to "locate" people, to give them an identity that delineates their obligations and determines the contours of their relationships, thereby providing personal and political stability, limits, and order.

Feminists do not deny that "through his or her membership in a variety of social groups . . . the individual identifies himself or herself and is identified by others." It would be most surprising, even impossible, for those with the political understanding feminists have of gender "socialization" or "conditioning" (to use terms which for some reason sound almost quaint today), to think otherwise. To say that socialization, or embeddedness, is inevitable, however, is only a modest beginning. The process of identity formation within and between cultures takes a wide range of forms that lead to distinctly different ways of living together. Feminists are more interested than are communitarians in understanding *how* social selves are constituted, toward what ends, and with what costs and benefits for various individuals, groups, and relations. Given the experience of gender oppression, feminists are likely to work for understandings of the self that acknowledge human interdependence, social responsibility, and an end to "gender obsession." Further, knowledge of the historical reality of social change and the present need for it tempers a possible resignation by showing that the individual can usefully gain some distance from the community, can critique and evaluate, and can work to create alternative cultures that will foster individuals with new concepts of themselves and others. Such choice and critical distance are viewed differently by feminists and communitarians because of their different evaluations of how fragile and destructive certain social bonds are.

The political challenge made by feminists to abstract individualism rejects the communitarian vision. Liberalism's ideal is criticized for encouraging people to think of themselves first, for fostering egoism and rewarding selfishness, and for drawing a picture of the self that is incomplete where it is not inaccurate. But the complacent communitarian reliance on "place," as the next sections will further show, is also rejected for failing to address, and therefore to solve, the issues at the heart of feminism.

Because of his assumptions regarding original asociality, self-absorption, and indolence and his analysis of modern egoism, Rousseau's goal is to find institutions, values, and motivations that will in fact "embed" people in various identity-providing associations that foster cooperation and interdependence. Rousseau's thought, like that of contemporary communitarians, does not begin with or centrally address the *problems* of social identity rooted in gender (he does better with class). He shares more with contemporary communitarian desire for "a particular space within an interlocking set of social relationships" than with feminist determination to "renegotiate" roles and relationships according to the demands of gender equality. Like later communitarians, Rousseau is influenced by the model of the ancient Greek *polis* to a degree that is incompatible with feminist understandings of a liberatory reconstruction of society: one "that both encourages a sense of community and group solidarity and respects individual autonomy."[24]

Grounded in women's experiences, feminist analysis does not see the self as so unconnected as to make individual autonomy dangerous, so rapacious

132 *Feminism and Communitarianism*

as to make meeting material needs an impossible means for encouraging solidarity, or so asocial as to make chosen communities untenable.

2. SOCIAL RELATIONS

2a. Understanding Liberalism

Communitarianism

[According to liberalism] the social world [is] nothing but a meeting place for individual wills, each with its own set of attitudes and preferences and who understand that world solely as an arena for the achievement of their own satisfaction.[25]

[T]he liberal portrait of human nature . . . construe[s] the human essence as radically individual and solitary, as hedonistic and prudential, and as social only to the extent required by the quest for preservation and liberty in an adversary world of scarcity.[26]

[For individualists] No binding obligations and no wider social understanding justify a relationship. It exists only as the expression of the choices of the free selves who make it up. And should it no longer meet their needs, it must end.[27]

Feminism

Western liberal democratic thought has been built on the concept of the "individual" seen as a theoretically isolatable entity. This entity can assert interests, have rights, and enter into contractual relations with other entities. But this individual is not seen as related to other individuals in inextricable or intrinsic ways. This individual is assumed to be motivated primarily by a desire to pursue his own interest, though he can recognize the need to agree to contractual restraints on the ways everyone may pursue their interests.[28]

According to both feminists and communitarians, the liberal vision of interpersonal relations follows from its atomism: the boundaries of human relations are drawn by the nature of the self, understood in liberalism as competitive, privatistic, hedonistic, prudential, isolated, and self-interested. Liberal assumptions theoretically limit the potential bonds that can and should be created between people to ones that are voluntary, self-interested, instrumental, and contractual. Parties to contracts, however, like their interests, remain essentially separate. According to feminist and communitarian portraits of liberal theory, people see themselves, rightly, not primarily as members of a group with a common good and shared values, but as individuals with independent identities and separate, often opposed interests. Relationships are more akin to "mere associations" than to full-fledged communities because they are based solely on "congruent private interests" and are not capable of progressing beyond this base.[29] That social world which does exist is minimal, because the individual of liberal theory does not seem to want, to need, or to be able to form deep connections with others; in fact, in a world perceived to be in a condition of scarcity, others may even be enemies, clashing in what is aptly called the social "arena." Self-interest both forces individuals into a social setting and restricts how social that setting can be.

The liberalism on which Rousseau focuses is again the same kind that is addressed by contemporary communitarians and feminists. The object of much of Rousseau's attention is social relationships founded upon self-interest, relationships which he so negatively characterizes as inherently limited, unstable, and divisive. Although Rousseau is said to be a "social contract" theorist, his evaluation of both the compact that establishes and legitimates civil society and the contracts that establish obligations within society differ crucially from those of Hobbes and Locke. As he sees it, the liberal contract aims at regulating and facilitating the social and commercial dealings of self-absorbed individuals, while his contract aims at stepping away from the self-interest that overwhelms modern individuals and modern theory.

While there seems to be no significant difference in the Rousseauean, communitarian, and feminist understandings of the liberal view of social relationships, such harmony once again abruptly ends when they critique it. To the extent that it is true that "[t]he central issue for political theory is not the constitution of the self but the connection of constituted selves, the pattern of social relations,"[30] differences here may reflect fundamentally different political perspectives.

2b. Critiques of the Liberal View

Communitarianism

[O]ur great modern free world is all too often a world in which men and women do not exist for others; . . . in which altruistic behavior is discouraged in the name of bargaining efficiency and utility accounting. . . . In this world, there can be no fraternal feeling, no general will, no selfless act, no mutuality, no species identity, no gift relationship, no disinter-

Feminism

To see contractual relations between self-interested or mutually disinterested individuals as constituting a paradigm of human relations is to take a certain historically specific conception of "economic man" as representative of humanity. And it is, many feminists are beginning to agree, to overlook or to discount in very fundamental ways the ex-

ested obligation, no social empathy, no love or belief or commitment that is not wholly private.[31]

Liberal theory . . . deprives us of any ready access to our own experience of communal embeddedness. . . . It explains our inability to form cohesive solidarities, stable movements and parties that might make our deep convictions visible and effective in the world.[32]

perience of women. . . . To the extent that some of our relations should be seen as contractual, we should recognize how essentially limited rather than general such relations are.[33]

Atomism cannot . . . represent non-peer relationships like those of parent and child, teacher and student, or any where one person takes care of the interest of another.[34]

Communitarians find at least two things troubling in the liberal account of human relations. First, because the relations between people are portrayed as superficial, extrinsic, and utilitarian, individuals remain essentially alone, private. Altruism, fraternity (sic), mutuality, empathy, and disinterestedness are discouraged, penalized, or dissolved by liberal ideology and liberal social and economic structures, while narrowly self-interested acts are encouraged and rewarded. Consequently, "[u]nder such conditions many individuals will be incapable of achieving genuine community, either because the pressures to live the life of an autonomous chooser of ends will undermine their own attempts at commitment, or because they will be unable to rely upon the commitments of others."[35] The loss or absence of community, whether caused by or reflected in the philosophy of liberalism, is seen as both real and regrettable.

A second, and generally incompatible, communitarian critique of the liberal approach to human relations recognizes within liberal societies the existence and especially the validity of nonvoluntary, noncontractual ties and obligations—familial, communal, and national—and faults liberalism for inadequately accounting for them. The problem with liberalism in this reading is not the actual absence of community but the theoretical misrepresentation or neglect of concrete communal experiences. The incompleteness of liberal theory affects action and understanding, leaving people with motives too weak to protect communities, models too meager to assist efforts in creating and maintaining communities, and doubts too serious about the trustworthiness and altruism of others to support communal political activism.

The differences between the feminist and communitarian critiques here seem to be ones of emphasis and specificity. While this sounds like a relatively minor divergence, the differences, when examined, reveal very distinct political agendas.

The stress in feminist analysis is on how very few actual relations the liberal account covers, rather than on the actual lack of noncompetitive, other-concerned, interdependent relations in society. Positive relations of dependency, of care, of cooperation, and between unequals all exist but are omitted in varying ways in the liberal account, despite the fact that these are the relations in which we spend most of our lives: as children or parents, teachers or students, clients or helpers, employers or employees.

This criticism, which thus far is very similar to at least one strain of the communitarian commentary, is more precise in naming what and who is left out. Feminists argue that what liberal analysis most systematically neglects are the experiences of women and children, and of the private realm with which they are primarily identified. Given the earlier feminist argument that the supposedly neutral, abstract individual of liberal theory is, to the extent that there is reality to the model, a (privileged) male, it follows that the social relations of liberal theory are, to the extent that they reflect reality, those between men or seen from a male perspective. "If the epitome of what it is to be human is thought to be a disposition to be a rational contractor, human persons creating other human persons through the processes of human mothering are overlooked. And human children developing human personhood are not recognized as engaged in a most obviously human activity."[36] The recognition this neglect generally receives from (nonfeminist) communitarians is minimal, and thus its importance is minimized: "it is an interesting question, *not addressed here*, whether this first [Marxist] communitarian critique speaks to the experience of women: Are necessity and private interest their only bonds with one another?"[37]

Further, feminists point out that this omission of women, children, and the "private" is an "oversight" with real costs. For example, "it is a great distortion of the [traditional] place of married women to see them as self-interested, autonomous beings competing for the satisfaction of their interests. This way of viewing them will not lead to a recognition of the real needs such women have."[38]

This feminist attention to women's lives can be connected to another point made by feminists and not found, or not emphasized, in the communitarian literature. Not only is it argued that narrowly self-interested relations should be understood as one limited variety of human experience but liberalism's very understanding of self-interest is challenged as too restricted: "[W]hen people think about what they want, they think about more than just their narrow self-interest. When they define their own interests and when they act to pursue those interests, they often give great weight both to their moral principles and to the interests of others."[39]

There is more in the communitarian critique that feminists find deeply troubling. In considering nonvoluntary, noncontractual relations, communitarians tend to speak of "the family" as a universal, unproblematical, and undifferentiated unit, and to link it with political community and nation. By lumping the familial with the political, communitarians make it too easy to assume that the two do or should serve the same ends and consist of similar relationships. Yet analogies such as these have brought particular harm to women, by providing, for example, "evidence" of the need for a (male) head of household and by turning childrearing into the task of "republican motherhood." By neglecting to differentiate the relations *within* families, communitarians render invisible power differences correlated with age and gender, as well as many of the problems to which they contribute, including the numerous forms of domestic violence. By not discussing family structures as they have varied across time and from culture to culture communitarians implicitly leave the heterosexual, patriarchal family as the norm. The family of communitarian theory is too often that which serves male advantage. Thus, while feminists, like communitarians, do take issue with liberalism for its neglect of the family, feminists are more interested in bringing the familial experiences of women and children into the conversation, and the attention they want paid to the family is far more critical.

The emphasis in Rousseau's critique is very definitely on the defects and dangers of self-interested relations, relations he thinks pervade the family as deeply as they pervade politics and business. If the isolation and separation of the individual in the state of nature informs Rousseau's thought from one direction, the isolation and separation of the individual in bourgeois society informs it as strongly from another. Rousseau's verdict is gender-neutral: like communitarians he sees women as being just as corrupted by selfishness as men. But he sees the consequences of this as gender-differentiated: women's selfishness is said to have more dire consequences than men's for children, families, culture, and politics.

By omission, Rousseau's critique bears more resemblance to that of communitarians than that of feminists. He seems to discern few gradations between pure self-interest and unadulterated community. He thinks each of these "extremes" can have some realm in which to operate, but seems not to reckon with the complex middle ground in which most women, simply by virtue of their family roles, live. His assault on self-interestedness, especially with respect to women, reinforces the notion of the sacrificial mother (even as it recognizes the political benefits this brings), without evidence that he understands what this means for women's lives.

2c. Alternatives to Liberalism

Communitarianism

So to see ourselves as deontology would see us is to deprive us of those qualities of character, reflectiveness, and friendship that depend on the possibility of constitutive projects and attachments. And to see ourselves as given to commitments such as these is to admit a deeper commonality than benevolence describes, a commonality of shared self-understanding as well as "enlarged affection." As the independent self finds its limits in those aims and attachments from which it cannot stand apart, so justice finds its limits in those forms of community that engage the identity as well as the interests of the participants.[40]

Feminism

Instead of importing into the household principles derived from the marketplace, perhaps we should export to the wider society the relations suitable for mothering persons and children . . . relations . . . characterized by more care and concern and openness and trust and human feeling than are the contractual bargains that have developed so far in political and economic life, or even that are aspired to in contractarian prescriptions.[41]

We need a model that allows for organic connections, some more fundamental than others, among people, connections of dependency and interdependency of many kinds.[42]

The model of interpersonal relationships preferred by feminists to that of liberalism is not unitary, but "acknowledges many kinds of relations among people, and many kinds of social roles, and other kinds of interest than self-interest. . . . competition will be only one of the relations among people where determinations of justice apply." A model such as this acknowledges the diversity of human beings and human relationships, and that alone accords it superiority over liberalism's, which, as we have seen, especially ignores traditional women and children and the relationships in which they are involved. Women will "fit in [this new model] in a variety of ways and roles,"[43] because relationships between males will not be taken as the norm at the outset, because the complexity of human connections will not be reduced to a unitary ideal, and because it will be assumed that as sexism has differentiated the lives of the sexes, women too have lessons to teach about relationships.

One of the questions with which feminist political theory concerns itself is how to resolve the tension, most felt by women, between care for and obligations to others and care for and obligations to one's self. It is necessary to "envision a society that grants each of us our 'individual dignity' but does not allow us to lose sight of our connections to each other."[44] Women's roles have frequently meant obliteration and sacrifice of the self or redefinition of one's self and self-interest in terms of and in relation to others. The communitarian solution to liberalism's impoverished social life fails, however, to solve or even seriously address this enforced self-abnegation, and here Rousseau's scheme is virtually identical. Because communitarians, including Rousseau, see the social problem as fragmentation, their answer is connection. They favor tradition, as Rousseau applauds mores, because tradition offers place, security, coherence, and stability. But the problem for women has not been solitude and lack of commitment, and the feminist alternative is neither simply connection nor simply separation. A feminist vision of social relations cannot gloss over what various traditions have meant to people of color, to gays and lesbians, to the lower classes, and to women. Failure to give these matters the attention they demand invites more hierarchical and exclusionary practices to reassert themselves. A feminist vision also necessarily entails critical reevaluation and restructuring of such engendered institutions and practices as the family, the sexual division of labor, and the connections between private and public. Neither contemporary communitarians nor Rousseau see sexual differentiation as particularly problematic; in fact, it is often held up as a cure to *other* (read: important) social ills. At that point feminists and communitarians, Rousseau included, truly part ways.

3. POLITICAL COMMUNITY

3a. Understanding Liberalism

Communitarianism	*Feminism*
For liberal individualism a community is simply an arena in which individuals each pursue their own self-chosen conception of the good life, and political institutions	[L]iberal philosophers seek to develop a political theory that is independent of any substantive claims about the nature of the good life or of human happiness or

exist to provide that degree of order which makes such self-determined activity possible. Government and law are, or ought to be, neutral between rival conceptions of the good life for man, and hence, although it is the task of government to promote law-abidingness, it is in the liberal view no part of the legitimate function of government to inculcate any one moral outlook.[45]

fulfillment. Individuals are entitled to set their own ends. . . . They see the state as the neutral arbiter of conflicting social interests, whose task is to protect individual rights and so to defend against the tyranny of any individual or group.[46]

What liberalism professes to offer, according to Rousseau, communitarians, and feminists, is a limited, neutral state that provides the conditions of "liberty" and "protection" in which individuals can pursue their private interests and goods as they define them. MacIntyre agrees with Ronald Dworkin that "the central doctrine of modern liberalism is the thesis that questions about the *good life for man* or the ends of human life are to be regarded from the public standpoint as systematically unsettlable. . . . The rules of morality and law hence are not to be derived from or justified in terms of some more fundamental conception of the good for man."[47] This is also Sandel's conceptualization of "deontological liberalism": "society, being composed of a plurality of persons, each with his own aims, interests, and conceptions of the good, is best arranged when it is governed by principles that do not *themselves* presuppose any particular conception of the good."[48] Individuals have rights, and equal rights at that, and the task of the liberal state is to preserve them. It does this by protecting individuals from one another and by itself not interfering with what is properly an individual's private concern.

This political posture follows, as does the liberal view of social relations, from liberalism's atomism: separate, self-interested individuals demand a politics that imposes no ends but enables the fulfillment of the individual's independently chosen ones. "The standard liberal argument for neutrality is an induction from social fragmentation. Since dissociated individuals will never agree on the good life, the state must allow them to live as they think best, subject only to John Stuart Mill's harm principle, without endorsing or sponsoring any particular understanding of what 'best' means."[49]

Just as there is considerable agreement between Rousseauean, feminist, and communitarian understandings of liberalism's perspective on the self and social relations, so is there considerable agreement between them concerning liberalism's concept of political community. Perhaps most importantly, all note that liberalism accepts a politics of conflict that leads to the need for government as mediator. There are, however, some significant differences in emphasis among the three portrayals of liberalism. The aspect of liberal politics that gets most attention from feminists is the gap between neutrality in theory and partiality in practice, itself related to the larger problem of liberalism's public/private distinction and the role of government in each sphere. The aspect of the liberal state that gets most attention from communitarians is government's misguided role as a neutral "referee" of values. Rousseau's stress is often placed on the undesirable individualistic values bolstered by a liberal state in both its own deliberations and its general social influence. Examples include liberalism's minimal conception of citizenship and its acceptance of interest-group politics.

3b. Critiques of Liberalism

Communitarianism

Liberal democracy may not be a theory of political community at all. It does not so much provide a justification for politics as it offers a politics that justifies individual rights. It is concerned more to promote individual liberty than to secure public justice, to advance interests rather than to discover goods, and to keep men safely apart rather than to bring them fruitfully together. As a consequence, it is capable of fiercely resisting every assault on the individual—his privacy, his property, his interests, and his rights—but is far less effective in resisting assaults on community or justice or citizenship or participation.[50]

Feminism

Liberal theory does not provide the language or concepts to help us understand the various kinds of human interdependence which are part of the life of both families and polities, nor to articulate a feminist vision of "the good life."[51]

[R]ights oversimplify complex power relations . . . [T]he resort to rights can be effectively countered by the resort to competing rights . . . [R]ights formulated to protect the individual against the state, or the weak against the strong, may be appropriated by the more powerful.[52]

[T]he liberal notion of "the private" has included what has been called "woman's sphere" as "male property" and sought not only to preserve it from the interference of the public realm but also to keep those who "belong" in that realm—women—from the life of the public.[53]

For communitarians, the liberal political world, in which all that people share is protection from one another by an impartial state, leaves people without a common moral anchor, requires of them morally nothing higher than law-abidingness, and abdicates its responsibility for moral education. "Liberalism teaches respect for the distance of self and ends. . . . By putting the self beyond the reach of politics, it makes human agency an article of faith rather than an object of continuing attention and concern, a premise of politics rather than its precarious achievement. This misses the pathos of politics and also its most inspiring possibilities."[54] According to communitarians, liberal politics follows from and reinforces atomistic individualism. The successes of the liberal state concern only its ability to protect the self-interested and isolated self, via structures and practices such as property rights, privacy claims, and interest-group politics. Social skills and feelings are not consciously cultivated, deeply restricting the style and substance of political life.

While communitarians find liberalism's politics inadequate, feminists find it at times mythical and at times positively injurious to women. More fully, communitarians speak as if liberalism were basically good at doing what it set out to do, but argue that it does not set out to do the right things. While feminists, too, question whether liberal principles can or should be the ones guiding the state, they also challenge liberalism for its failure in practice to do for both sexes what in principle it sets out to do.

Feminists evaluate liberalism's politics from a vantage point that reveals dynamics not attended to by communitarians. Catharine MacKinnon discusses how "liberal neutrality" in fact amounts to "substantive misogyny."[55] In the face of existing sexual inequality, a politics that, in the name of neutrality, refuses to take sides is in reality taking sides with the more powerful, men, allowing them to maintain their dominance through a state policy of noninterference. Feminist critics of liberal politics challenge its pretense to (gender) neutrality in a second way: feminists wonder how a state can be considered neutral that has upheld sexual segregation in employment, continues to prefer the nuclear heterosexual family over all other familial arrangements in public policy, considers affirmative action reverse discrimination, and refuses, on "privacy" grounds, to "interfere" in cases of domestic abuse, even while it outlaws "private" sexual acts between consenting adult members of the same sex.

Further, granting "rights" to the less powerful, a time-honored liberal solution, receives mixed reviews from feminists. True, gaining rights is a victory over those who would prefer little restraint on the potential exploitation of women.[56] But problems remain: private (male) power is often untouched by and impervious to (women's) formal rights; social and economic factors can limit the exercise of women's rights; and appeals to rights tend to treat the sexes (and individuals generally) as adversaries, thus reinforcing a problematical politics.

As Marxist feminists might prefer to put it, liberal rights are fictitious cover-ups veiling the class rule of men. "Marxist feminists would have us recognize that a system of economics and gender rooted in capitalist, male-dominated structures underlies much of liberal ideology, from the notion of independent rational man to the conception of separate private and public realms, from the value of individualism to the equation of freedom with free trade."[57] In fact, many feminists present a view of the liberal state as male-dominated, a concept parallel to the Marxist notion of a class-dominated state. One understanding of the destructiveness of the patriarchal liberal state, not subscribed to only by Marxist feminists, is offered by Hartsock:

> The masculine gender carried by power intensifies the tensions of community and leads to the construction of an even more conflictual and false community than that formed by means of exchange. It is a community both in theory and in fact obsessed with revenge and structured by conquest and domination. . . . These dynamics of conquest and domination mean that the gain of one participant can come only at the expense of the other's submission, humiliation, or even death.[58]

Because it is infused with patriarchal principles and processes, feminists would necessarily insist not on a state that reasserts *its* rights in the moral domain, as communitarians desire, but one that reassesses its own ethics.

Rousseau's critique of liberal politics shares the communitarian concern with the absence of a common moral anchor, an absence that allows self-interest to be the dominating force in political life as elsewhere and heralds the politics of conflict, exploitation, and deception. Participation in the liberal state does not require moving beyond self-interest; in fact it could not require this, since, according to Rousseau, in the liberal polity neither the family nor education provides the training necessary for such full-fledged citizenship.

Rousseau shares with feminists and communitarians a deep concern about the social and political consequences of a polity based on individual advantage. Rousseau states most boldly that there *is* no political community when self-interest is the guiding principle. Like many other communitarians, he sees the rise of self-interest as causally connected to the decline of a common moral sense in political communities, and thus looks to a resurrection of the latter as a solution to the problems of liberal politics. Feminists see the consequences of the liberal state as significantly different for the two sexes and urge attention to women's communities and networks for both insight into liberalism and ideas for alternatives to self-interested individualism. Here it becomes clear how criticisms of liberalism that are "gender-blind" are also "gender-biased"; the problems of liberalism most specific to women are ignored in the gender-blind critiques, and the call for a return to "a common moral vision" or, more often today, to "traditional values," is a gender-biased solution which does not speak from or to the lives of many women.

3c. Alternatives to the Liberal View

Communitarianism

The application of that measure [of goodness] in a community whose shared aim is the realization of the human good presupposes . . . a wide range of agreement in that community on goods and virtues, and it is this agreement which makes possible the kind of bond between citizens which, on Aristotle's view, constitutes a *polis*. That bond is the bond of friendship. . . . Indeed from an Aristotelian point of view a modern liberal political society can appear only as a collection of citizens of nowhere who have banded together for their common protection. They possess at best that inferior form of friendship which is founded on mutual advantage. . . . They have abandoned the moral unity of Aristotelianism.[59]

Feminism

A valuable alternative conception of politics . . . is perhaps best called the democratic one, and it takes politics to be the collective and participatory engagement of citizens in the determination of the affairs of their community. The community may be the neighborhood, the city, the state, the region, or the nation itself. What counts is that all matters relating to the community are undertaken as "the people's affair."[60]

[T]he conception of power as dominance is partial and misleading . . . one must not take the question of who rules whom to be the most critical political issue.[61]

There are so many visions of political community that perhaps it is impossible to represent them fairly here. Communitarian schemes range from MacIntyre's conventionalist Aristotelianism and Sandel's revitalized civic republicanism to Barber's Rousseauean participatory democracy. Feminist visions run the gamut from Sara Ruddick's maternal politics to Marge Piercy's small-town ecologically minded democracies and Jaggar's socialist feminist state. And Judith Sklar has shown us that Rousseau's theory itself encompasses multiple political visions. There is overlap as well as diversity among these theorists, most obvious in their frequent advocacy of democratic and of socialist communities. Too often, however, the overlap is merely nominal. Focusing only on the common ground of democracy and socialism may conceal the different and often incompatible sets of political concerns and arrangements behind feminist and communitarian versions of each. One illustration of how feminists, communitarians, and Rousseau diverge in their visions of community is the striking contrast in their attitudes toward ancient Greece.

MacIntyre's *After Virtue* has three chapters exclusively devoted to ancient Greece. It is fair to say that his picture of community is very strongly and positively affected by the ancient Greek polities, even if he does not accept them as flawless. (There is, however, precious little evidence of his finding any fault with them.)

These "heroic societies," as MacIntyre calls them, are marked by certain "key features": "Every individual has a given role and status within a well-defined and highly determinate system of roles and statuses." "[T]here is for each status a prescribed set of duties and privileges. There is also a clear understanding of what actions are required to perform these and what actions fall short."[62]

As Okin notes, "one is left with the impression that it is [MacIntyre's] conscious intention to make the reader forget about the exclusionary nature of Aristotle's views about who could lead 'the good life for a human being,' " or who was capable of Aristotle's highest form of friendship. "[H]is benign interpretation de-emphasizes both the social hierarchy of heroic societies and the heavy sanctions that reinforced it."[63]

Rousseau's political preference is for a democratic community of virtuous citizens similar to, familiar with, and interested in one another. But only for men is direct political participation urged, even while women are given disproportionate responsibility (blame) for the state of the community. Rousseau's use of the ancient Greeks is neither as critical as feminists' nor as uncritical as MacIntyre's. Interestingly, Rousseau seems more approving of the lives of Greek women than those of Greek men. Overlooking the severely oppressed condition of women in Greek societies, Rousseau cites sev-

Feminism and Communitarianism **145**

eral Greek women as exemplars of public and private virtue. Appearing in a positive light in Rousseau's works are pictures of Spartan women (supposedly) commanding men "for the glory of the state and public happiness" (SD, 89), women more concerned with military victory than with the lives of their own sons (*Emile*, 40), and praise for the practice of some Greeks of utterly confining women in the private sphere (*Emile*, 366).

Once again, then, the gloss painted on a picture of hierarchy, exclusion, and degradation by MacIntyre and Rousseau comes at precisely those points where feminists would scour the surface and reveal all the undercoats. In this case the difference is so striking that feminists seem quite justified in their lack of enthusiasm for communitarianism.

[T]he Greek understanding of politics and power rested more directly and explicitly than ours on the division between women and men, between the household, a private and apolitical space, and the *polis*, a public and political space. This division was, moreover, a division between a realm of necessity and a realm of freedom, a realm held to be characterized by inequality and a realm seen as populated by equals, a realm described as dominated by the body and a realm where the soul or intellect was held to be dominant. All of this both rested on and reinforced a profound misogyny.[64]

Feminists should be wary of communitarian calls for moral unity. Such calls may signal a readiness to accept grave social inequalities and an insensitivity to the enriching power of differences.

CONCLUSION

The writers explored here all prefer a more communal theory and practice than is found in liberalism. A final, more subterranean, issue helps explain the distance between feminist and communitarian thought: their motives for rejecting liberalism.

MacIntyre's *After Virtue* is informed by the "grave disorder" of moral anomie, which "perhaps . . . a very few—recognised as a catastrophe" (2, 3). The concerns at the center of his enterprise seem most directly to involve and be felt by moral theorists—truly a "very few." The "catastrophe" is that there is "no rational way of securing moral agreement in our culture" (6). That we are experiencing a moral decline is shown by our "complacency" about "moral pluralism," when what we really have is "an unharmonious melange of ill-assorted fragments" of viewpoints (10). Given the cultural power of "emotivism," we are quite comfortable with the view that "all moral judgments are *nothing but* expressions of preference, expressions of attitude or feeling," despite the fact that this "Weberian vision of the world cannot be rationally sustained" (19, 11, 103). MacIntyre's concern is with "modern moral theorists" who are faced with "insoluble problems . . . [by] modern moral utterance and practice" (104–5), who are searching for "impersonal . . . standards of justice or generosity or duty" (9). It is not clear that MacIntyre's problem is necessarily so remote from the political concerns that inform feminism, but the inference from his writing is that feminist issues are not relevant to a search for justice or virtue. Immoral misogynist behavior must, again, take a back seat, this time to moral agreement in theory. It is then not surprising that his "vindication" of Aristotelian ethics and politics, and the "way of life" they entail (111), seems so politically uncritical from a feminist perspective.

Much the same can be said of Michael Sandel's *Liberalism and the Limits of Justice*. He tells us at the outset that the limits of (liberal) justice he argues for "are not practical but conceptual" (1). His enterprise of showing the incoherence of a "concept of a subject given prior to and independent of its objects" has as its end the refutation of the liberal "claim for the primacy of justice" (7). Feminists are not necessarily unconcerned about the theoretical consistency of liberalism, or whether the right is prior to the good. But unlike Sandel, feminists find the limits of liberal justice most dramatically visible in the "practical" world; little would be gained, from a feminist perspective, if liberalism were made more tidy conceptually and left as dirty in practice.

Christopher Lasch writes in 'The Communitarian Critique of Liberalism" that "it was the impoverishment of public life under liberalism, the relegation of all the important questions to the obscurity of private life, that gave rise in the first place to a communitarian critique of liberalism" (183). Lasch's summary helps explain why feminists and communitarians cooperate less with each other than they ideally could. First, as his comment indicates, communitarianism does not necessarily challenge either the division of social life into public and private spheres or the hierarchical relationship between them—both of which are very much contested by feminists. Next, communitarians often contrast the present-day "impoverishment of public life" with the "rich" politics of premodernity, and many find in antiquity the defining model for such a "rich" politics, despite the fact that most ancient polities excluded women (and many men) from participation and despite the fact that "history simply does not support" the view "that when members of a society have settled roots and established traditions, they will tolerate the speech, religious, sexual, and associational preferences of minorities."[65]

Finally, the authors of *Habits of the Heart* speak thus of the "tensions" analyzed in their text:

> We strongly assert the value of our self-reliance and autonomy. We deeply feel the emptiness of a life without sustaining social commitments. Yet we are hesitant to articulate our sense that we need one another as much as we need to stand alone, for fear that if we did we would lose our independence altogether.[66]

The standpoint from which this is written is that of the traditional male, endless usages of "we" and "our" notwithstanding. This is the male who is more comfortable asserting his autonomy than acknowledging his need for or debt to others, most fearful of all of losing what he calls his "independence." Traditional woman's starting point is the opposite: she is more comfortable acknowledging her need for others than asserting her autonomy, most fearful of losing her connections to others. Indeed, the individual stories in *Habits of the Heart* show this to be true, and still the point is missed. The authors continue to treat the male experience as the norm, rendering women's experiences invisible, outside the mainstream of supposedly universal human experience. That which could be learned from women's unique experiences with community, positive and negative, is lost.

It is astonishing that in the long lists of modern woes cited by communitarians one almost never finds items such as the feminization of poverty (by the year 2000 virtually all "officially" poor people in the United States will be women or children), rape (perpetrated on perhaps one out of every four women and compromising the freedom of all women), domestic violence (half of all married women can expect at least one violent episode at the hands of their mates), pornography (an $8-billion-a-year industry in the United States alone), child abuse, or sexual harassment. If any one of these is mentioned, it is too often as a mere symptom of a "real" or "bigger" problem that has nothing to do with male domination.

Given the sexism, racism, and homophobia pervasive in most cultures and our educational systems, unless people start out explicitly committed *not* to discriminate, they usually end up discriminating. This understanding of how oppression is maintained is, of course, the basis of affirmative action policies. Communitarianism lacks feminist consciousness and commitment to resolving problems of gender hierarchy. Thus, it usually ends up ignoring and therefore perpetuating those problems: it ends up with a white male vision, as "unintentional" and as thorough as that found anywhere. Feminists do indeed find a "perilous ally"[67] in communitarianism, whether it is Plato's, Rousseau's, or MacIntyre's, and will continue to as long as communitarianism is isolationist in its politics. Because patriarchal values and institutions continue to pervade and maintain communitarian visions, those of us committed to feminism need to continue to put energy into consciousness-raising and education and most definitely must persist in developing full-fledged visions of our own. We are clearly not in a "postfeminist" age.

Rousseau is part of a tradition, and we learn more about both him and the tradition by studying them together. Because of the dire consequences of antifeminist communities, it is important to direct our intellectual and political energy against them; "it is important to give irritation or anger some kind of shape."[68]

EIGHT

GENDER BIAS IN POLITICAL THEORY: (UN)SEEING AND (UN)DOING

Step for a few minutes into a world where everything changes when one thing changes—a world in which women dominate men. For simplicity's sake, look only at one subfield of one academic discipline in this topsy-turvy world: political theory. The history of political theory is peopled entirely by women: Aristonia and Platonia in antiquity, Saints Thomasina and Augustinia in medieval times and, in the modern period, Nicole MacVillain, Janice Locket, Donna Hobbles, Jeanne-Jacqueline Trousseau, Jane Stuart Miller, and Carla Marcus. Even the less prominent figures, such as Jeanette Bodine and Roberta Fillmore, are women.[1]

Looking at college curricula and textbooks on political theory, those few who notice such things wonder why there have never been any great male theorists, and they guess that this reflects the general superiority of the female intellect. Certainly they have heard that idea expressed often enough; they have heard it called upon as an explanation for everything from women's higher scores on standardized tests to men's underrepresentation among Nobel Prize winners, from women's virtual monopoly on positions of political and economic power to men's virtual absence among the "greats" of literature, music, and the other creative arts. But one day some men have the unusual opportunity to get together and formulate some questions, questions that eventually culminate in a thorough reappraisal of the history of political theory.

These friends (there would have to be some basis for trust among those willing to be so frank, so disloyal) studied the great political tradition together, with their gaze focused on claims concerning gender, the grounds on which such claims were defended, and their ramifications. This itself was no small task, given that they had been trained to glide over such problems in favor of ones supposedly more central. They stopped repeatedly to ponder how it was that scholars found the treatment of men—of half the human species!—a trivial aside, irrelevant to understanding or evaluating someone's political thought. Yet ink was generously spent over such problems as the distinctions between the early and late Carla Marcus and the similarity between Jeanne-Jacqueline Trousseau and the fictitious Savvy Victor in her text *Emily*.

With constantly renewed astonishment, they found in text after text that women were the real subjects of political theory and activity. Men were a secondary object of scrutiny: their inferiority was defined by their difference from the female norm; their nature was described in terms of the tasks women, or the culture women created, needed them to perform; and control over them was justified by the threat they posed to this matriarchal world order. Perhaps most commonly, men were said to lack whatever qualities a given philosopher regarded as making people complete, unique, divine, or happy. To be male and to be human were portrayed as mutually exclusive, and what being male came down to was serving women and children, and joining in the judgment of one's sex as irremediably defective.

Until they got together, these courageous and seditious men had each wondered privately which was the problem: men or political theory. In their talks they discovered—the first of a long train of ultimately very revealing commonalities—that each of them had tried to read the semisacred texts as if men, or at least some men, were included as actors in the fullest senses. Many had tried to suppose that the degrading statements about males referred to *other* men. This effort was fruitless and self-defeating. The declarations seemed to them as untrue of other men as of themselves. Entrenched gender identification made it tough to imagine even an "exceptional" man's assuming a role so clearly marked out for a female. Passages about how the fully human person should treat her husband always got in the way as well. Further, as they later realized, this strategy of trying to read some men into the texts only served to perpetuate division among men and allow derogatory, antimale sentiments to go unchallenged. Finally, it is hard to keep thinking of yourself as an exception when virtually nobody else does.

Many of these men had also tried translating "women" into "people" as

Gender Bias in Political Theory   **151**

they read, as if just willing these texts to be unbiased could make them so. They soon discovered, however, that the sexism of the world's most esteemed political theorists was not simply a matter of semantics, not some detachable appendage, but an intrinsic part of their work. You couldn't just "add men and mix," as they later expressed it. How, for example, could they imagine that Aristonia had women *and* men in mind as citizens, when the leisure women had at their disposal to dedicate to the polis was a direct result of the domestic enslavement of men? How could they assume that an endorsement of representative government for women meant or could mean representation of and by men, when women were the subjects and actresses in politics by virtue of being heads of households, representatives and beneficent mistresses of their husbands and children? No—men could not just be added. What was required, in these cases, was a more comprehensive understanding of what experiences prepare one for political action and what domestic and economic structures enable and encourage people to participate.

This group of men brought to their common reading a long history of sensitivity to nuance. What was new was that they were using that sensitivity to understand and judge and change their own plight, rather than, as in the past, to understand and accommodate others. As they were freed from the confinement of the previously ubiquitous female bias, they were almost overwhelmed by their new understanding of how deeply men were injured in female-dominated societies and by the deluge of new ideas, of fresh perspectives, in virtually every debate. They were determined not to part ways with their sensitivity, not to lose touch in their own theorizing with how thoroughly despicable, how terrible, it is to have not only themselves but any group described and defined in such insulting, negative, derogatory, matronizing, narrow, static, arrogant, and self-serving terms, terms then used to justify and perpetuate mistreatment of that group in practice.

Not everything they found was so depressing. One of their most rewarding and remarkable discoveries was that there *were* great male philosophers. Their discoveries of lost figures and forgotten ideas were accompanied by tremendous intellectual and emotional excitement, that powerful combination that the other sex seemed so eager to dismiss. In this process they learned something about internalized oppression—about how much they themselves had come to believe in male inferiority—when they discovered their joy and surprise at finding that, despite all the forces conspiring to keep men uneducated and domesticated throughout history, men did write political theory: profound, playful, passionate theory. Interestingly, like the works of those few women who wrote in support of sexual equality, the works of these men remained unpublished. Or, if published, remained out of print. Or, if in print, were untranslated. Or, if translated, remained unstudied. Or, if studied, were not written about, for graduate students don't get jobs and professors don't get published by researching what are widely considered minor figures and marginal topics. This is where what might once have seemed to them a series of unconnected and coincidental events began to be seen as a pattern, a system, a union of forces working against men by design.

Think how exciting it was when these daring fellows realized that Walter Stonecraft, despite his virtual invisibility in standard histories of political theory, wrote a treatise at least as innovative and as representative of early liberal philosophy as those by Janice Locket or Jane Stuart Miller. Yet even in 1992 people failed to mark, much less celebrate, the bicentenary of his *Vindication of the Rights of Man*.[2] And Simon deRover performed similar feats in existential philosophy, turning from Jeanne-Pauline's theories about the free choice available to all people at all times to an existentialism that can account for and work against the social unfreedom of males. The fate of these theorists—their consignment to oblivion—taught the men about the extent to which some would go to allow women and only women to define the parameters and subjects of a theory. Think how empowering it was when the now self-proclaimed masculists challenged the commonly accepted notion that Jane Stuart Miller only wrote *On the Subjection of Men* because of the undue and unnatural influence of her overbearing and somewhat testerical husband Harry Taylor Miller. The absence of any mention of that text in numerous commentaries about her (much less any positive mention) helped them to see that even if you are female, utterly sincere, and well-respected, in a matriarchy you cannot write that men are equal to women without being ignored or ridiculed, or having your womanhood questioned. It was hard to acknowledge but harder still to ignore these lessons about the intensity of the forces working to keep men subordinate, and the intensity with which men would have to work to liberate themselves. And they must certainly have tingled with nervous excitement over the fact that even in those dark Middle Ages men spoke out in defense of their sex, as Chris deZan did in *The Book of the City of Gentlemen*. Such male luminaries existed, and were part of the great history not only of political theory but of resistance to sexism.

Gender Bias in Political Theory

As they continued to read together and to analyze the forces behind the silencing of these voices, the masculists became increasingly convinced that the gender problem in political thought was due to matriarchy, its disdain for anything associated with the male, including men themselves, and its willingness to sacrifice the male for the interests of women. The shameful treatment of men in the history of theory was only finally comprehensible as one of many manifestations of female domination. Now masculists began to pop up everywhere, analyzing, deconstructing, and revisioning what had once seemed obvious and uncontroversial. They started building on each other's work, finding similarities, making connections, and adding their own contributions. It was easy, for example, to link the bias in political theory to the bias in public policy, for in both the norm that defined problems and constructed remedies was a female one. Similarly, the trivialization of men by philosophers corresponded to the gender gap in American politics, for in both cases men became a mere puzzle for strategists to solve—that is, to manage for female advantage. When they reached this masculist understanding, *it* seemed so incontrovertible and obvious that they couldn't remember how they had ever seen the world any other way. It felt the way it feels when you first get glasses after years of squinting, or, better, the way it feels when you finally and suddenly solve a complex mystery story despite the author's numerous attempts to confuse and mislead you. "Of course," you say. "I should have seen that."

These men had dutifully studied row upon row of works regarded—by those women said to know them best—as the most insightful, truthful, impartial, and universally applicable. Yet at the end, with a boldness often thought to be reserved for women, they challenged the motives, truth, and objectivity of virtually every woman in the history of theory, as well as the women who interpreted them, and the women who regarded the equal inclusion of works by men as sacrilege, "a distortion of our cultural heritage."

When they asked who was included in the "our" whose cultural heritage was to be cherished and preserved, these men's libbers declared that because of sexism every culture actually contains at least two cultures, one female and one male. (It would take more time before the intersections of sex with race, class, sexuality, and nationality broke this down further, and longer still before some wondered if things hadn't then been broken apart.) They went so far as to assert that men's culture was as rich, complete, inspiring, and worthy of study and emulation as was women's. Some, though we are assured only a radical and strident minority, even considered men's heritage to be superior. The masculists talked of finding in political theory written by men less concern with glory and exclusion, less tolerance of abuse and violence, and attention not only to what divides people but also to what connects them. They claimed that men had been less corrupted by power and less trained in dominance and conquest than women had been (though I can only guess at some of what they meant), and that this difference had led to understandings of the self, and of personal and social relationships, built less on greed and more on compassion, less on jealousy and more on trust.

Well, it *is* true that in *The Republican* Platonia makes the rather damning assertion that in every occupation the female is superior to the male. I have double-checked, and it is also clear that Aristonia did say of men that their rationality was incomplete, and thus they should serve their female superiors. Even those we call saints, yes, these too are guilty. Perhaps you, like me, hadn't noticed that Saint Thomasina felt it necessary to ask in her great compendium of theological questions, "Whether the Men Should Have Been Made in the First Production of Things?"[3] I'm not sure I grasp their point entirely, but the men's libbers have said that Nicole MacVillain should be criticized for seeing in men that which women should fear and conquer. Janice Locket they read as still living in her own primitive state of nature. Donna Hobbles, for all they cared, could be the next victim of her "war of all against all," for she ignored the more cooperative history of men when she claimed that aggressiveness is just part of human nature. Jeanne-Jacqueline Trousseau . . . well, what do *you* think should be the fate of the supposedly great democrat who says "Man is born to serve and please woman," but reassures us that this does not mean the sexes are unequal?!

WHICH END IS UP?

In the hands of male chauvinists and certain comedians, gender reversal is a tactic used to undermine feminism by making it look ridiculous, almost sacrilegious. In the hands of feminists, however, gender reversal is used not to advocate as an ideal the oppression of men but to help us see the invisible, the unconscious. When we're asked our reaction to a woman's saying "No husband of mine is going to work!" we realize how extraordinary are the ordinary and unnoted expressions of male control over women. When someone suggests that if men got pregnant all methods of birth control would be 100 percent effective, we come to see how powerfully but invisibly sexism influences policy and research agendas. When someone suggests, as I have done here, that theorizing done by women, reducing man to woman's inferior and servant, might be something less than perfectly objective, it helps us to see the extent to which we have unquestioningly accepted the very questionable decrees of male political theorists about both their own impartiality and about women's marginality.

Gender bias, like most of the all-too-numerous varieties of discrimination, comes in a range of forms. Too often we recognize and address as sexist only the most obvious statements and actions that limit and stigmatize individual women because they are women, members of a group which is itself caricatured, misrepresented, and maligned. This lack of subtlety in analysis and action does more than present some risk for gender equality; it guarantees havens for misogyny perfectly capable of sustaining systematic male domination.

One of the more blatant forms of gender bias is that which reserves for men all of the "best" traits, jobs, ambitions, and roles and assigns and attributes to the nature and province of women those which are deemed secondary and inferior. In Aristotle women have deficient rationality, live in a permanent state of being ruled, and do not participate in public deliberations. Left to men like himself, unswayed of course by mere opinion, are the most revered capacities—to reason and to govern—and the most highly esteemed and powerful positions in which to develop and exercise them. In Freud women's lack of a penis destines them to possess deficient moral reasoning. It is left to men like himself, uninfluenced by womb envy, to reach the heights of moral development. If being created directly by God is taken as the source of human dignity, then woman's secondary creation, as depicted in Genesis 2, is used as the source of her inferiority and subordination. If being able to rise above the bodily, the sensual, or the physical is the mark of the fully human, then woman's capacity to bear children excludes her from full humanity and binds her to an inferior realm. With minor variations on the theme, and despite their frequent contradictions with each other, political philosophy reissues such immoral, misogynist, self-righteous edicts century after century. The inability of theorists to agree on what essentially differentiates women and men, and with what social and political consequences, is an indication that what is primary, what really matters, is keeping the sexes polarized and women subordinated, and that whatever arguments come most easily or work best in a given historical era and philosophical framework will be employed. Women's ambitions, capacities, desires, and interests, that is to say, are not really the subject of independent, rigorous, and sincere inquiry, but are an afterthought, described in terms of whatever complements the idealized male subject. And it is utterly critical that we not lose sight of this ugly inequality when it is disguised, more or less cleverly, in terms of "different but equal," or when the inequality is said to be superficial, and balanced by women's irresistible and indirect power.

In a related form of gender bias, theories not only ascribe to women a secondary and inferior nature and function but present women as a serious threat to men and the social order (as "order" is defined by and serves men), a threat men rightly attempt to conquer. One of women's roles in Augustine is as temptress, an aspect of the devil's evil designs. Nietzsche's heroic overman creates values and battles conventionality; his woman is but a "dangerous plaything." The connection between the perception of women as threatening and violence against women could not be clearer than in Nietzsche, for in *Thus Spake Zarathustra*, after describing woman as dangerous, a plaything, base in her soul, and superficial, he writes: "Do you go to women? Do not forget the whip!" Thus spake misogyny.

Disdain for and bias against women in the history of theory also takes the form of silence. Just as whites too often fail to notice the absence of people of color at certain gatherings, and as the able-bodied rarely note the absence of access ramps, until feminism entered the academy few seemed to notice or attribute significance to the absence of women in the philosophies that are supposed to help us understand ourselves and our relations with each other. Plato's *Republic* vividly illustrates the consequences of women's being silenced in philosophical dialogue. In book 1, for example, Cephalus explains that while most bemoan old age, "longing for the pleasures of youth and reminiscing about sex, about drinking bouts and feasts," he finds that age brings "escape . . . from a sort of frenzied and savage master . . . great peace and freedom. . . . When the desires cease to strain . . . it is possible to be rid of very many mad masters."[4] Cephalus's explanation of why most bemoan old age is based entirely on the experience of free Greek men. Greek women, free or enslaved, rarely participated in feasts and festivities, and acts of premarital and extramarital sex were among the worst crimes a woman could commit. The dialogue is silent about what it means to be destined for a life of seclusion and domestic service, to be sent off, perhaps sold while you are yet a teenager, to an older husband chosen for you by your father and with whom you may not even be acquainted. It is not clear what frenzied desires were ever allowed mastery in the lives of young Athenian women. Growing old means different things for men and women in sexually differentiated societies. The end of childbearing, changes in child-rearing duties, and caring for an aging husband may have been more definitive of aging for Athenian women than was the loss or diminution of the capacity to overindulge in food, liquor, and sex. But such experiences are entirely excluded from the dialogue.

This does not mean, of course, that the topics of the *Republic* are exclusively "male" issues. They are, however, discussed exclusively on the basis of the experiences of free males. The more radical a system of sex roles, the greater the dangers of not having gender-inclusive knowledge. When we understand only what privileged men think and feel about aging, for example, our social policy priorities, medical research agendas, and cultural lore are flawed, at best serving and representing a part of the whole, at worst ignoring, injuring, and invalidating the rest. To the extent Whitehead is correct that "all philosophy is a footnote on Plato," all philosophy is a patriarchal conversation, both in the questions that have been blessed with the stamp of importance and the viewpoints considered worthy opponents. The leaving out of certain information privileges the perspective of a part of humanity and mutes, marginalizes, or delegitimizes other voices.

Exclusion, then, in fact speaks loud and clear. It bestows upon us a tradition in which what certain men have valued is institutionalized and justified, whether that be military valor, as in Homeric times, or acquisitive victory in the marketplace, as for several modern philosophers. Liberalism conceives of the human person as an atomistic individual, rationally maximizing their self-interest. Marxism looks at capitalism and sees the worker as exploited and alienated through wage slavery. Neither liberalism nor Marxism take as particularly relevant the unpaid mother, among other female figures, sometimes rationally, sometimes not so rationally, contributing to the well-being of others.

A last form of male bias is a bias against feminist theory itself. Before feminism, as some would have it, there was no one and nothing granting academic acceptability to particular methods, subjects, disciplines, styles, or results. Now upstart feminists are trying to impose their biases on everyone, threatening true discourse with their power to grant medals of political correctness, bullying objectivity into submission. I must say that I sometimes take momentary comfort in this vision as I daydream of revenge, but it is a far cry from reality with respect to both what feminism is doing and the power that it possesses to do it. Before we take pity on the poor powerless but objective scientists being harassed by feminist censors, we should at least ask whether this isn't a red herring. The clamor over political correctness is an attempt to derail feminism by portraying it as destructive of everything that is good and dear in the academy; an attempt that, if successful, will permit—even urge—us to avoid grappling with the sexism, racism, and homophobia pervasive in our institutions and practices. Feminism, rather than sexism, is made out to be the problem.

Calling feminist theory "unscholarly" or "ideological" is an accusation that refuses to consider the possibility that patriarchy is a bias. Dale Spender offers one only slightly exaggerated portrayal of what is at stake in academia's resistance to feminism:

> Am I, a woman of the limited, non-authoritative, emotional, deviant and wrong sex, unschooled in the art-and-science of philosophy, being so presumptuous as to fly in the face of centuries of established philosophical tradition and to suggest that there is a fundamental, philosophical question about the nature of human existence that my "superiors" have not addressed? If no such question has arisen in the philosophical circles of the masters, can I not see that it must not be important—that is, if it is indeed a *real* question and not just a product of my sense of grievance and embitteredness, because I happen to be born of the wrong sex?[5]

Feminist theory is sometimes said to be biased because it has already concluded that men oppress women, and do so wrongly. This implies that with the lone exception of women's studies, or perhaps also some of its relatives, such as ethnic studies, professors hold no substantive positions, or, if they do, keep them out of the classroom. While it's not a requirement for tenure or promotion, one would hope that after years of study, most professors would hold substantive positions on some of the issues they discuss and would share their findings with their students. And every discipline and every subfield within a discipline has foregone conclusions, not only in notions about what to study and how to study it, but in norms of what a "balanced ecosystem" is, a "healthy body," an "acceptable risk," and a "free election." Political theory is not just formal debate on artificial and hypothetical issues and situations. It has to address real problems—and women's oppression is one of them. Theory is filled with substantive moral and political positions, from relativism, Marxism, and pluralism to communitarianism, liberalism, and realism. In every case, feminism included, theoretical skills are brought to bear on the relevant set of issues, arguments are made and weighed on various sides, refutations are considered, and conclusions are reached.

Even in the most traditional view of the tasks and methods of political theory, feminist theory has a legitimate place. Arguments about women's nature, role, and status are found throughout the history of philosophy, from Plato to Rawls, or, better yet, from Sappho to Daly. Further, it has always been part of political inquiry to ask questions about human nature, convention, legitimate authority, ideology, majority tyranny, civil disobedience, and citizen rights and duties. Even this most time-honored list of topics makes clear that gender is both a legitimate object of political theorizing itself and an important source of information required for addressing other questions. We needn't totally reconceive the field to see that it has been biased in its choice of questions, subjects, and examples. As Le Doeuff puts it, "[T]he project of philosophy and that of feminist thinking have a fundamental structure in common, an art of fighting fire with fire and looks with looks, of objectifying and analyzing surrounding thought, of regarding beliefs as objects that must be scrutinized, when the supposedly normal attitude is to submit to what social life erects as doctrine."[6]

Lest this sound too much like the argument that Marxists and capitalists all put on their shoes the same way, let me point out one last difference. Having taught both feminist theory and traditional theory, I think that one of the reasons many people question whether feminist theory is indeed theory is that so many students come out of feminist theory courses committed to political change: the material has a deep impact, personally, politically, and intellectually. But why should we not consider this impact something about feminist theory that makes it particularly exemplary rather than unacademic? Why do we pledge allegiance to the idea that what happens in the classroom is "only academic"? We underestimate both our contribution and our potential, as women once did in describing themselves as "just housewives."

Having breezed through what a reversed gender bias might look and feel like, and a few of the forms gender bias can take, I'd like to close with some quick thoughts about the more difficult and important issue of what an unbiased political theory might look like and inquire into. In the university, theory classes and theory journals would approach from a more comprehensive perspective the figures we are used to finding there, considering as relevant their ideas on gender and the impact these have on their theory in general. These figures, moreover, would no longer dominate the scene: they would be regarded only as contributors to a broader conversation about political life. Filling out the picture would be political thinkers such as Sappho, Christine de Pizan, Mary Wollstonecraft, Simone de Beauvoir, Harriet Taylor, Emma Goldman, Frances Wright, Margaret Fuller, the Grimké sisters, Susan B. Anthony, Charlotte Perkins Gilman, Virginia Woolf, Mary Daly, Adrienne Rich, Bell Hooks, Marilyn French, Angela Davis, Catharine MacKinnon, and Audre Lorde, to cite just a few.[7] It's extraordinary, but there's a whole other intellectual history out there of which we have all been robbed, a history that puts the tradition we know in proper perspective, as only part of the story. With an unbiased curriculum we would get a less distorted and more heterogeneous picture, for the costs of omission are wide and deep.

An unbiased political theory would know that the personal is political and the political is personal. That is, the range of questions considered to be part of the discipline would be expanded, and the information used to answer them would be wider-ranging. What might we find, for example, if studies in balances of power scrutinized not only relations between different branches of government but also relations between the sexes? What else would we learn about how power is maintained, and at what costs, if our insights were derived not only from political tyrannies but also from domestic violence? From childrearing? From the legal and social status of gay men and lesbians? What practices would such queries force us to reconsider?

What changes when we treat the bearing and rearing of children as the socially necessary labor it is, essential to survival and well-being, instead of treating it as nonproductive, nonpolitical, private, and natural? What can we learn when we apply public values and concepts such as self-interested rationality, consent, and one person/one vote to the family? Alternatively, what does the world look like when concepts such as nurture, family, trust, common good, and accommodation are applied to politics? The division of life into public and private has been a safeguard against totalitarianism but has also worked to women's disadvantage: failing to protect her against abuse, defining her out of politics, and leaving her domestic labor unpaid. What institutional safeguards can protect the freedom of *both* sexes?

Political theory as if women mattered—that is what we should be constructing. Political theory as if every individual mattered, as if the need to be accountable for contributing to well-being were treated as self-evident. So very much is at stake. As Adrienne Rich expressed it:

What does a woman need to know, to become a self-conscious, self-defining human being? Doesn't she need a knowledge of her own history; . . . of the creative genius of women of the past—the skills and crafts and techniques and visions possessed by women in other times and cultures, . . . doesn't she need an analysis of her condition, a knowledge of the women thinkers of the past who have reflected on it, a knowledge too of women's world-wide individual rebellions and organized movements against economic and social injustice . . . ? Without such education, women have lived and continue to live in ignorance of our collective context, vulnerable to the projections of men's fantasies about us as they appear in art, in literature, in the sciences, in the media, in the so-called humanistic studies. . . . [E]nforced ignorance has been a crucial key to our powerlessness.[8]

Political theory freed from sexism will use women's lives as a source for theory and as a check upon it. And that theory will be accessible enough to be of greater usefulness.

As a student I read (or tried to read) political theory as if the great thinkers were including me, or at least my kind, in their grand schemes. Seeing the history of justifications for women's limitation, victimization, and exclusion was extremely dismaying—even demoralizing. I wondered why the historical conversation about gender was so impoverished and so monotonous, and why no one in any of my classes gave any sign of having noticed that all these theorists seemed to detest women and to generate theories out of that hatred. Finally I found the taint from sexism so pervasive, infecting so much beyond sexual relations, that trying to rid theories of their sexism came to feel, in Mary Daly's words, like trying to rid the KKK of its racism.[9]

The long-standing and still ongoing feminist reappraisal of political theory has shown that the historical conversation about gender has in fact not been unchallenged. The trouble is, we've only been hearing half the conversation. There is in feminist theory a revisioning of the landscape: a profound change in the questions we must ask and the answers we can live with. The male bias in mainstream political theory truly is pervasive. Feminism provides us with an opportunity for such theory to be more than it has been: more comprehensive, open to more voices, and more concerned with justice for more people. We must struggle constantly to keep that opportunity alive and growing.

NOTES

1. INTRODUCTION

1. Thérèse Levasseur and Rousseau were companions from about 1745 until his death in 1778. The secondary literature treats her with more scorn and dismissive characterizations than does Rousseau himself. (This is a phenomenon with precedents dating back perhaps to the case of Socrates and Xanthippe.) His understanding of his own life is available to us in his *Confessions*.
2. People are much too easily forgiving of others' unwillingness to challenge their own and society's sexism. This eagerness to excuse it, as in attributing it to something "obviously" outside an author's control or even vision, itself helps perpetuate inequality.
3. Michèle Le Doeuff, *Hipparchia's Choice: An Essay Concerning Women, Philosophy, Etc.* (Cambridge: Basil Blackwell, 1991), 63.
4. One version of this argument can be found in Patricia J. Williams's excellent book, *The Alchemy of Race and Rights: Diary of a Law Professor* (Cambridge: Harvard University Press, 1991), 47.
5. Gender receives considerable treatment in *Emile*, the *Second Discourse*, *Julie*, and the *Letter to d'Alembert*.
6. Useful collections of works by or about women theorists are too few; among them are Dale Spender, ed., *Feminist Theorists: Three Centuries of Key Women Thinkers* (1983; New York: Pantheon, 1984); Dale Spender, *Women of Ideas—and What Men Have Done to Them* (London: Routledge & Kegan Paul, 1982); Alice Rossi, ed., *The Feminist Papers: From Adams to de Beauvoir* (New York: Bantam, 1973). Many original works of women theorists are beginning to reappear. There is still a shortage of them; they still rarely appear in anthologies in political philosophy; and there are still few book-length interpretations of them.
7. See Rousseau's unpublished and fragmentary *Sur les Femmes*, OC 2:1254–55.
8. For treatments of the different schools of feminist thought the following are useful: Alison M. Jaggar, *Feminist Politics and Human Nature* (Totowa, N.J.:

164   *2. Producing Gender*

   Rowman and Allanheld, 1983); Rosemarie Tong, *Feminist Thought: A Comprehensive Introduction* (Boulder, Colo.: Westview, 1989); Josephine Donovan, *Feminist Theory* (New York: Frederick Ungar, 1985); Hester Eisenstein, *Contemporary Feminist Thought* (Boston: G. K. Hall, 1983); and Sylvia Walby, *Theorizing Patriarchy* (Cambridge: Basil Blackwell, 1990).
9. Those interested in reviewing some of the most standard objections to treating gender as a philosophical subject, and responses to those objections, can refer to Jane English, "Is Feminism Philosophy?" *Teaching Philosophy* 3 (Fall 1980): 397–403.
10. Le Doeuff, *Hipparchia's Choice*, 42.
11. For my purposes here I use the term "antifeminism" broadly, to indicate opposition to feminism (or to the means necessary to attain sexual equality), as the opposition understands itself or as self-identified feminists understand it. Texts by feminists on antifeminism include Andrea Dworkin, *Right-Wing Women* (New York: Putnam, 1978); Zillah Eisenstein, *Feminism and Sexual Equality: Crisis in Liberal America* (New York: Monthly Review Press, 1984); and, Rebecca Klatch, *Women of the New Right* (Philadelphia: Temple University Press, 1987).

2. PRODUCING GENDER

1. Women's responses to *Emile* in the eighteenth century were *not* entirely negative. One reason for this is that Rousseau's writings were frequently perceived as acknowledging the importance of women's traditional social and familial roles. See, for example, P. D. Jimack, "The Paradox of Sophie and Julie: Contemporary Response to Rousseau's Ideal Wife and Ideal Mother," in *Woman and Society in Eighteenth-Century France*, ed. Eva Jacobs, W. H. Barber, Jean Block, F. W. Leakey, and Eileen Le Breton (London: Athlone Press, 1979), 152–65; and Anne Harper, "The Family and the State in Rousseau's *Emile, or On Education*" (Ph.D. diss., University of Michigan, 1986).
2. Victor Wexler, " 'Made for Man's Delight': Rousseau as Antifeminist," *American Historical Review* 81 (April 1976): 266.
3. Ron Christenson, "The Political Theory of Male Chauvinism: J. J. Rousseau's Paradigm," *Midwest Quarterly* 13 (April 1972): 294.
4. Susan Moller Okin, "Rousseau's Natural Woman," *Journal of Politics* 41 (May 1979): 395.
5. Jane Roland Martin makes this causal argument in "Sophie and Emile: A Case Study of Sex Bias in the History of Educational Thought," *Harvard Educational Review* 51 (August 1981): 357–72.
6. Roger D. Masters, *The Political Philosophy of Rousseau* (Princeton: Princeton University Press, 1968), 15.
7. For example, the idea of a "basic" elementary school, where children of several ages learn together at individualized paces in various subjects is challenging the structure which rigidly requires all to achieve certain things by certain ages or be "left back" a grade.

8. It is interesting to note that in Plato's *Republic*, to which Rousseau implicitly compares the *Emile*, tales of the Styxes as "hateful rivers," fear of which makes one "malleable and soft" (387b–c), are banned from the city.
9. Simone de Beauvoir, *The Second Sex* (1949; New York: Alfred A. Knopf, 1970), 30–33. Today feminists are much more likely to challenge the "facts" treated by de Beauvoir as immutable biological givens, arguing that biological differences themselves are often the product of social and economic differences. See, for example, Alison M. Jaggar, "Human Biology in Feminist Theory: Sexual Equality Reconsidered," in *Beyond Domination: New Perspectives on Women and Philosophy*, ed. Carol Gould (Totowa, N.J.: Rowman & Allenheld, 1984), 21–42.
10. I thank Michael Weinstein for helping me clarify this point.
11. Christenson, "The Political Theory of Male Chauvinism," 294.
12. Condemnation of education employing appeals to authority may recall the ancient and medieval warnings against arguments from authority. The latter, however, were concerned with unquestioning acceptance of opinions as a barrier to the discovery of truth. Rousseau, on the other hand, focuses on the slavishness and conformity resulting from subjection to opinion. That is, he looks more at the loss of personal freedom than the failure to grasp "truth."
13. Leo Strauss, "On the Intention of Rousseau," in *Hobbes and Rousseau*, ed. Maurice Cranston and Richard S. Peters (Garden City, N.Y.: Anchor Books, 1972), 274–75. See also *Emile*, 39.
14. Allan Bloom, Introduction to *Emile*, 11, emphasis added. Also see Richard S. Peters, *Essays on Educators* (London: Allen & Unwin, 1981), 17–20, where he discusses how Emile is coerced and manipulated by the "concealed authority of the tutor."
15. For both the idea and the language here I thank Edward Goerner.
16. See *Emile*, 46, where Rousseau applauds those women who "brave the empire of fashion" and become "worthy mothers."
17. See, for example, Rosemary Agonito, *History of Ideas on Woman: A Source Book* (New York: Putnam, Capricorn Books, 1977), 83–84.
18. Thomas Hobbes, *Leviathan, or, The Matter, Forme and Power of a Commonwealth Ecclesiasticall and Civil* [1651], ed. Michael Oakeshott (New York: Collier Books, 1974), 52.
19. Gabriel Compayre, *Rousseau and Education from Nature* (New York: Putnam, Capricorn Books, 1921), 83–84.
20. While I would like to credit a particular individual by name, I can only thank an anonymous reader for helping me put this question so succinctly.
21. Jean-Jacques Rousseau, *The Reveries of the Solitary Walker*, trans. Charles E. Butterworth (New York: New York University Press, 1979), 83–84.
22. William T. Bluhm, "Freedom in *The Social Contract*: Rousseau's 'Legitimate Chains,' " *Polity* 16 (Spring 1984): 363–64.
23. It is possible to cite other similarities between the two educational programs. For example, in "The Family and the State in Rousseau's *Emile*," Harper explores how both sexes are educated to be virtuous, not erudite.

3. ANATOMY AND DESTINY

1. Joyce Trebilcot, "Sex Roles: The Argument from Nature," *Ethics* 85 (April 1975): 251. "Societal factors" include such related things as education, legislation, family structures, and economic and political systems, among others both more and less sweeping and subtle. I would replace the "encourage" in Trebilcot with "enforce," and would hazard a guess, based on her writings since this early piece, that she would not disagree.
2. "Traditional" is a troubling if widely used term. I use it because of and in line with the popular understanding of it: a heterosexual married couple with children, with a sexual division of familial labor parallel to that in society as a whole. I am aware, however, that the term wrongly implies the existence of only one tradition in human history. This erroneous inference is precisely what conservatives would have people draw.
3. Alison Jaggar, "Political Philosophies of Women's Liberation," in *Feminism and Philosophy*, ed. Mary Vetterling-Braggin, Frederick Elliston, and Jane English (Totowa, N.J.: Littlefield, Adams, 1977), 6. Jaggar maintains this view in her more recent "Human Biology in Feminist Theory," 22.
4. See, for example, Janet Radcliffe Richards, *The Sceptical Feminist* (London: Routledge & Kegan Paul, 1980); and Nancy Holmstrom, "Do Women Have a Distinct Nature?" in *Women and Values: Readings in Recent Feminist Philosophy*, ed. Marilyn Pearsall (Belmont, Calif.: Wadsworth, 1986), 25–42.
5. Nanerl Keohane, " 'But for Her Sex . . . ': The Domestication of Sophie," *University of Ottawa Quarterly* 49 (July 1979): 392.
6. See Ashley Montague, *The Natural Superiority of Women* (New York: Collier Books, 1974).
7. Joel Schwartz, *The Sexual Politics of Jean-Jacques Rousseau* (Chicago: University of Chicago Press, 1984), 3.
8. Ibid., 155.
9. Ibid., 3.
10. Ibid., 51.
11. If there are certain tasks which must be performed for the smooth and legitimate operation of society, and if people have no natural inclinations to perform them, being naturally lazy and asocial, then arrangements must be made to "induce" people to carry them out. One obvious, and, to Rousseau, obviously unacceptable option is to establish a slave class. Another option, common in our day, is to establish legal penalties for failure to comply with certain obligations; witness, for example, our government's program to track down fathers owing child support. It may be that Rousseau sees sex roles as a less odious, and more legitimate (by his standards) means by which to ensure that specific social functions are fulfilled and that people want to act as they ought.
12. Christenson, "The Political Theory of Male Chauvinism," 298.
13. Lynda Lange, "Rousseau and Modern Feminism," *Social Theory and Practice* 7 (Fall 1981): 275n. 43.

14. Aristotle, *Politics*, trans. Ernest Barker (Oxford: Oxford University Press, 1975), 35.
15. See Marc F. Plattner, *Rousseau's State of Nature: An Interpretation of the Discourse on Inequality* (Dekalb: Northern Illinois University Press, 1979), chapter 3; and Masters, *The Political Philosophy of Rousseau*, 5.
16. See Genevieve Lloyd, "Rousseau on Reason, Nature, and Women," *Metaphilosophy* 14 (July/October 1983): 308–26.
17. Susan Moller Okin, *Women in Western Political Thought* (Princeton: Princeton University Press, 1979), 130. Also see Martin, "Sophie and Emile." Okin sees Rousseau as a functionalist only in his discussions about women. Martin, I think correctly, sees functionalism as his approach to both sexes.
18. Judith Sklar does note that "Emile is not illiterate, even though his intellectual equipment is not very complex." *Men and Citizens: A Study of Rousseau's Social Theory* (Cambridge: Cambridge University Press, 1969), 24.
19. SD, 216 (Note L). In light of Rousseau's critique of civil society, the arts, and commerce, it is interesting to see the patriarchal family grouped with them.
20. Mary Wollstonecraft, *A Vindication of the Rights of Woman* [1792], ed. Carol Poston (New York: W. W. Norton, 1988), 43.
21. Agonito, *History of Ideas on Woman*, 115.
22. A useful summary of these themes is given by Caroline Whitbeck, "Theories of Sex Difference," in *Women and Philosophy: Toward a Theory of Liberation*, ed. Carol Gould and Marx Wartofsky (New York: Putnam, 1976), 54–80.
23. Le Doeuff, *Hipparchia's Choice*, 24.
24. The legislator's claim of divine sanction and Rousseau's civil religion seem obvious examples of noble lies. William Bluhm, in "Freedom in *The Social Contract*," argues that even Rousseau's concept of civil freedom may be but a useful political myth. For general discussions of Rousseau's views on lying, see Bluhm, "Freedom in *The Social Contract*"; and Ann Hartle, *The Modern Self in Rousseau's Confessions: A Reply to St. Augustine* (Notre Dame: University of Notre Dame Press, 1983), especially chapter 1. Rousseau discusses lying in *The Reveries of a Solitary Walker*, Fourth Promenade.
25. Andrea Dworkin, "Biological Superiority: The World's Most Dangerous and Deadly Idea," in *Letters from a War Zone: Writings, 1976–1989* (New York: E. P. Dutton, 1989), 112–13, emphasis added.

4. FAMILIES AND POLITICS

1. This chapter is from an article originally coauthored with Anne Harper. Her contribution is central to the discussions of wet nurses and the duties of fathers.
2. Rousseau's discussion of mother-child relations in the state of nature is noteworthy for a number of reasons; for example, it takes the fact that we are born dependent as relevant, and it assumes female independence from males in childrearing. It is certainly intriguing that mothers tending to children is not thought by him necessarily to entail lasting emotional attachment on either side

4. Families and Politics

or to lead to any desire for additional interpersonal relations. He seems to understand the bond between mother and child as superficial, perhaps like bonds between corrupt social people, which also entail little attachment and fail to lead to community. It is still questionable, however, whether this understanding does full justice to the reality of a nursing, teaching, protective mother, even in his state of nature.

3. The period called "childhood" is not stable across historical periods or classes. Among lower-class families of late eighteenth-century France, childhood was remarkably short by our standards. "Children in poor families had to work instead of play. From the age of four, they were considered able to work; and they were set to gathering wood, feeding chickens, or helping to card wool. . . . Children left the family at very young ages—nine to twelve—to work as apprentices and servants." Cissie Fairchilds, "Women and Family," in *French Women and the Age of Enlightenment*, ed. Samia Spencer (Bloomington: University of Indiana Press, 1984), 106. Further, "Work constituted the very fabric of the lives of most French women during the eighteenth century. At least ninety percent of them, from the age of fourteen on, spent most of their waking hours engaged in one or another form of work" (Elizabeth Fox-Genovese, "Women and Work," in *French Women and the Age of Enlightenment*, ed. Spencer, 111).
4. Fairchilds, "Women and Family," 97 and 98.
5. Matthew Josephson, *Jean-Jacques Rousseau* (New York: Harcourt, Brace, 1931), 123–24.
6. Ibid., 126.
7. Bloom, Introduction to *Emile*, 4–5. The sexist pronouns are Bloom's; Rousseau thought it was equally possible for both sexes to be bourgeois in this sense, and equally undesirable, as will be explained later.
8. This view of childhood is discussed in D. G. Charlton, *New Images of the Natural in France: A Study in European Cultural History, 1750–1800* (Cambridge: Cambridge University Press, 1984), chapter 8.
9. See Cissie Fairchilds, *Domestic Enemies: Servants and Their Masters in Old Regime France* (Baltimore: Johns Hopkins University Press, 1984).
10. Fox-Genovese, "Women and Work."
11. Jimack, "The Paradox of Sophie and Julie," 161.
12. Fairchilds, "Women and Family," 100. See also George D. Sussman, *Selling Mother's Milk: The Wet-Nursing Business in France, 1715–1914* (Urbana: University of Illinois Press, 1982), 73–97.
13. See Athol Fugard's play *"Master Harold"—and the Boys* (New York: S. French, 1982), where a white South African is disturbed by his relationship with the black servants who have cared for him as a child. Adrienne Rich has written of this same problem as it affected white Southerners in the United States brought up by mammies whom they were later taught to despise as black people. See her *Of Woman Born: Motherhood as Experience and Institution* (New York: W. W. Norton, 1976). While he does not focus on race, Rousseau sees the social dangers to all parties of allowing people for whom one has no respect to be the primary caretakers of one's children.

14. Likewise, Rousseau considers it a sign of social decay when citizens pay others to do their jobs, or pay taxes instead of doing the work themselves (SC, 101–2).
15. See John Locke, *Some Thoughts Concerning Education*, in *The Educational Writings of John Locke*, ed. James L. Axtell (Cambridge: Cambridge University Press, 1968).
16. In SC, 65–67, Rousseau asserts that all legitimate states are based on the rule of law.
17. This would explain why Rousseau considers the fertility rate a sign of the health of the state (SC, 95–96).
18. Lange, "Rousseau and Modern Feminism," 246–47.
19. These quotes are taken from a roundtable discussion among contemporary conservatives in "Sex and God in American Politics," *Policy Review* (Fall 1984): 15–17. The first quote is from Phyllis Schlafly, the second from Rabbi Seymour Siegel, and the last from Midge Decter.
20. I thank an anonymous reader for this wording of the issue.
21. Schwartz, *The Sexual Politics of Jean-Jacques Rousseau*.

5. THE JUSTICE OF SEX ROLES

1. Schwartz, *The Sexual Politics of Jean-Jacques Rousseau*, chapter 4.
2. Okin, "Rousseau's Natural Woman," 402.
3. Zillah Eisenstein, *The Radical Future of Liberal Feminism* (New York: Longman, 1981), 80.
4. Ibid., 64, 76–77, and 80. As discussed in chapter 1, Rousseau is not an advocate of bourgeois individualism.
5. Marilyn Frye discusses what she terms "male parasitism" in "Some Reflections On Separatism and Power," in her *Politics of Reality: Essays in Feminist Theory* (Trumansburg, N.Y.: Crossing Press, 1983), 95–109.
6. Sarah Hoagland, "On the Reeducation of Sophie," in *Women's Studies: An Interdisciplinary Collection*, ed. Kathleen O'Connor Blumhagen and Walter D. Johnson (Westport, Conn.: Greenwood Press, 1978), 18–19.
7. Keohane, "But For Her Sex," 395.
8. Okin, "Rousseau's Natural Woman," 410.
9. Ibid., 409.
10. Ibid., 410.
11. Keohane, "But For Her Sex," 399, emphasis added.
12. Richard Fralin, "The Evolution of Rousseau's View of Representative Government," *Political Theory* 6 (November 1978): 524–25.
13. Lynda Lange, "Rousseau: Women and the General Will," in *The Sexism of Social and Political Theory*, ed. Lorenne M. G. Clark and Lynda Lange (Toronto: University of Toronto Press, 1979), 50.
14. Keohane, "But for Her Sex," 397.

6. ROUSSEAU AND FEMINIST REVOLUTION

1. It means many things to address gender as a political category. My main point is that such categorization is not inevitable, and that it serves the political interests of men.
2. Among the feminist commentaries that find the least to salvage in Rousseau are Okin, *Women in Western Political Thought*; Z. Eisenstein, *The Radical Future of Liberal Feminism*; and Christenson, "The Political Theory of Male Chauvinism."
3. In *Modern Political Theory and Contemporary Feminism* (New York: SUNY Press, 1991), Jennifer Ring captures nicely what is at stake in moving away from notions of static human nature(s).
4. The limits of a Marxist understanding of human nature for feminist theory are explored in Jaggar's *Feminist Politics and Human Nature*. Marx's theory may be narrower than Rousseau's, in ascribing fewer factors as causal. Good use is made of Marx in feminist theorizing on human nature by Nancy Holmstrom, "Do Women Have a Distinct Nature?"
5. For examples of court cases unpholding the legitimacy of such restrictions, see *Bradwell v. Illinois*, 83 U.S. 130 (1873), *Minor v. Happersett*, 38 U.S. 162 (1874), *Muller v. Oregon*, 208 U.S. 412 (1908), *Goesaert v. Cleary*, 335 U.S. 464 (1948), and *Hoyt v. Florida*, 368 U.S. 57 (1961).
6. It may well be the case that *all* antifeminists view the personal as political. I have made this argument in "Legal Anti-feminisms: Judicial Defenses of Sexual Differentiation," presented at the meeting of the American Political Science Association in 1988. Andrea Dworkin makes this case even more forcefully and convincingly in *Intercourse* (New York: Free Press, 1987), chapter 8. Antifeminists, however, view both the public and the private with patriarchal blinders on.
7. See Jean Hampton, *Hobbes and the Social Contract Tradition* (Cambridge: Cambridge University Press, 1986), chapter 9.
8. I have reviewed Schwartz's book in the *Review of Politics* 47 (April 1985): 300–303.
9. Arthur Melzer, *The Natural Goodness of Man: On the System of Rousseau's Thought* (Chicago: University of Chicago Press, 1990), 248.
10. As Polemarchus said in Plato's *Republic*, 327c, "Could you really persuade if we don't listen?"
11. Schwartz, *The Sexual Politics of Jean-Jacques Rousseau*, 4.
12. Alexander Hamilton, James Madison, and John Jay, *The Federalist Papers* (New York: New American Library of World Literature, 1961), no. 48.
13. Rossi, *The Feminist Papers*, 10 and 11.
14. Hamilton, Madison, and Jay, *The Federalist Papers*, no. 47.
15. See Jane Mansbridge, *Beyond Adversary Democracy* (New York: Basic Books, 1980), for the distinction between adversary and unitary democracy.
16. Wollstonecraft, *A Vindication of the Rights of Woman*, 62.
17. Daniel Pekarsky, "Education and Manipulation," *Philosophy of Education Pro-*

ceedings (1977): 354–55. Pekarsky is speaking of the morality and utility of teachers' manipulating their students; however, the dynamics would seem to apply to the topic I am discussing as well. It is interesting that so little of a serious nature is written about women's restriction to manipulation as a form of power.

18. Helen Andelin, *Fascinating Womanhood* (New York: Bantam Books, 1963), 252, 265, and 294–95.
19. Ibid., 5.
20. Jean Starobinski, *Jean-Jacques Rousseau: Transparency and Obstruction* [1971], trans. Arthur Goldhammer (Chicago: University of Chicago Press, 1988), 5, emphasis added.
21. Schwartz, *The Sexual Politics of Jean-Jacques Rousseau*, 84 and 24.
22. Ibid., 43 and 25.
23. Rita Freedman, *Beauty Bound* (Lexington, Ky.: D. C. Heath, 1986), 80–81.
24. This contrasts interestingly with the means traditionally given men to restrain women. For example, in Sir William Blackstone's *Commentaries on the Laws of England*, men are legally responsible for the wrongs of women, and accordingly are granted the right of "restraining her, by domestic chastisement" (book 1, chapter 15). In Rousseau, women of course have no such right, nor access to any but appropriately "feminine" recourses. They may not even be left with the self-worth necessary to challenge another's behavior. This observation is most certainly not intended to be an endorsement of physical violence by either sex.
25. Charlotte Perkins Gilman, *Women and Economics: A Study of the Economic Relation between Men and Women as a Factor in Social Evolution* [1898], ed. Carl Degler (New York: Harper & Row, 1966), 333.
26. Schwartz, *The Sexual Politics of Jean-Jacques Rousseau*, 142–43.
27. Virginia Woolf, *Three Guineas* (1938; New York: Harcourt Brace, 1966), 15.
28. Wollstonecraft, *A Vindication of the Rights of Woman*, 27.
29. I cite just two examples, both from U.S. case law. In the famous 1873 case *Bradwell v. Illinois* (83 U.S. 130, 21 L.Ed. 442), upholding a law prohibiting women from practicing law in Illinois, Justice Bradley wrote: "The harmony, not to say identity, of interests and views which belong, or should belong, to the family institution is repugnant to the idea of a woman adopting a distinct and independent career from that of her husband." If women sacrifice their career ambitions and talents, according to this opinion, then harmony reigns. In the 1971 case *Reed v. Reed* (404 U.S. 71, 92 S.Ct. 251, 30 L.Ed.2d 225), the court that overruled an Idaho law that gave preference to males over equally entitled females in estate administration nevertheless thought there was "positive value" in the law because it contributed to "avoiding intrafamily controversy." That is, when there's a disagreement, the man automatically wins, and then everyone is happy. For more on the concept of a rape culture see Dianne Herman, "The Rape Culture," in *Women: A Feminist Perspective*, 2d ed., ed. Jo Freeman (Palo Alto, Calif.: Mayfield, 1979), 41–63.
30. Gloria Steinem, *Revolution from Within: A Book of Self-Esteem* (Boston: Little, Brown, 1992), 48.

31. de Beauvoir, *The Second Sex*, xx.
32. Elisabeth Badinter, *The Unopposite Sex: The End of the Gender Battle* (New York: Harper & Row, 1986), 88.
33. Ibid., 89.
34. Jane Addams, "The Modern City and the Municipal Franchise for Women," in *Woman Suffrage: Arguments and Results* (New York: National Woman Suffrage Association, 1910).
35. Mary Daly, *Beyond God the Father: Toward a Philosophy of Women's Liberation* (Boston: Beacon Press, 1973), 18.
36. Jack Nagel, *Participation* (Englewood Cliffs, N.J.: Prentice-Hall, 1987), 14–15. Is it the perspective of an individualist that makes the results seem paradoxical?
37. Steinem, *Revolution from Within*, 157.
38. Le Doeuff, *Hipparchia's Choice*, 35.

7. FEMINISM AND COMMUNITARIANISM

1. When I refer to "male" or "female" values, "masculine" and "feminine," etc., I am referring to what has been socially assigned to and associated with one gender or the other. I am referring not to biological categories but to social constructs.
2. Michael Walzer, "The Communitarian Critique of Liberalism," *Political Theory* 18 (February 1990): 6.
3. See Barbara Ehrenreich, "On Feminism, Family, and Community," *Dissent* (Winter 1983): 103–6; James Huffman, "Liberalism and Community in Feminist Legal Theory" (Paper presented at AMINTAPHIL Conference on Liberalism and Community, Salt Lake City, Utah, October 1990); and Iris Young, "The Ideal of Community and the Politics of Difference," *Social Theory and Practice* 12 (Spring 1986): 1–26. These three critiques present an array of viewpoints.
4. See Jean Bethke Elshtain, "On Feminism, Family, and Community," *Dissent* (Fall 1982): 442–49; and M. Elizabeth Albert, "In the Interest of the Public Good? New Questions for Feminism," in *Community in America: The Challenge of Habits of the Heart*, ed. Charles Reynolds and Ralph Norman (Berkeley and Los Angeles: University of California Press, 1988), 84–96.
5. I thank Bob Strikwerda for his insight into the philosophical and political applications of the notion of parallel play. Sometimes being parents does directly help our "other" work!
6. Christopher Lasch, "The Communitarian Critics of Liberalism," in *Community in America*, ed. Reynolds and Norman, 175.
7. Alasdair MacIntyre, *After Virtue: A Study in Moral Theory* (Notre Dame: University of Notre Dame Press, 1981), 232–33.
8. Benjamin Barber, *Strong Democracy: Participatory Politics for a New Age* (Berkeley and Los Angeles: University of California Press, 1984), 33.
9. Marilyn Friedman, "Feminism and Modern Friendship: Dislocating the Community," *Ethics* 99 (January 1989): 275.

10. Mary Dietz, "Context Is All: Feminism and Theories of Citizenship," *Daedalus* 116 (Fall 1987): 5.
11. Jaggar, *Feminist Politics and Human Nature*, 42.
12. Not everyone agrees that these features of the self are necessarily part of liberalism. There is a significant effort to counter the charges against liberalism, particularly those made by communitarians. See for example, Walzer, "The Communitarian Critique of Liberalism"; Will Kymlicka, "Liberalism and Communitarianism," *Canadian Journal of Philosophy* 18 (June 1988): 181–95; and Allen Buchanan, "Assessing the Communitarian Critique of Liberalism," *Ethics* 99 (July 1989): 852–82. See also Susan Wendell, "A (Qualified) Defense of Liberal Feminism," *Hypatia: A Journal of Feminist Philosophy* 2 (Summer 1987): 65–94.
13. Kymlicka, "Liberalism and Communitarianism," 181.
14. Chantal Mouffe, "American Liberalism and Its Critics: Rawls, Taylor, Sandel and Walzer," *Praxis International* 8 (July 1988): 198.
15. MacIntyre, *After Virtue*, 32.
16. Seyla Benhabib and Drucilla Cornell, "Introduction: Beyond the Politics of Gender," in *Feminism as Critique*, ed. Seyla Benhabib and Drucilla Cornell (Minneapolis: University of Minnesota Press, 1987), 12.
17. Dietz, "Context Is All," 1.
18. Michael J. Sandel, *Liberalism and the Limits of Justice* (Cambridge: Cambridge University Press, 1982), 179.
19. MacIntyre, *After Virtue*, 204–5.
20. See Walzer, "The Communitarian Critique of Liberalism."
21. Good examples of this include Naomi Scheman, "Individualism and the Objects of Psychology," in *Discovering Reality: Feminist Perspectives on Epistemology, Metaphysics, Methodology, and the Philosophy of Science*, ed. S. Harding and M. Hintikka (Dordrecht: Reidel, 1983); Sara Ruddick, "Maternal Thinking," *Feminist Studies* 6 (Summer 1980): 342–67; and Holmstrom, "Do Women Have a Distinct Nature?"
22. MacIntyre, *After Virtue*, 32.
23. Benhabib and Cornell, "Introduction: Beyond the Politics of Gender," 12–13.
24. Ann Ferguson, *Sexual Democracy: Women, Oppression, and Revolution* (Boulder, Colo.: Westview Press, 1991), 217.
25. MacIntyre, *After Virtue*, 24.
26. Barber, *Strong Democracy*, 213.
27. Robert Bellah, Richard Madsen, William Sullivan, Ann Swidler, and Steven Tipton, *Habits of the Heart: Individualism and Commitment in American Life* (Berkeley and Los Angeles: University of California Press, 1985), 107.
28. Virginia Held, "Non-Contractual Society: A Feminist View," *Canadian Journal of Philosophy* 13 (1987): 124–25.
29. Buchanan, "Assessing the Communitarian Critique of Liberalism," 856–57.
30. Walzer, "The Communitarian Critique of Liberalism," 21.
31. Barber, *Strong Democracy*, 71–72.

32. Walzer, "The Communitarian Critique of Liberalism," 10.
33. Held, "Non-Contractual Society," 113 and 115.
34. Elizabeth Wolgast, *Equality and the Rights of Women* (Ithaca: Cornell University Press, 1980), 154.
35. Buchanan, "Assessing the Communitarian Critique of Liberalism," 866.
36. Held, "Non-Contractual Society," 120.
37. Walzer, "The Communitarian Critique of Liberalism," 8.
38. Wolgast, *Equality and the Rights of Women*, 155–56.
39. Jane Mansbridge, *Beyond Self-Interest* (Chicago: University of Chicago Press, 1990), ix.
40. Sandel, *Liberalism and the Limits of Justice*, 181–82.
41. Held, "Non-Contractual Society," 122.
42. Wolgast, *Equality and the Rights of Women*, 147.
43. Ibid., 156–57.
44. Albert, "In the Interest of the Public Good?" 88.
45. MacIntyre, *After Virtue*, 182.
46. Jaggar, *Feminist Politics and Human Nature*, 174 and 200.
47. MacIntyre, *After Virtue*, 112.
48. Sandel, *Liberalism and the Limits of Justice*, 1.
49. Walzer, "The Communitarian Critique of Liberalism," 16.
50. Barber, *Strong Democracy*, 4.
51. Mary Shanley, "Marital Slavery and Friendship: John Stuart Mill's *The Subjection of Women*," *Political Theory* 8 (May 1981): 229–47.
52. Carol Smart, *Feminism and the Power of the Law* (London: Routledge, 1989), 144–45.
53. Dietz, "Context Is All," 4.
54. Sandel, *Liberalism and the Limits of Justice*, 183.
55. Catharine MacKinnon, *Feminism Unmodified: Discourses on Life and Law* (Cambridge: Harvard University Press, 1987), 15.
56. Williams, *The Alchemy of Race and Rights*, chapter 8.
57. Dietz, "Context Is All," 8.
58. Nancy Hartsock, *Money, Sex, and Power: Toward a Feminist Historical Materialism* (Boston: Northeastern University Press, 1983), 177.
59. MacIntyre, *After Virtue*, 146.
60. Dietz, "Context Is All," 14.
61. Hartsock, *Money, Sex, and Power*, 224.
62. MacIntyre, *After Virtue*, 115.
63. Susan Moller Okin, *Justice, Gender, and the Family* (New York: Basic Books, 1989), 45 and 49.
64. Hartsock, *Money, Sex, and Power*, 187.
65. Amy Gutmann, "Communitarian Critics of Liberalism," *Philosophy and Public Affairs* 14 (Summer 1985): 319.
66. Bellah et al., *Habits of the Heart*, 151.
67. Friedman, "Feminism and Modern Friendship," 277.
68. Le Doeuff, *Hipparchia's Choice*, 13.

8. GENDER BIAS IN POLITICAL THEORY

1. I am deeply indebted to Gerd Brantenberg, author of *Egalia's Daughters: A Satire of the Sexes* (Seattle: Seal Press, 1985). Her book, creatively depicting a whole society in which women dominate, gave me the idea of trying a reversal aimed at a more specific target. After using her book in teaching feminist theory, it also made me a believer in the usefulness of reversals as an educative tool. A good source for finding such texts is Sarah Lefanu, *Feminism and Science Fiction* (Bloomington: Indiana University Press, 1988).
2. Maria Falco noticed the gap with regard to Wollstonecraft and in 1992 organized panels on her work at the meetings of the Indiana Political Science Association and the American Political Science Association. Falco also has plans to edit a volume on Wollstonecraft. See also Virginia Sapiro's recent *Vindication of Political Virtue: The Political Theory of Mary Wollstonecraft*. Chicago: University of Chicago Press, 1992.
3. There was also in popular lore a Saint Nickelless, whose husband, Mr. Claws, was never allowed to reveal his first name or to join in any reindeer games.
4. Plato, *The Republic*, 329c–d. This example is from my "Plato's *Republic*: I as Male Dialogue," forthcoming.
5. Spender, *Women of Ideas*, 7.
6. Le Doeuff, *Hipparchia's Choice*, 29.
7. There now exists a Society for the Study of Women Philosophers, founded in 1987. Information about their meetings can be gotten from advertisements in *Hypatia: A Journal of Feminist Philosophy*, from the American Philosophical Association, or from the Society for Women in Philosophy.
8. Adrienne Rich, "Taking Women Students Seriously," in her *On Lies, Secrets, and Silence: Selected Prose, 1966–1978* (New York: W. W. Norton, 1979), 240.
9. Mary Daly, "The Qualitative Leap beyond Patriarchal Religion," in *Women and Values: Readings in Recent Feminist Philosophy*, ed. Marilyn Pearsall (Belmont, Calif.: Wadsworth, 1986), 199.

BIBLIOGRAPHY

Addams, Jane. "The Modern City and the Municipal Franchise for Women." In *Woman Suffrage: Arguments and Results*. New York: National Woman Suffrage Association, 1910.
Agonito, Rosemary. *History of Ideas on Woman: A Source Book*. New York: Putnam, Capricorn Books, 1977.
Albert, M. Elizabeth. "In the Interest of the Public Good? New Questions for Feminism." In *Community in America: The Challenge of Habits of the Heart*, edited by Charles Reynolds and Ralph Norman, 84–96. Berkeley and Los Angeles: University of California Press, 1988.
Allan, D. J. "Nature, Education and Freedom According to Jean-Jacques Rousseau." *Philosophy* 12 (April 1937): 191–207.
Andelin, Helen. *Fascinating Womanhood*. New York: Bantam Books, 1963.
Aristotle. *Politics*. Translated by Ernest Barker. Oxford: Oxford University Press, 1975.
Atkinson, Ti-Grace. *Amazon Odyssey*. New York: Hyperion Press, 1974.
Badinter, Elisabeth. *The Unopposite Sex: The End of the Gender Battle*. New York: Harper & Row, 1986.
Barber, Benjamin. *Strong Democracy: Participatory Politics for a New Age*. Berkeley and Los Angeles: University of California Press, 1984.
Bellah, Robert; Madsen, Richard; Sullivan, William; Swidler, Ann; and Tipton, Steven. *Habits of the Heart: Individualism and Commitment in American Life*. Berkeley and Los Angeles: University of California Press, 1985.
Bellhouse, Mary L. "Femininity and Commerce in the Eighteenth Century: Rousseau's Criticism of a Literary Ruse by Montesquieu." *Polity* 13 (Winter 1980): 285–99.
Benhabib, Seyla, and Cornell, Drucilla. "Introduction: Beyond the Politics of Gender." In *Feminism as Critique*, edited by Seyla Benhabib and Drucilla Cornell, 1–15. Minneapolis: University of Minnesota Press, 1987.

Berman, Marshall. *The Politics of Authenticity*. New York: Atheneum, 1970.

Bloom, Allan. "Rousseau on the Equality of the Sexes." In *Justice and Equality Here and Now*, edited by Frank S. Lucash. Ithaca: Cornell University Press, 1985.

Bluhm, William T. "Freedom in *The Social Contract*: Rousseau's 'Legitimate Chains.'" *Polity* 16 (Spring 1984): 359–83.

Boyd, William. *The Educational Theory of Jean Jacques Rousseau*. New York: Russell & Russell, 1963.

———, ed. and trans. *The Emile of Jean Jacques Rousseau: Selections*. New York: Teachers College, 1962.

Brantenberg, Gerd. *Egalia's Daughters: A Satire of the Sexes*. Seattle: Seal Press, 1985.

Broome, J. H. *Rousseau: A Study of His Thought*. London: Edward Arnold, 1963.

Buchanan, Allen. "Assessing the Communitarian Critique of Liberalism." *Ethics* 99 (July 1989): 852–82.

Burgelin, Pierre. "L'Education de Sophie." *Annales de la Société Jean-Jacques Rousseau* 35 (1959–62): 113–37.

———. "The Second Education of Emile." *Yale French Studies* 28 (1961–62): 106–11.

Charlton, D. G. *New Images of the Natural in France: A Study in European Cultural History, 1750–1800*. Cambridge: Cambridge University Press, 1984.

Charpentier, John. *Rousseau, the Child of Nature*. London: Methuen, 1931.

Charvet, John. "Individual Identity and Social Consciousness in Rousseau's Philosophy." In *Hobbes and Rousseau*, edited by Maurice Cranston and Richard S. Peters, 462–83. New York: Anchor Books, 1972.

Christenson, Ron. "The Political Theory of Male Chauvinism: J. J. Rousseau's Paradigm." *Midwest Quarterly* 13 (April 1972): 291–99.

Compayre, Gabriel. *Rousseau and Education from Nature*. New York: Putnam, Capricorn Books, 1921.

Cranston, Maurice. "Rousseau on Equality." *Social Philosophy and Policy* 2 (Autumn 1984): 115–24.

Daly, Mary. *Beyond God the Father: Toward a Philosophy of Women's Liberation*. Boston: Beacon Press, 1973.

———. "The Qualitative Leap beyond Patriarchal Religion." In *Women and Values: Readings in Recent Feminist Philosophy*, edited by Marilyn Pearsall, 198–210. Belmont, Calif.: Wadsworth, 1986.

de Beauvoir, Simone. *The Second Sex*. 1949. New York: Alfred A. Knopf, 1970.

DeJean, Joan. "*La Nouvelle Héloïse*, or the Case for Pedagogical Deviation." *Yale French Studies* 63 (1982): 98–116.

Dietz, Mary. "Context Is All: Feminism and Theories of Citizenship." *Daedalus* 116 (Fall 1987): 1–24.

Donovan, Josephine. *Feminist Theory*. New York: Frederick Ungar, 1985.

Dworkin, Andrea. "Biological Superiority: The World's Most Dangerous and Deadly Idea." In *Letters from a War Zone: Writings, 1976–1989*, 110–16. New York: E. P. Dutton, 1989.

———. *Intercourse*. New York: Free Press, 1987.

Ehrenreich, Barbara. "On Feminism, Family, and Community." *Dissent* (Winter 1983): 103–6.
Eisenstein, Hester. *Contemporary Feminist Thought*. Boston: G. K. Hall, 1983.
Eisenstein, Zillah. *Feminism and Sexual Equality: Crisis in Liberal America*. New York: Monthly Review Press, 1984.
———. *The Radical Future of Liberal Feminism*. New York: Longman, 1981.
Ellrich, Robert. *Rousseau and His Reader: The Rhetorical Situation of the Major Works*. Chapel Hill: University of North Carolina Press, 1969.
Elshtain, Jean Bethke. "On Feminism, Family, and Community." *Dissent* (Fall 1982): 442–49.
———. *Public Man, Private Woman: Women in Social and Political Thought*. Princeton: Princeton University Press, 1981.
English, Jane. "Is Feminism Philosophy?" *Teaching Philosophy* 3 (Fall 1980): 397–403.
Fairchilds, Cissie. *Domestic Enemies: Servants and Their Masters in Old Regime France*. Baltimore: Johns Hopkins University Press, 1984.
———. "Women and Family." In *French Women and the Age of Enlightenment*, edited by Samia Spencer, 97–110. Bloomington: University of Indiana Press, 1984.
Ferguson, Ann. *Sexual Democracy: Women, Oppression, and Revolution*. Boulder, Colo.: Westview Press, 1991.
Fox-Genovese, Elizabeth. "Women and Work." In *French Women and the Age of Enlightenment*, edited by Samia Spencer, 111–27. Bloomington: University of Indiana Press, 1984.
Fralin, Richard. "The Evolution of Rousseau's View of Representative Government." *Political Theory* 6 (November 1978): 517–36.
Freedman, Rita. *Beauty Bound*. Lexington, Ky.: D. C. Heath, 1986.
Friedman, Marilyn. "Feminism and Modern Friendship: Dislocating the Community." *Ethics* 99 (January 1989): 275–90.
Frye, Marilyn. *The Politics of Reality: Essays in Feminist Theory*. Trumansburg, N.Y.: Crossing Press, 1983.
Fugard, Athol. *"Master Harold"—and the Boys*. New York: S. French, 1982.
Gilligan, Carol. *In a Different Voice: Psychological Theory and Woman's Development*. Cambridge: Harvard University Press, 1982.
Gilman, Charlotte Perkins. *Women and Economics: A Study of the Economic Relation between Men and Women as a Factor in Social Evolution*. 1898. Edited by Carl Degler. New York: Harper & Row, 1966.
Gutmann, Amy. "Communitarian Critics of Liberalism." *Philosophy and Public Affairs* 14 (Summer 1985): 308–22.
Hampton, Jean. *Hobbes and the Social Contract Tradition*. Cambridge: Cambridge University Press, 1986.
Harper, Anne. "The Family and the State in Rousseau's *Emile, or On Education*." Ph.D. diss., University of Michigan, 1986.
Hartle, Ann. *The Modern Self in Rousseau's Confessions: A Reply to St. Augustine*. Notre Dame: University of Notre Dame Press, 1983.

Hartsock, Nancy. *Money, Sex, and Power: Toward a Feminist Historical Materialism*. Boston: Northeastern University Press, 1983.
Held, Virginia. "Non-Contractual Society: A Feminist View." *Canadian Journal of Philosophy* 13 (1987): 111–37.
Herman, Dianne. "The Rape Culture." In *Women: A Feminist Perspective*, 2d ed., edited by Jo Freeman, 41–63. Palo Alto, Calif.: Mayfield, 1979.
Hoagland, Sarah. "On the Reeducation of Sophie." In *Women's Studies: An Interdisciplinary Collection*, edited by Kathleen O'Connor Blumhagen and Walter D. Johnson, 13–20. Westport, Conn.: Greenwood Press, 1978.
Hobbes, Thomas. *Leviathan; or, The Matter, Forme and Power of a Commonwealth Ecclesiasticall and Civil*. 1651. Edited by Michael Oakeshott. New York: Collier Books, 1974.
Holmstrom, Nancy. "Do Women Have a Distinct Nature?" In *Women and Values: Readings in Recent Feminist Philosophy*, edited by Marilyn Pearsall, 25–42. Belmont, Calif.: Wadsworth, 1986.
Huffman, James. "Liberalism and Community in Feminist Legal Theory." Paper presented at AMINTAPHIL Conference on Liberalism and Community, Salt Lake City, Utah, October 1990.
Jaggar, Alison M. *Feminist Politics and Human Nature*. Totowa, N.J.: Rowman and Allanheld, 1983.
———. "Human Biology in Feminist Theory: Sexual Equality Reconsidered." In *Beyond Domination: New Perspectives on Women and Philosophy*, edited by Carol Gould, 21–42. Totowa, N.J.: Rowman and Allanheld, 1984.
———. "Political Philosophies of Women's Liberation." In *Feminism and Philosophy*, edited by Mary Vetterling-Braggin, Frederick Elliston, and Jane English, 5–21. Littlefield, Adams, 1977.
Jimack, P. D. "The Paradox of Sophie and Julie: Contemporary Response to Rousseau's Ideal Wife and Ideal Mother." In *Woman and Society in Eighteenth-Century France*, edited by Eva Jacobs, W. H. Barber, Jean Bloch, F. W. Leakey, and Eileen Le Breton, 152–65. London: Athlone Press, 1979.
John, G. "The Moral Education of Emile." *Journal of Moral Education* 11 (1981): 18–31.
Josephson, Matthew. *Jean-Jacques Rousseau*. New York: Harcourt, Brace, 1931.
Kelly, Christopher. "Rousseau and His Readers." *Political Science Reviewer* 12 (Fall 1982): 315–36.
Keohane, Nanerl. " 'But for Her Sex . . . ': The Domestication of Sophie." *University of Ottawa Quarterly* 49 (July 1979): 390–400.
———. *Philosophy and the State in France*. Princeton: Princeton University Press, 1980.
Kymlicka, Will. "Liberalism and Communitarianism." *Canadian Journal of Philosophy* 18 (June 1988): 181–95.
Lange, Lynda. "Rousseau: Women and the General Will." In *The Sexism of Social and Political Theory*, 41–52, edited by Lorenne M. G. Clark and Lynda Lange. Toronto: University of Toronto Press, 1979.

———. "Rousseau and Modern Feminism." *Social Theory and Practice* 7 (Fall 1981): 245–77.
Lasch, Christopher. "The Communitarian Critique of Liberalism." In *Community in America: The Challenge of Habits of the Heart*, edited by Charles Reynolds and Ralph Norman, 173–84. Berkeley and Los Angeles: University of California Press, 1988.
Le Doeuff, Michèle. *Hipparchia's Choice: An Essay Concerning Women, Philosophy, Etc.* Cambridge: Basil Blackwell, 1991.
Lefanu, Sarah. *Feminism and Science Fiction*. Bloomington: Indiana University Press, 1988.
Lemos, Ramon M. *Rousseau's Political Philosophy: An Exposition and Interpretation*. Athens: University of Georgia Press, 1977.
Lloyd, Genevieve. *The Man of Reason: "Male" and "Female" in Western Philosophy*. Minneapolis: University of Minnesota Press, 1984.
———. "Rousseau on Reason, Nature, and Women." *Metaphilosophy* 14 (July/October 1983): 308–26.
Locke, John. *Some Thoughts Concerning Education*. In *The Educational Writings of John Locke*, edited by James L. Axtell. Cambridge: Cambridge University Press, 1968.
Lovejoy, A. O. "The Supposed Primitivism of Rousseau's Discourse on Equality." *Modern Philology* 21 (1923): 165–86.
MacIntyre, Alasdair. *After Virtue: A Study in Moral Theory*. Notre Dame: University of Notre Dame Press, 1981.
MacKinnon, Catharine. *Feminism Unmodified: Discourses on Life and Law*. Cambridge: Harvard University Press, 1987.
McMillan, Carol. *Women, Reason and Nature: Some Philosophical Problems with Feminism*. Princeton: Princeton University Press, 1982.
Mansbridge, Jane. *Beyond Self-Interest*. Chicago: University of Chicago Press, 1990.
Marshall, Terence E. "Rousseau Translations: A Review Essay." *Political Theory* 10 (February 1982): 103–23.
Martin, Jane Roland. *Reclaiming a Conversation: The Ideal of the Educated Woman*. New Haven: Yale University Press, 1985.
———. "Sophie and Emile: A Case Study of Sex Bias in the History of Educational Thought." *Harvard Educational Review* 51 (August 1981): 357–72.
———. "Taking Sophie Seriously." *Proceedings of the Annual Meeting of the Philosophy of Education Society* 39 (1983): 53–56.
Masters, Roger D. *The Political Philosophy of Rousseau*. Princeton: Princeton University Press, 1968.
Meek, Ronald. *Social Science and the Ignoble Savage*. New York: Cambridge University Press, 1976.
Melzer, Arthur. *The Natural Goodness of Man: On the System of Rousseau's Thought*. Chicago: University of Chicago Press, 1990.
Meyer, P. H. "The Individual and Society in Rousseau's *Emile*." *Modern Language Quarterly* 19 (1958): 99–114.

Montague, Ashley. *The Natural Superiority of Women*. New York: Collier Books, 1974.
Morgan, Marabelle. *The Total Woman*. New York: Pocket Books, 1973.
Mouffe, Chantal. "American Liberalism and Its Critics: Rawls, Taylor, Sandel, and Walzer." *Praxis International* 8 (July 1988): 193–206.
Nagel, Jack. *Participation*. Englewood Cliffs, N.J.: Prentice-Hall, 1987.
Norgren, Jill. "Child Care." In *Women: A Feminist Perspective*, 3d ed., edited by Jo Freeman, 139–53. Palo Alto, Calif.: Mayfield Publishing, 1984.
Ogden, Henry V. S. "The Antithesis of Nature and Art, and Rousseau's Rejection of the Theory of Natural Rights." *American Political Science Review* 32 (August 1938): 643–54.
Okin, Susan Moller. *Justice, Gender, and the Family*. New York: Basic Books, 1989.
———. "Rousseau's Natural Woman." *Journal of Politics* 41 (May 1979): 393–416.
———. "Women and the Making of the Sentimental Family." *Philosophy and Public Affairs* 11 (Winter 1982): 65–88.
———. *Women in Western Political Thought*. Princeton: Princeton University Press, 1979.
Osborne, Martha Lee. *Woman in Western Thought*. New York: Random House, 1979.
Pekarsky, Daniel. "Education and Manipulation." *Philosophy of Education Proceedings* (1977): 354–62.
Peters, Richard S. "The Paradoxes in Rousseau's *Emile*." In Richard S. Peters, *Essays on Educators*, 15–31. London: Allen & Unwin, 1981.
Piercy, Marge. *Woman on the Edge of Time*. New York: Fawcett Crest, 1976.
Plato. *The Republic*. Translated by Allan Bloom. New York: Basic Books, 1968.
Plattner, Marc F. *Rousseau's State of Nature: An Interpretation of the Discourse on Inequality*. DeKalb: Northern Illinois University Press, 1979.
Rapaport, Elizabeth. "On the Future of Love: Rousseau and the Radical Feminists." In *Women and Philosophy: Toward a Theory of Liberation*, edited by Carol Gould and Marx Wartofsky, 185–205. New York: Putnam, Capricorn Books, 1976.
Rich, Adrienne. *Of Woman Born: Motherhood as Experience and Institution*. New York: W. W. Norton, 1976.
———. "Taking Women Students Seriously." In Adrienne Rich, *On Lies, Secrets, and Silence: Selected Prose, 1966–1978*, 237–45. New York: W. W. Norton, 1979.
Richards, Janet Radcliffe. *The Sceptical Feminist*. London: Routledge & Kegan Paul, 1980.
Ring, Jennifer. *Modern Political Theory and Contemporary Feminism*. New York: SUNY Press, 1991.
Roche, Kennedy F. *Rousseau: Stoic and Romantic*. New York: Harper & Row, 1974.
Rossi, Alice, ed. *The Feminist Papers: From Adams to de Beauvoir*. New York: Bantam, 1973.
Rothenberg, Paula. "The Construction, Deconstruction, and Reconstruction of Difference." *Hypatia: A Journal of Feminist Philosophy* 5 (Spring 1990): 42–57.
Ruddick, Sara. "Maternal Thinking." *Feminist Studies* 6 (Summer 1980): 342–67.

Salkever, Stephen G. "Rousseau and the Concept of Happiness." *Polity* 11 (Fall 1978): 27–45.
Sandel, Michael J. *Liberalism and the Limits of Justice.* Cambridge: Cambridge University Press, 1982.
Scheman, Naomi. "Individualism and the Objects of Psychology." In *Discovering Reality: Feminist Perspectives on Epistemology, Metaphysics, Methodology, and the Philosophy of Science,* edited by S. Harding and M. Hintikka. Dordrecht: Reidel, 1983.
Schwartz, Joel. *The Sexual Politics of Jean-Jacques Rousseau.* Chicago: University of Chicago Press, 1984.
Sénéchal, Anicet. "Jean-Jacques Rousseau, Secrétaire de Madame Dupin, d'après des Documents Inédits, avec un Inventaire des Papiers Dupin Dispersés en 1957 et 1958." *Annales de la Société Jean-Jacques Rousseau* 36 (1963–1965): 173–290.
"Sex and God in American Politics." *Policy Review* (Fall 1984): 10–19.
Shanley, Mary. "Marital Slavery and Friendship: John Stuart Mill's *The Subjection of Women.*" *Political Theory* 8 (May 1981): 220–47.
Sklar, Judith. *Men and Citizens: A Study of Rousseau's Social Theory.* Cambridge: Cambridge University Press, 1969.
―――. "Rousseau's Images of Authority." In *Hobbes and Rousseau,* edited by Maurice Cranston and Richard S. Peters, 333–65. New York: Anchor Books, 1972.
Skillen, Anthony. "Rousseau and the Fall of Social Man." *Philosophy* 60 (1985): 105–21.
Smart, Carol. *Feminism and the Power of the Law.* London: Routledge, 1989.
Spender, Dale, ed. *Feminist Theorists: Three Centuries of Key Women Thinkers.* 1983. New York: Pantheon, 1983.
―――. *Women of Ideas—and What Men Have Done to Them.* London: Routledge & Kegan Paul, 1982.
Springborg, Patricia. *The Problem of Human Needs and the Critique of Civilization.* London: Allen & Unwin, 1981.
Starobinski, Jean. *Jean-Jacques Rousseau: Transparency and Obstruction.* 1971. Translated by Arthur Goldhammer. Chicago: University of Chicago Press, 1988.
Steinem, Gloria. *Revolution from Within: A Book of Self-Esteem.* Boston: Little, Brown, 1992.
Strauss, Leo. "On the Intention of Rousseau." In *Hobbes and Rousseau,* edited by Maurice Cranston and Richard S. Peters, 254–90. Garden City, N.Y.: Anchor Books, 1972.
Sussman, George D. *Selling Mother's Milk: The Wet-Nursing Business in France, 1715–1914.* Urbana: University of Illinois Press, 1982.
Tenenbaum, Susan. "Woman through the Prism of Political Thought." *Polity* 15 (Fall 1982): 90–102.
Tong, Rosemarie. *Feminist Thought: A Comprehensive Introduction.* Boulder, Colo.: Westview, 1989.
Trebilcot, Joyce. "Sex Roles: The Argument from Nature." *Ethics* 85 (April 1975): 245–55.

Walby, Sylvia. *Theorizing Patriarchy*. Cambridge: Basil Blackwell, 1990.
Walzer, Michael. "The Communitarian Critique of Liberalism." *Political Theory* 18 (February 1990): 6–23.
Wendell, Susan. "A (Qualified) Defense of Liberal Feminism." *Hypatia: A Journal of Feminist Philosophy* 2 (Summer 1987): 65–94.
Wexler, Victor. " 'Made for Man's Delight': Rousseau as Antifeminist." *American Historical Review* 81 (April 1976): 266–91.
Whitbeck, Caroline. "Theories of Sex Differences." In *Women and Philosophy: Toward a Theory of Liberation*, edited by Carol Gould and Marx Wartofsky, 54–80. New York: Putnam, 1976.
Williams, Patricia J. *The Alchemy of Race and Rights: Diary of a Law Professor*. Cambridge: Harvard University Press, 1991.
Wolgast, Elizabeth. *Equality and the Rights of Women*. Ithaca: Cornell University Press, 1980.
Wollstonecraft, Mary. *A Vindication of the Rights of Woman*. 1792. Edited by Carol Poston. New York: W. W. Norton, 1988.
Woolf, Virginia. *Three Guineas*. 1938. New York: Harcourt, Brace, 1966.
Young, Iris. "The Ideal of Community and the Politics of Difference." *Social Theory and Practice* 12 (Spring 1986): 1–26.

INDEX

Adams, Abigail, 99
Adams, John, 99
Addams, Jane, 111
Affirmative action, x, 141
Andelin, Helen, 102
Anthony, Susan B., 160
Antifeminism, 7, 8, 9, 28, 37, 38, 46, 56, 62, 67, 71, 73, 74, 88, 91, 92, 93, 103, 104, 108, 114, 122, 148, 158, 164 n., 170 n. *See also* Biological determinism; Male values/perspective; Patriarchy; Sexism; Sexual differentiation/roles
Aquinas, Thomas, 6, 149, 154
Aristotle, 6, 43, 85–86, 92, 122, 130, 143, 144, 146, 149, 151, 154, 155
Astell, Mary, 88
Atomism, 125, 126, 132, 134, 139, 141
Augustine, 149, 156
Authenticity, 22, 23, 102, 115

Baer, Judith, xii
Barber, Benjamin, 144
Biological determinism, 8, 37, 46–47, 48, 52–53; Rousseau's rejection of, 37–38, 43, 57, 71, 91–92, 114. *See also* Antifeminism; Sexual differentiation/roles
Bloom, Allan, 25, 60
Bluhm, William, 33, 167 n.

Children, 14, 15, 46, 47, 48, 49, 57, 59, 70, 86, 111, 114, 135, 137, 168 n., breast-feeding of, 61–64; childcare, 62–64, 71, 160; parent-child relations, 61–67, 167–68 n.; physical weakness of, 42; in state of nature, 58, 61. *See also* Families; Fathers; Mothers; Parents
Citizens(hip), 46, 48, 59, 65, 68, 78, 84, 103, 112, 122, 140, 142, 169 n.
Civil society, distributing benefits and burdens in, 20, 70, 85, 86–88; and self-interest, 85
Class, 19, 128, 129, 131, 138, 142, 153
Collaborative research, ix–xvi
Collins, Patricia Hill, x
Communitarian(ism), criticisms of liberalism, 126–29, 133–36, 140–43; relation to feminism, 9, 121–47; and sexual differentiation, 94–117; view of the self, 130; view of social relations, 137–38. *See also* Community; Feminism; Liberalism
Community, 17, 28, 57, 66, 93–94, 131; destruction of, 9, 54, 63–64, 89, 95, 102, 105, 113, 115–16, 134, 145; establishment of, 7, 8–9, 52, 56, 61, 69, 70, 71, 93; and (in)equality, 73, 94, 111, 116, 121–23, 142, lesbian, 127, 128; maintenance of, 21, 24–25, 26, 69, 86, 134; relation to freedom, 33–34; and sexuality, 108. *See also* Communitarian(ism); Education; Families
Competition, 59, 68, 72, 132, 137
Confessions, 44
Conscience, 23, 25, 26

185

Daly, Mary, x, xi, 159, 160, 161
Davis, Angela, 160
de Beauvoir, Simone, 17, 128, 152, 160
Dependence, 14, 16, 17, 19, 22, 28; and justice, 77–79; and opinion, 23; and physical strength, 39. *See also* Independence; Interdependence; Subjugation
de Pizan, Christine, 128, 152, 160
de Pompadour, Madame, 68
Desires, 27–29, 55; sexual, 107–9
Difference, 35, 111, 124, 145; and (in)equality, 74, 95, 110, 111, 116, 156
Division of labor, 20, 78; inattention to, 98–99; rationale for, 94; sexual, 36, 38, 51, 52, 54, 81, 83, 84, 86, 91. *See also* Sexual differentiation/roles
Dworkin, Andrea, 53
Dworkin, Ronald, 139

Education, 48, 115; class-specific, 19; of desires, 27, 29; and freedom, 12–13; as guided by preparation for future, 16, 19, 45; negative education, 31; as political, 29, 30–31, 33, 46, 82; religious, 23; sex education, 67; sexually differentiated, 8, 11, 36, 54; and social change, 18–19, 22, 28; for social roles/community, 17, 21, 32, 52; utility as standard in, 15, 45; women's demands for, 69. *See also* Children
Ego, 101, 126; as amour-propre, 103; male ego, 104–6; as self-love, 58–59, 115. *See also* Egoism; Will
Egoism, 50, 56, 59, 63, 67, 70, 83, 125, 131. *See also* Ego; Self-interest
Eisenstein, Hester, xi, xiii
Eisenstein, Zillah, xvi, 78
Emile, 4, 18, 30, 34, 39, 50, 51, 52, 65, 66
Equality, 131; and community, 73, 94, 106, 116; and indirect power, 98; liberal, 70, 71–72; moral vs. physical, 40
Exploitation, 28, 32, 39, 51, 58, 71, 73, 79, 89, 94, 95, 104, 109, 142. *See also* Dependence; Subjugation

Families, 8, 47–48, 56; aristocratic, 59–60, 66–67, 70; bourgeois, 60–61, 66–67, 70; destruction of, 68; development of, 63, 92; equality in, 68; as "haven," 57, 70, 81, 84; reconstruction of, 62; and the state, 69; "traditional," 56, 57, 166 n.; variety of models of, 116–17. *See also* Children; Fathers; Mothers; Parents
Fathers, 58, 59, 60, 64–65, 68, 81, 87, 166 n. *See also* Men
Femininity, 105, 109, 113, 115, 124. *See also* Masculinity; Women
Feminism, 135, 143–45; communitarian feminism, 123–24; criticisms of communitarianism, 127–28, 131–32, 133–36, 138, 140–43; criticisms of liberalism, 126–29; and families, 72–74; feminist ethics, 100; feminist movement, 5, 129; liberal feminism, 5, 61, 70, 71–72, 88, 124; radical feminism, 75, 93; view of the self, 130–31; view of social relations, 137–38. *See also* Communitarian(ism); Feminist theory; Liberalism
Feminist theory, 159; history of, xi, 163 n., 17; reappraising the history of philosophy, 6, 9, 54–55, 149–61. *See also* Feminism
Ferguson, Ann, xiv
First Discourse, 32, 59, 76, 106, 115
Formey, Jean, 10
Fralin, Richard, 84
Freedom, 50, 77; as equilibrium between powers and desires, 12, 18, 27, 28, 32, 46, 58, 88; feeling free, 32; as guide in education, 12; and individualism, 78, 126; limits on, 20, 24, 29; relation to community, 33–34; social freedom, 12, 18, 31; in state of nature, 12, 33
French, Marilyn, 160
Freud, Sigmund, 155
Friedan, Betty, 19, 88
Friendship, 103, 105, 137, 143
Frye, Marilyn, xiv, xvi, 169 n.
Fuller, Margaret, 160

General will, 34, 82, 83–84, 111, 133
Gilligan, Carol, 93, 112
Gilman, Charlotte Perkins, 19, 106, 160
Goldberg, Steven, 93
Goldman, Emma, 160
Grimké, Angelina, 160
Grimké, Sarah, 160

Index

Habit, 22, 23, 25, 47, 58, 63, 66, 69
Happiness, 13, 15, 27, 29, 32, 34, 46, 48, 88, 115
Hartsock, Nancy, ix, 142
Heterosexual relationships, 102, 136, 141. *See also* Marriage
Hobbes, Thomas, 28, 29, 70, 93, 133, 149, 154
Homosexual relationships, 127, 128, 138, 141, 160; homophobia, 147, 158. *See also* Community
Hooks, Bell, xiii, xvi, 160
Human condition, 56, 58–59, 70, 92
Human nature, 4, 31, 50, 125, 132; and feminism, 91–92, 128

Imagination, 27
Inconsistencies, apparent in Rousseau's writings, 3, 4, 8, 10, 11, 13–14, 19, 23–24, 39, 77–78, 82, 85; vs. real consistency, 11, 14–18, 24–26; Rousseauean responses to charges of, 77–88
Independence, 12, 23, 71, 147; economic, 18–21; and freedom from opinion, 22, 24; in state of nature, 58. *See also* Dependence; Interdependence
Individualism, 7, 70–71, 106, 114, 128, 138; and communitarianism, 95; and freedom, 79; negative consequences of, 102; Rousseau's critique of, 93, 129, 136, 140, 142. *See also* Atomism; Egoism; Self-interest
Interdependence, 12, 18, 33, 42, 45, 56, 58, 59, 61, 71, 72, 78, 80, 93, 131, 137. *See also* Community; Dependence; Independence

Jaggar, Alison, 37, 144
Justice, 137, 146; and advantage, 85–88; and dependence, 77–79; and participation, 82–85; and subjugation, 79–82

Lange, Lynda, 84
Lasch, Christopher, 146–47
Laws, 65, 66, 67, 83, 96, 139, 141
Laws of nature, 51, 82
Le Doeuff, Michèle, xiii, 4, 159
Letter to d'Alembert, 55

Levasseur, Thérèse, 3, 163 n.
Liberalism, 9, 70, 73, 78, 157; and community, 106; and sex roles, 88, 116; view of political community, 138–40; view of the self, 125–26; view of social relations, 132–33. *See also* Communitarian(ism); Feminism
Lies, 52, 167 n.
Locke, John, 28, 47, 65, 92, 133, 149, 152, 154
Lorde, Audre, 160
Louis XV, 68
Luxury, 27

Machiavelli, Niccolò, 149
MacIntyre, Alasdair, 9, 127, 129, 139, 143, 144–45, 146, 148
MacKinnon, Catharine, 141, 160
Male values/perspective, 32, 35, 44, 72, 122, 135, 147–48, 157, 172 n. *See also* Antifeminism; Sexism
Manipulation, 114, 171 n.; in education, 25, 29, 165 n., 43, 50; of environment, 41; of men by women, 45, 81, 101–4; negative consequences of, 102–3, 105–6, 107–9. *See also* Power
Marriage, 97; adultery in, 60, 68; aristocratic vs. bourgeois, 67–70; arranged, 60, 68; contract, 70; violence in, 105, 136, 141, 160. *See also* Families
Marx, Karl, 7, 92, 135, 149, 150, 157, 158, 159; Marxist feminism, 142
Masculinity, 97, 104, 105, 107; overvaluing of, 109–10. *See also* Femininity; Men
Master/slave, 13, 17, 19, 31–32, 35, 65
Masters, Roger, 12
Maximin strategy, 28
Melzer, Arthur, 97
Men, 47, 141; direct power of, 36; as economic actors, 18–21, 78, 112; as husbands, 70; military service for, 15, 17, 87, 111, 112, 115–16; motivating, 42, 81, 97, 103, 104, 107; nature of, 38, 48; physical differences among, 39; physical training of, 13–14, 18, 52; as pleasing to women, 81–82; and public opinion, 22–23, 25; rationality in, 43–46; social roles of, 36, 112. *See also* fathers; Masculinity

Military service: as male duty, 15, 17, 87, 111, 112, 115–16; as social role, 17; women's fitness for, 40
Mill, John Stuart, 88, 116, 139, 149, 152
Morality, 39, 56, 58, 68, 129, 139, 141; gendered moral codes, 86; in state of nature vs. civil society, 86
Mores *(les moeurs)*, 25, 82–83, 95, 96, 129, 138
Morgan, Marabel, 102
Mothers, 47, 58, 59, 62, 64, 71, 87, 135, 137, 167–68 n.; maternal instinct, 46, 47. *See also* Women

Nagel, Jack, 112
Natural savage, 15, 17, 20, 31, 32, 40, 44, 50, 78. *See also* State of nature
Necessity, 23, 27, 39, 52
Needs, 43; true needs, 20, 28
Nietzsche, Friedrich, 156

Obedience, 22, 40, 66, 97
Oligation, 70, 93, 130, 134
Okin, Susan Moller, 144

Parents, 59, 61–67; in state of nature, 61. *See also* Fathers; Mothers
Participation, 4, 33–34, 142; and all-male assembly, 111–12, 144–45; and justice, 82–85, 130; and socialization, 112, 116, 126
Pateman, Carole, x, 88
Patriarchy, 94, 99, 104, 128, 142, 153, 158. *See also* Antifeminism; Male values/perspective; Sexism
Perfectibility, 31, 43
Physical education, 13–18; hardships and, 13, 14, 16; and relation to mental development, 16; and relation to self-sufficiency, 14, 16; and relation to women's relative physical weakness, 17, 40–42. *See also* Education
Piercy, Marge, 144
Pity, 28
Plaskow, Judith, xiii, xiv
Plato, 9, 122, 148, 149, 154, 156–57, 159, 165 n.
Political legitimacy, 4, 24, 40, 70, 72–73, 76, 77, 82, 108, 117, 166 n.; and advantage, 85–88; and obligation, 93; and representation, 84
Political theory, 158–59
Power, 108, 143; balance of, 98, 99, 100, 160; indirect, 82, 95–98, 156; and inequality, 80, 115; men's over women, 81, 98, 113; women's over men, 81, 98, 99. *See also* Manipulation
Pregnancy, 46, 47
Pride, 27, 28, 29, 32, 106, 125
Public opinion, 22–26, 86; and conformity, 22; and social attachment, 25; and socialization, 48–49
Public/private, 32, 36, 37, 38, 39, 48, 55, 57, 73, 75, 82–84, 87, 88, 93, 106, 107, 112, 117, 140, 146, 160
Publius, 99

Race, 127–28, 138, 153; and civil rights movement, 127; and racism, 5, 114, 127, 147, 156, 158, 161, 168 n.
Rawls, John, 159
Reason, 22, 23, 25; in liberal theory, 125–26; in original state vs. civil society, 43, 85–86. *See also* Men; Women
Representation, 82, 84, 111, 151. *See also* Participation
Reproduction, 46–48, 69. *See also* Sex differences; Women
Rich, Adrienne, 160–61
Rights, 140, 141–42
Robinson Crusoe, 18, 24
Rousseau, Jean-Jacques: as antifeminist, 94–117; centrality of his views on gender, 7, 8, 37, 52, 75, 88; as compatible with feminism, 91–94, 129; and environmentalism, 41, 129; explanations of his views on gender, 36–37, 39; feminist critiques of, 53–54, 88–89, 94–117, 138; as functionalist, 44, 75, 167 n.; as nonrationalist, 44; philosophy of education, 14; political problem addressed by, 59, 71, 79; rhetorical strategies of, 50, 51–53, 55, 129. *See also titles of individual works*

Sandel, Michael, 127, 139, 143, 146
Sappho, 159, 160
Sartre, Jean-Paul, 4–5, 152
Savoyard Vicar, 23

Schlafly, Phyllis, 92
Schwartz, Joel, 37, 41, 73, 95–96, 97, 98, 100, 103, 107
Second Discourse, 4, 59, 76
Self-absorption, 17, 35, 56, 58, 66, 69, 71, 133; and family, 83; and illness, 16
Self-development, 32, 33, 51; mental, 43, 44; physical, 41
Self-interest, 26, 47, 60, 65, 69, 70, 71, 80, 81, 83, 105, 117, 132, 135–36; checks upon, 26; vs. community, 8, 31, 67, 93; overcoming, 70; in state of nature, 58. *See also* Egoism; Individualism
Sex differences, 36, 37, 51, 54; feminist ideas about, 38, 41–42, 52; in intellect, 42–46; and nature, 55; in physical strength, 39–42; political (ir)relevance of, 17, 37, 40, 50; in reproduction, 46–48. *See also* Biological determinism; Sexual differentiation/roles
Sexism, 4, 108, 127–28, 137–38, 143, 147–48, 158; forms of, 155–58; resistance to, 115, 152, 161. *See also* Antifeminism; Male values/perspective; Patriarchy
Sexual differentiation/roles, 36; and complementarity, 46, 52, 94, 110, 156; and forms of power, 81; and interdependence, 84; social utility of, 38, 40, 51, 55–56, 57, 71, 75, 89, 94, 121. *See also* Community; Education; Feminism
Sexuality, 58, 67, 87, 127–28, 153; and community, 108; objectification of women's, 106–9; in state of nature, 68, 87
Sklar, Judith, 144
Smith, Hilda, xiv
Social Contract, 4, 24, 51–52, 77, 80, 95
Social contract, 40, 70, 77, 83, 133; contractual relations, 132, 133–34, 137
Socrates, 163 n.
Spender, Dale, xvi, 158
Starobinski, Jean, 102
State, 48, 139; common good in, 72, 122; and family, 69; liberalism and, 126, 139, 140, 141, 142
State of nature, 12, 20, 47, 58, 63, 86, 103; asociality in, 42, 45, 50, 58, 94, 97; families in, 47, 92; and freedom, 19, 31–32; and happiness, 20; indolence in, 31, 42, 97; isolation in, 18, 31, 63, 67, 70, 73, 87, 94, 125; reason in, 43, 44; and self-preservation, 78; and true needs, 28, 50. *See also* Natural savage
Strauss, Leo, 24
Subjugation, 49, 90, 99, 106, 109, 155; and justice, 79–82. *See also* Dependence; Women
Suffering, 15, 34, 88

Taylor, Harriet, 128, 152, 160
Thetis, 16
Tong, Rosemarie, xi
Tradition(s), 125, 127, 138
Tyranny, 100, 139, 160

Virtue, 23, 41, 65, 81, 86, 115–16
Voltaire, 10

Walzer, Michael, 122–23
Will, 66, 83–84, 106; independent, 80
Wollstonecraft, Mary, 10, 49–50, 88, 100, 107–8, 128, 152, 160
Women: arguments against economic dependence of, 19–20; as household manager, 19, 21, 36, 46; and indirect power of, 9, 36; nature of, 38, 40, 47, 48, 49, 55; physical weakness as a tool of, 42; as pleasing to men, 80–82; privatization of, 38, 47–48, 82, 122, 156; and public opinion, 23–26; rationality in, 43–46, 51; relative physical weakness of, 17, 39–42, 87; silencing of, 110–13, 122, 153, 156; subjugation of, 45, 155; traditional contributions of, 21, 35, 78, 93, 112, 113, 164 n.; as wives, 47, 69. *See also* Femininity; Mothers
Woolf, Virginia, 19, 107, 160
Wright, Frances, 160

Xanthippe, 163 n.

www.ingramcontent.com/pod-product-compliance
Lightning Source LLC
Chambersburg PA
CBHW022056290426
44109CB00014B/1127